West End

Punsbourn

Wormle...

Wor...

Beaumont Green

Newgate Street

Appleberry Stree

Cheshunt

Hammond Str...

Common

Flamsted

Goffs Oak

Cheshunt Ho.

Coffley

The Medicinal Water or Northhall Wells

Love Green

CHESHUN

Berryfi...

mmon

Cattle Gate

Theobalds...

Little Hook Gate

Hillocks Hook

Pond

New Pond

White Webbs Gate

Bulls

ocker
ge

The Flash

Crofs

Bels...

Clay Hill

New River

Tuke

Brook

The Cuffley Story

Patricia Klijn & Michael Clark

TEWIN ORCHARD
2005

The Cuffley Story

Published by Tewin Orchard 2005

1 Upper Green Tewin Welwyn Hertfordshire AL6 0LX

ISBN 0-9549508-0-1

Designer Emma Pitrakou. Printed and bound in China

For our parents, Olive and Fred Fenshom, Joan and Bernard Clark, who gave us our Cuffley childhoods

Please contact Patricia Klijn via 01707 874828 initially if you have any new material or old family snapshots that include views of Cuffley.
Our material has inevitably been biased to our own family collections and circles of friends, but we welcome your input to correct this imbalance.
We are particularly grateful to **The Hertfordshire Natural History Society,** Annabel Whittet, the staff of Kallkwik, Welwyn Garden City for their very helpful copy work, our ever willing printer Jeremy Kuo, the many people who have contributed information or permission to use material, (see page 256), and the sponsors:

LISBET RAUSING

Hertfordshire Biological Records Centre

Hertfordshire County Council

Contents

Molly Vivian Hughes (right) in the 1890s by kind permission of Oxford University Press. The Gray family vacated half their cottage for the recently widowed Molly and her three boys on their arrival from nearby Barnet in 1920.

In 1920 Molly Hughes and her family came to live on the right side of the cottage at 58 Tolmers Road. The picture, *top left*, shows the whole cottage in 1918 when the Gray family rented the entire building, having moved there from Hill Farm at the top of Plough Hill. *Below, left:* the cottages at breakfast time during the winter of 1968, taken from 45a Tolmers Road. *Above, right:* the only known picture of Molly with her sons, left to right, Barnholt, Vivian (oldest) and Arthur, East Ridgeway, about 1937.

Chapter One

The Hughes Legacy

Before Mary Vivian Hughes came to Cuffley as a widow in 1920 with her three sons, she had been a teacher in schools in Darlington and West Kensington, written Latin text books with a colleague and travelled to America.

It was during the 1930s that the books of her early life were published, namely, *A London Child of the 1870s*, *A London Girl of the 1880s* and *A London Home in the 1890s*. These chronicles of childhood and early married life are an important part of the social history of her times: readable, poignant and detailed. There were other books too, full of history and anecdotes, *America's England (1930)*, *London at Home (1931)* and *City Saints (1932)*.

But it was a later title that made her important in

the history of Cuffley when it was published in 1940: *A London Family between the Wars*. Here in a nutshell is a lively description of the village as it was, before shops, housing development and trains to Hertford. The railway terminated at Cuffley, most shopping had to be fetched from Enfield, other than bread and milk, and the true centre of Cuffley was at the top of Plough Hill.

Molly Hughes, as she was better known, lived in one of the semi-detached cottages at the corner of Oak Lane with Tolmers Road, squashed in with her three schoolboy sons and the books that had sustained this well-educated woman all her life. On moving to Cuffley she had taken a post as inspector of schools and travelled the country in this role. Working hard on her writing as well, she was determined that all her boys should go to Oxford or Cambridge as her husband had wanted. *A London Family between the Wars* was reissued as a paperback in 1979 by the Oxford University Press

4

By 1937 both the Grays and the Hughes had moved to new houses built for them in East Ridgeway. Joan Gray was married that year to Bernard William Clark and Molly presented them with a cedar garden seat as a wedding present. Joan continued to prepare runner beans from the garden into her 90s, sitting on the same seat outside Oak Cottage, 44 Hill Rise. Joan's mother Maud Gray, *(right)*, featured in Molly's book *'A London Family Between the Wars'* as 'Mrs Semi-detached' and the families always kept in touch in later years. When she was in her 80s Molly went to live with Arthur in Ireland. He regularly visited Jack, (Joan's brother), and Marie Gray when he visited England in later years.

and the cheerful cover of a Spencer Gore painting (although of a cottage at Letchworth) ensured a new generation of Cuffley people could enjoy her work. Molly was able to commission the building of a new home for the family on the East Ridgeway corner as it joins The Ridgeway as 'Fronwen' which was built by Mr Chinchen, disguised as Mr K in the *'London Family'* book.

It is the intriguing uncovering of these disguises in Molly's book that led us to the daughter of 'Mrs Semi-detached', who lived in the other half of the Hughes home in Tolmers Road. Joan Clark, or Joan Gray as she was then, remembers Mrs Hughes vividly as 'a plump figure in a knitted cap who knew lots of unusual nursery rhymes and stories.' As children living so close-by, Joan and her brother Jack enjoyed the company of the lively family and recall that an interconnecting door was left, but later firmly locked, between the two households. Many years later when Joan married she was given a

garden seat from Molly Hughes and she remained friends with the family. It is as Joan Clark, mother of the co-author of this book that Cuffley knows her today. It is through the sons of Molly Hughes, Barnholt, Vivian and Arthur that the story continues. In 1948 Vivian wrote of his impressions of Cuffley as he remembered it in the 1916 - 1920 period. Never before have these reminiscences been published and they have been in Jack and Joan's care all these years. Perhaps even more remarkable are the drawings and paintings he produced, capturing the rural scenes, farms and The Plough in sketches and watercolours. Reproduced throughout the book are his paintings, again never before published, one in fact of Hill Farm which was another of Joan Gray's homes as a child. Jack Gray, her brother was a schoolfellow of Arthur Hughes.

From Arthur we learn more of his mother's earlier work. "In her early married life she wrote *From Baptism to Holy Communion and Christ's First*

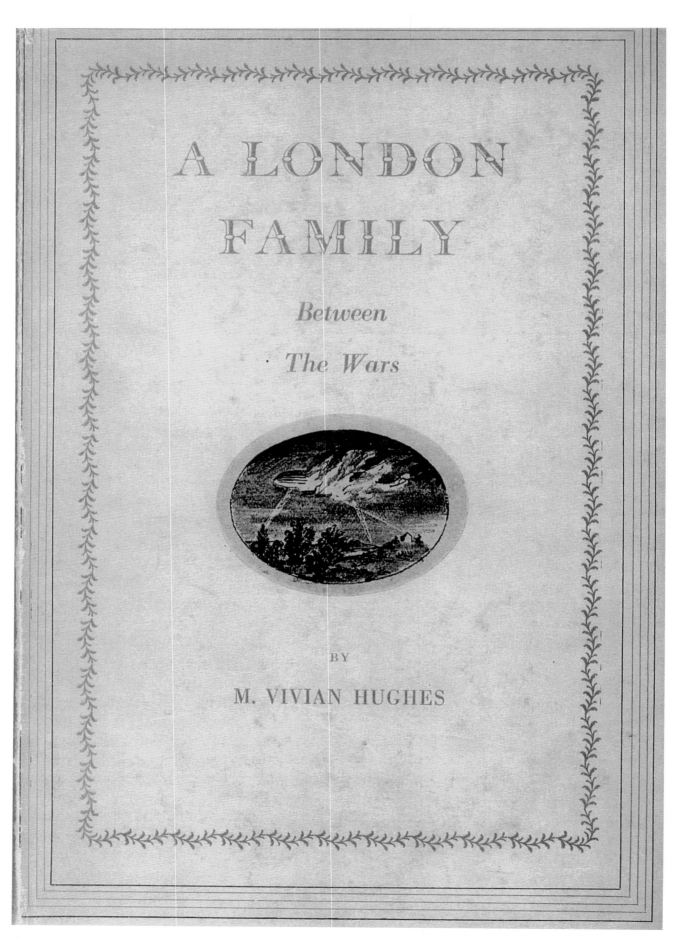

A LONDON
FAMILY

Between

· *The Wars*

BY

M. VIVIAN HUGHES

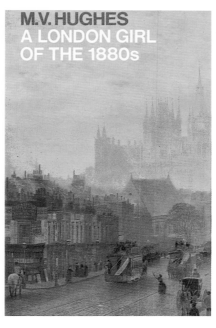
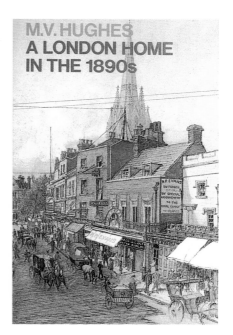

Facing page: the original cover of Molly Hughes book about life in Cuffley in the 1920s and 1930s, published in 1940. The first airship shot down over Britain is featured in the drawing, (see p 64). *Above:* Molly's trilogy of books about her family life during the reign of Queen Victoria which preceeded the Cuffley title. These were reproduced in paperback in the 1970s by the original publishers, Oxford University Press, who have kindly given us permission to reproduce these front covers with other copyright material here.

Missionaries, published by the "National Society" (she was a deeply religious woman, if a bit unconventional - and steeped in the Bible). Her best book in this vein was *Hidden Interests in the Bible* also published by the National Society. Another book was *Scripture Teaching To-day*, published by the SCM"

In a letter written from his home in Dublin to Jack Gray in 1987, Arthur says how delighted he is that his mother's *London Family* trilogy is not only available in paperback but in Talking Books and LARGE PRINT (his capitals).

In an earlier letter in 1985 he had said: 'My brother Vivian wrote his notes on Cuffley in 1948, describing it as he remembered it between 1916 and 1920. Vivian's notes may be of interest today, but he hasn't my mother's lightness of touch. His main interest, you may have gathered was trains!'

Vivian's reminiscences follow, retaining his use of capital letters, punctuation and dashes.

The Birth Of A Dormitory

Cuffley Thirty Years Ago

Whatever may be the uses of history, one of its fascinations is the fact that it enables us to imagine the early and more dramatic stages of things which have become commonplace. This is most noticeable in the case of the growth of Greater London during the last fifty years. Yet it is a curious fact that, though there are abundant records of the earlier history of the home counties, and many periodicals and works of reference dealing with their remoter past, the more recent and more sweeping changes are in danger of passing unrecorded.

London is fringed with residential districts which fifty years ago were no more than villages -- they were not even undeveloped suburbs, but genuine elements in a rural life, to which the advent of the railway made at first but little difference. The new

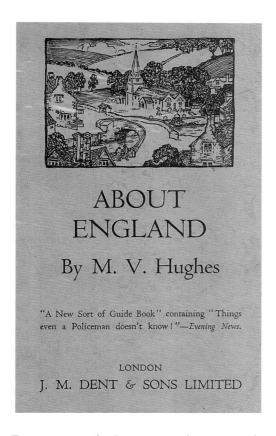

Facing page: the Lynton Lamb cover to the original 1934 first edition of Molly Hughes' first book of personal reminiscences. She had already written non-fiction books for J M Dent, (including her popular travel guides, *About England* (1927), *America's England* (1930) and *The City Saints* (1932). Lamb (1907-1977) was a very successful illustrator in the last century and worked on production for the London office of the Oxford University Press. He is described in Alan Horne's *The Dictionary of 20th Century British Book Illustrators* and Chris Beetles also gives a catalogue biography in *The Illustrators, 1780-1993*. Molly also wrote school text books.

Right: the paperback cover of the 1979 edition of Molly's account of Cuffley featured Spencer Gore's painting of 100 Wilbury Road: 'Harold Gilman's house' in Letchworth. The house was designed by Barry Parker (1867-1947) and Raymond Unwin (1863-1940). Their garden city architecture is almost identical to the style of Molly's first Cuffley home. (By kind permission of Oxford University Press and Leicester Museum & Art Gallery.)

Our first home in Cuffley
(from a sketch by Vivian)

Following the family's arrival in 1920 at 58 Tolmers Road, Cuffley, Vivian Hughes began to draw his new surroundings. He sketched their home in the spring of 1921, *above* and *facing page,* (Catalogue 31). Mervyn Miller, in his *Letchworth* (1989) illustrates this style of housing particularly well. From page 67 he describes Courtenay Crickmer's work and his 1908 trademark 'M' double gable houses. Crickmer's work is perhaps the finest produced outside the Parker & Unwin Garden City architects' immediate circle.

houses - homes of retired people living on pensions, investments or commercial gains, or business men with secure city jobs - were occasional and experimental, and the house-agent and speculative builder had to wait some years before, in commercial jargon, the place was "ripe for development".

Among such places is Cuffley, in the South East corner of HERTS, between Potters Bar and Cheshunt. At present it has the usual attractions of an outer suburb, being separated from the main urban conglomeration by a belt of genuine agricultural country, yet enjoying, at least in the "rush" hours, a frequent train and bus service. From the ridgeway towards Potters Bar there are extensive views embracing North London and Epping Forest, and the general upland character of the county gives it a healthy climate - not the least cause of its appeal.

Yet those who have known Cuffley only as an

attractive, but essentially modern, suburb with the usual miscellany of comfortable houses and labour-saving bungalows, and an abundance of well cared for and well stocked gardens, can have little idea of what Cuffley connoted some thirty-two years ago, when I first visited the place shortly after the German Zeppelin was brought down by Leefe Robinson in the field behind the "Plough" Inn, i.e. in September 1916. The "Zep" raid, a wide-spread one over the South of England, took place on Saturday September 2nd, and Leefe Robinson's spectacular chase ending in victory at Cuffley late that night was watched by thousands from their windows and streets in North London, and over the following weekend a record number visited the little HERTS village, causing quite a strain on the railway staff and such catering facilities as Cuffley offered. Since, in fact, little change was made between Sep. 1916 and Sep. 1920, when I went to live there with my mother and younger brothers, a description of its

main features and the occupations of its inhabitants as I remember them during 1920 and 1921, coupled with additional facts gleaned from still older inhabitants, may serve to give a fair picture of pre-suburban Cuffley.

Cuffley in September 1920 consisted of the "Plough Inn", St. Andrew's Church, four cottages, two of which still stand, by the village green and water pump, which was always covered with straw in winter to keep it from freezing. At the foot of the hill, by the triangular green, where the road to Cheshunt leaves the Northaw Road, was the school house and the tiny hall which did duty as the Church of England school, until the authorities made other arrangements for the education of Cuffley children. Finally, in respect of older buildings, there were eight farms in the district, namely: Upper Hanyards, Lower Hanyards, Brook Farm (alias Pantiles), Cuffley Hill Farm, Castle Farm, Wells Farm, Colesdale and Soper's. All of these survive as

interesting and picturesque links with the past with the exception of two - Cuffley Hill Farm, and Lower Hanyards. These two were characteristic of early Cuffley and their demolition, to make way for modern bungalows, was a sad but no doubt inevitable landmark in the process of changing a village into a suburb. Hill Farm stood opposite the "Plough" and was an attractive, rambling building, that had been altered internally and externally by various owners. It had the tarred wooden boarding, and weathered tiles, which are a striking feature of many HERTS farms and cottages. It possessed a fine old timber barn, standing on the north side behind the elms which still flank the green.

Lower Hanyards, though less conspicuously situated, afforded a more striking contrast to things modern, as it was close to the railway station (see illustrations). A small, but strongly built and well proportioned brick house, reputed to be over three hundred years old, it was charmingly backed by tall

A Letchworth Garden City postcard (sent on 23 December 1906 from Southend-on-Sea in Essex to Miss M Locke, Bedford House, Aylesbury, Buckinghamshire) features a watercolour by Frank Dean of 'Garden City: general view from Norton'. The architecture is very reminiscent of the Cuffley cottages built in or just off Tolmers Road where the Hughes' family came to live.

elms, and its thatched barn was the first, and at first sight the only, building, as it obscured the house, to greet the traveller who left the station by the footpath on the Cuffley side. This path is still the normal exit for most of the inhabitants of Cuffley, and is in fact the property of the railway, but the barn and the tree-trunks on which we used to sit and eat our sandwiches when prospecting for a house in the summer of 1920, made way for Tolmers Gardens, a new crescent of bungalows about 1928. The approach to the farm was by a track from a gate on the Cheshunt road, and ran parallel to the then new Tolmers Road, which was one of the first instalments of the Cuffley Garden Estate, and which remains "unadopted", with a decidedly patchy surface, as the hundreds who now live on it know to their cost. One cannot have everything, however, and the risk of road accidents to children playing in Tolmers Road must be small. The owner of Cuffley Hill Farm also owned Lower Hanyards and in 1920

was renting it to some people from London.

There had been a ninth farm - Brickwall Farm - which though itself demolished by 1920, had left one interesting and still functioning souvenir. For the "Cabin" - long since enlarged and now Cuffley's Victory Centre with a long record of employment for dances, theatrical shows, concerts and very many other activities, was simply the old barn of Brickwall, and it is as a picturesque scene that I remember it, when one Sunday afternoon I sketched it sitting on what remained of the brick wall, in which was situated the only post-box. (See this painting of Vivian's on p 245).

Close to the "Cabin" was an army hut, which had been acquired, shortly before we went to Cuffley, by a sister of the owner of the Hill Farm. In it she set up a grocery, branch post office and telephone exchange. She also owned the Cabin and hired it for dances, whist-drives and other entertainments. This lady has only recently left Cuffley, and has long

Vivian drew with coloured pencils and watercolours through the 1920s. Our catalogue of his Cuffley work (page 238) lists the pictures from his brother Arthur's gift to Joan & Jack Gray during the decade 1920 - 1930. This quickly produced watercolour shows the field layout, hedge and the cottages in Oak Lane, off Tolmers Road, above the fenced railway embankment. Tolmers Road is on the left, (Catalogue 41).

been one of its most interesting and best-known personalities. Hers was for many years the only shop in the district. Bread was delivered by a Potters Bar bakery, and was also obtainable from a tiny shop in Northaw, 2 miles away. Other shopping was usually done at Enfield to which the trains ran hourly. It was not till about 1933 that the cross-country bus to Waltham Cross and Potters Bar was instituted.

The first of the modern residences was Ridgeway House, built in 1906, and inhabited in 1920 by the authoress of some historical novels dealing with Hertfordshire. It is still, to my mind, one of the most attractive houses in the district, and is situated on the outskirts of Holmwood (Vivian's spelling) on the North side of the Ridgeway, commanding fine views towards Ponsbourne. Other houses along the Ridgeway followed at considerable intervals of time and space: Holmwood House in 1912, Carbone House in 1913. These and three other new houses along East Ridgeway comprised all the new houses

in Upper Cuffley, but there were one or two more in the process of construction.

In 1913 "The Cuffley Tenants Ltd" began building some two-storey semi-detached houses, or cottages, close to the railway just beyond the station. In all eight were built around a cul-de-sac leading out of Tolmers Road, and it was one of them which became our new home in Cuffley in 1920. The scattered situation of the newer houses and the abundance of fine trees in the district, e.g the elms around Lower Hanyards, or flanking "Plough" Hill, or the varied trees along East Ridgeway, tended to camouflage any modern buildings, and even now despite the felling of some veterans Cuffley is well favoured with trees.

Plans for developing the district into a garden city had been drawn up about the beginning of the century, and Ebenezer Howard, whose book "Garden Cities of Tomorrow", appearing about 1895, inspired the creation of Letchworth, was at

Two views of Lower Hanyards Farm in watercolour studies by Vivian Hughes dated 1922,
(Catalogue 13 and 9). The tall elms were at the top of the rise of Tolmers Road up from what is now Station
Road. The entrance to the station is out of sight on the right. Vivian was keenly interested in the railways and
a little sketch book of trains he made at Cuffley was given to Jack Gray, but has since been lost.

one time interested in similar proposals for Cuffley.
Had "Green Belt" restrictions, such as are now at
last receiving official sanction, been rigorously
imposed on London at that time, the plan might well
have succeeded, and Cuffley might have been a
small garden city with its own industries, instead of
becoming a dormitory. At any rate elaborate plans
for a "Cuffley Garden Estate" appeared about 1900,
with provision for an industrial zone, as well as
recreation grounds with band-stands and other
amenities, which have not been realised.

The part played by the railway in the development
of this, as of other suburbs, was of course a vital
one, and the fact that railway facilities were long
non-existent in this part of the county is one reason
for its largely unspoilt character, as compared with
that of many districts within the same radius from
the City. Not that the present railway, with its
simple, rural-type stations and occasional impressive
viaducts is in any way a disfigurement, but the

logical aim of railway companies was to obtain
addition-revenue from suburban development. As it
was, however, the costly nature of the new loop line
from Enfield to Stevenage, with its two-mile tunnel
at Ponsbourne, extensive embankments and four
long viaducts necessitated its being completed in
stages. The first section, from Grange Park Junction
to Cuffley, was not opened until April 4th, 1910.
The rest of the line was opened for goods traffic in
March 1918, but not for passenger trains until June
2nd, 1924.

Bricks for the long tunnel were manufactured at a
special works erected on Darnicle Hill south of the
tunnel mouth - and an agreement was made that the
factory with its chimney be demolished on
completion of the work. The railway company had
at one time proposed to erect a station near Darnicle
Hill, to serve the villages of Newgate Street and
Goffs Oak, but were induced by the owners of the
Cuffley Garden Estate to select instead the site

Molly was born in October 1866 at Little Monkham, Epping Forest, Essex. She retired from Cuffley to live in Ireland initially with Arthur's family. She later moved to Durban in South Africa, to live with Barnholt's family, where she is buried. She died in 1956, aged 90.

where the line crosses the Cheshunt Road near the foot of the steep hill to Goffs Oak, for a station, destined for fourteen years to be the terminus for passenger trains.

One might feel inclined to parody Churchill's famous words, by saying that seldom in the annals of railway history have so many trains run so many miles for so few passengers. It must be remembered however that had it not been for the 1914-18 war, the line might well have been opened to Hertford by 1915. The original train service is interesting. Bradshaw (May 1910) shows 14 down trains from London on weekdays, at the rate of about one every hour, and about the same number up to London, the earliest "Up" being after 8am, and the last "Down" arriving at Cuffley at 7.37pm! On Sundays there were but three trains a day, the arrivals at Cuffley being at 11.14am, 3.44pm and 7.07pm.

As far as passenger receipts were concerned, it was the weekend traffic which was more remunerative,

and the Railway Company tried to attract this type of passenger by means of a poster depicting a shepherd in a smock under the invitation "Come to Cuffley", and by a series of guides to weekend rambles. Nor were these efforts unsuccessful. The proprietress of the "Plough" Inn - one of the oldest inhabitants - has told me that in the blackberrying season the Saturday and Sunday trains would be packed, and that in those days, i.e. before 1914, most of the cottages, of which there were more then than in 1920, would provide tea. Even before the coming of the railway the Plough was a favourite Sunday evening rendezvous for Enfield people, and in the days when every squire and farmer had a pony and trap, Cuffley had no transport problems. Even in 1921 the horse was commoner than the car and I well remember getting a lift to Hertford in a Newgate Street market gardiner's (sic) cart, there being no trains beyond Cuffley, and no bus nearer than Cheshunt, 3 miles away.

Coloured pencil studies by Vivian Hughes of the rear of Lower Hanyards Farm, (Catalogue 12), and the Triangle junction in Station Road (*opposite*) facing Brickwall Farm, (Catalogue 30). Only the barn (*centre*) remained, but this old building was to become very important to village social life as the 'Cabin' in later years. The caption is in Vivian's own handwriting.

The 1914-1918 War, though it retarded building development, advertised Cuffley in other ways. Apart from the Zeppelin affair, which first "put Cuffley on the map", the Ponsbourne tunnel had been, providentially, completed in time to afford an air-raid shelter, unofficial of course, to which hundreds from North London would trek night after night, lugging their bedding and other comforts along the track from the station to the tunnel mouth a mile further on, to return to work by the first up train.

In May 1917 there were four season-ticket holders from Cuffley, two of them being the two young sons of the owner of Carbone House, who were then attending a school in Enfield. In 1920 the season ticket holders could be counted on one's fingers, two of them being my younger brothers who travelled all the way to Merchant Taylor's School, then in Charterhouse Square, E.C. The rest were made up by two residents on the Ridgeway, one the father of the two boys; two of our neighbours on the Cuffley Tenants Estate, a bank-manager and a stockbroker; and, finally, one or two people from Goffs Oak. To-day there must be nearer two hundred seasons. We always imagined that the ticket-collectors at Finsbury Park and King's Cross regarded us with a certain amount of mild curiosity, and I was glad to have a chat quite recently with one of the Finsbury Park men who has been on the same job ever since 1920.

As stated above, Enfield became the main shopping centre for us more urban-minded people, and it was customary to talk about returning on "the one", or "the four" or "the six", according to which of the hourly trains one selected, minutes being irrelevant. Enfield doctors and dentists were likewise resorted to, and it was some four or five years before an Enfield lady doctor opened a small surgery at the "Cabin" on certain days of the week. Cars and motor vans were not common, and parcels

THE TRIANGLE, CUFFLEY.   AP. 7TH 1921.

were for many years conveyed from the station by a Goffs Oak carrier. Incidentally, hawkers, many of them interesting personalities, were then and still are a feature of the district. My mother regularly bought stationery from two such travelling vendors.

Whatever Cuffley lacked in urban amenities, was compensated by its simple but sociable amusements. The "Cuffley Ladies", led mainly by the wives of the few families then living on the "Garden Estate", held whist drives in the diminutive school. These were popular and well attended. In the summer there were often flower and vegetable shows, at which the children would give dramatic entertainments.

The vicar of Northaw, being also in charge of St. Andrew's, Cuffley, and the school, was often seen in the district and was popular with both the rural and urban elements. The older people especially missed him when he was moved to a busier parish. As most of the people on the Ridgeway were either retired from business or else something to do with the

Estate, and farmers and labourers were locally employed, the character and tastes of the district were predominantly those of a village. In 1920, and for some years after, there was no train late enough for us to do a London evening theatre, except on Saturdays. All the same, matinees and cinemas were within reach, for the occasional outing. Wireless was quite a novelty, and one of our first acquaintances in Cuffley was a German who used to invite us to listen in through his ear-phones. The Cabin and the School were the two main social centres. I well remember my first Christmas dance at the former - in December 1921, when the population had grown slightly. The floor was definitely overcrowded and one jostled everybody in a most friendly fashion. Prizes were always given both at these occasions and the whist drives, where they were competed for in deadly earnest.

In looking back one cannot help wondering at times whether the semi-rural way of life so

Vivian Hughes' watercolour painted in the summer of 1922 shows the village green with The Plough public house on the right. The long shadows and warm hues below the elms (left) and oak (right) give a sense of calm at the one-time centre of the village. The cast iron pump which supplied the water to Hill Farm, The Plough and the cottages here is just out of view on the left, (Catalogue 23).

congenial to us then, so long as we were pioneers was in reality a sham, destined to become more and more urban in character. It is true that the values of village life can only be experienced in a genuine village, i.e. a place which however near a large town, still does not mainly depend on that town for its livelihood. But it is also true that in Cuffley, and in many other similar outer suburbs, some of the village ideals still flourish, especially the social life. It is a matter for thankfulness that to-day there is the same, or an even greater enthusiasm, among most Cuffley people for local entertainments.

Dramatic shows, concerts, dances, Scouts, Guides, W.E.A. and Mother's Union are all as active here as in many rural districts which are far less accessible to the influence of films, wireless and other forms of escapist or mass produced amusements.

The following notes were added to the above manuscript by his younger brother Arthur and give *us a very brief insight into the life of the artist who painted the beautiful watercolours featured in this book. The paintings add so much to the history of Cuffley, illustrating as they do, the village as it was, the buildings that are no more and the countryside that is so much a part of Cuffley's heritage:*

'The above account was written by my brother I. Vivian Hughes (April 23rd 1900 - October 5th 1954). He was educated at Christ's Hospital, Horsham (1914-1915, 1 year on back with rheumatic fever) and Highgate School, late 1915 reading classics.

He won an open scholarship to Brasenose College, Oxford where he read "greats" and took honours and went into teaching. From early childhood he showed an aptitude for drawing.

His other interests were railways, especially the Old North London, Metropolitan and London Tilbury and Southend, and editing house magazines.'

Vivian's fir tree and cottages study at the entrance to Hill Rise, (Catalogue 27). This was originally the old farm track linking the green, The Plough and Hill Farm with Hanyards Farm. The fir trees survive on the sharp bend here. See also the pictures overleaf.

Chapter Two

Cuffley's Farms

When Vivian Hughes said that Cuffley consisted of little more than a village green surrounded by eight farms at the beginning of the last century he inferred that there was a largely farming population and what must have been a mixture of woods, hedgerows and fields very rich in wildlife. The entry for the parish in the *Victoria History of Counties of England, Hertfordshire* (Volume 2), 1908 reads: 'The people are agricultural; crops of wheat, beans and roots are raised, and a large supply of milk is sent up to London daily'.

Countless generations of farming families would have worried over the annual harvests, bred their own cattle, sheep and pigs. They would have attended market in Hertford or Enfield to buy or sell these animals. Keeping poultry was considered an

activity of the farmer's wife for pin money until intensive indoor rearing appeared in the last century. The farms sold milk and eggs to local people and vegetables were part of the field rotations as crop succeeded crop. Weather conditions dictated the wealth or lack of it for particular years and both Scottish and Welsh farming families bought farms in Hertfordshire during the depression in farming at the end of the 19th century.

We know from the account told to Fred Speakman of an Epping Forest poacher, Alfred Curtis, in his book *A Poacher's Tale* (1960), that bird catchers would travel out from the Lea Valley and London to take wild birds in the farm fields at Cuffley. The flocks of finches were particularly attractive because they could be netted or limed (where lime on branches would cruelly stick the feet of the birds to the wood until found and caged). This was illegal, but there was a lucrative caged bird trade in species such as goldfinches and linnets. Not being captive

(Continued on page 22)

Vivian Hughes' 17 March 1930 watercolour of the entrance to Hill Rise with Hanyards Farm in the distance, (Catalogue 40). The farm buildings are thought to have been the oldest in Cuffley. Inset are the more recent village pump study by Christine M Morter and the authors' photograph, both about 1967.

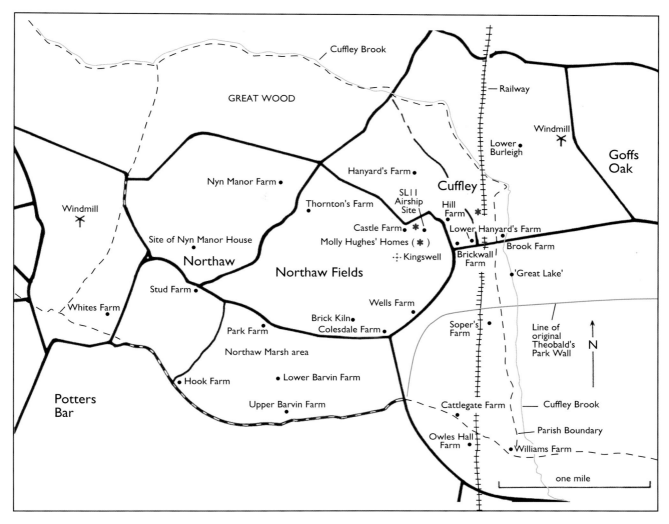

A selection of historic locations and the farms in the vicinity of Cuffley including the route of the Cuffley Brook, the original perimeter of the Theobald's Park wall as it extended into the Parish, the sites of windmills, and the two locations of Molly Hughes' homes. 'Northaw Marsh' and 'Great Lake' were titles coined by the bird watchers during the 1960s for two important wildlife water or wetland habitats.

'Northaw Marsh', (below, left), and the Lower Dell, (below right), facing the sand bank, September 1967, both by kind permission of Trevor James.

Hanyards Farm in 1967. It was demolished in 1971, thirteen years after its fields had been built over. A shop was located on the right side of the picture. The blocked windows on the 17th C timber framed farm house date from the window tax era, (1691 - 1851); the Lowens and Coulters farmed here in the 16th C, later Sam Peacock, John Elsom, Ben Law, John Moore and the Coutte family for A1 Dairies.

bred, many of these died, if not from the shock of capture, then by pining away their loss of flight and life in the wild.

Vivian Hughes also referred to the day-trippers who came by train to pick blackberries during the season. Many Cuffley families would also make for sites such as the 'White Road' leading from Carbone Hill into Northaw Great Wood, filling bags and baskets with berries from the abundant bushes along each side of the route. The railway embankments, where corn buntings would sing, also provided a ready source of 'pick-your-own' fruit. He listed eight farms in 1948, two of which had already been lost.

Of the rest, the oldest of these was Upper Hanyards which had an exceptional farm house. Only two colour pictures are known of this, both transparencies, taken shortly before it was demolished in 1971. The site dated back to the 15th century and the house had a 17th century timber

frame structure with bricked-up windows from the era of the window tax. By this time its fields had been built over, but the house should have been protected. Appropriately, if ironically, the modern site of where the fine old building, farm yard, barns and orchard once stood is named 'Hanyards End'.

The story of Cuffley's Farms is one of lost old country houses as well as fields developed for housing. It is of great regret that they were not preserved in a community which had no manor houses in this part of the Parish and had its origins in mixed farmland between attractive hills of woodlands and parks. Whilst most of the farming families have come and gone, the attractive country architecture of their homes should have survived them.

Upper Hanyards
The farm stood at the junction between Hanyards Lane and Hill Rise until the fields were sold up for housing in the 1950s and the farmhouse, as has been

The Hanyards Farm orchard in April 1967 just before it was built over at the same time as the mighty oak on the orchard margin (*shown overleaf*) was felled. A field oak on the boundary of the enclosure round Hanyards Farm, this tree was one of the largest and oldest in Cuffley. Numerous potatoes were baked and eaten at bonfires by children here in the 1950s when open fields linked Hill Rise with Tolmers Avenue.

described, the longest standing building in Cuffley, was demolished, despite its historic importance, in 1971. In spring the geese from Frank Bennett's corner house, which fed round the farm entrance, would become very territorial and menace children on the corner of the two roads.

It appears to have been the original farm for the village, before others were established, and worked the fields to the Home Wood, following the Cuffley Brook to Cuffley Hill and to the south and west boundaries formed by Plough Hill and Hill Rise. Gerald Millington and John Higgs (1983), note that this was the oldest farm in the Parish for which there are records. Manor Court Rolls of 1429 refer to the land of Thomas Lowyn at Cuffley and the family was probably farming here well before this date. The inventory of a descendent, William Lowen, (new spelling), 130 years later, indicates that the farm is Hanyards. Its original title 'Aviners' meant a trader in fodder and oats. In the inventory,

cattle and feed is listed, and later family inventories throughout the 16th century indicate that a very prosperous family lived here.

By 1700 the farm had expanded to four other houses with barns in the east of the Parish, as records show Cuffley Hill, Lower Hanyards and Brickwall Farms in existence. Coulter Close is named after a farmer at Hanyards who married into the Lowen family: Richard Coulter. He died in 1620. In the last two centuries Sam Peacock, John Elsom and Ben Law were recorded as farmers here and finally the A 1 Dairies established a milk depot managed by the Coutte family. The house and barns were surrounded on the east side by paddocks for the horses which drew the milk carts and there was an extensive old orchard. Milk was delivered throughout the village from this depot and there were regular visits by a blacksmith to keep the horses well shod.

As the horses gave way to electric vans the

(Continued on page 26)

23

This major oak *Quercus robur* was typical of so many in the Parish at one time and stood on the boundary of the Hanyards Farm orchard overlooking the rear gardens of houses in Hill Rise. It was felled in 1967. Old meadows have also been lost and ant-hills (*facing page*) are becoming a rare sight.

Trevor James' study of the meadows by 'Great Lake', looking across to Cuffley's railway viaduct
in the background. This was photographed in October 1976 and illustrates the rapid recovery of
the grass after a long drought. Following the appointment of a Minister to be responsible for the
drought, September had brought long awaited downpours. 1975 had also been a very dry year.

When Melvin Bedford (above) had to leave farming to become a milkman due to wheat dust intolerence the bottles he delivered had large necks and cardboard tops with perforated centres so that a drinking straw could be pushed through easily or the lid lifted out. He saw the A1 Dairies replaced by Express Dairies and many remember his lively wit and cheerful personality. He now lives in retirement with his wife Isabel at their cottage home in Epping Green.

milkmen regretted the loss of one feature of horse transport: the way the horses were trained to walk to the next gateway ready for the bottles to be delivered there. This had always saved the milkmen time and energy. The best known of the delivery men was the tall, thin 'Long George', and later, Melvin Bedford, a great character who was also known to notice where pheasants went up to roost during his winter rounds. Express Dairies later took over the milk distribution from here.

Albert and Mrs Coutte established a farm shop which faced into the yard and provided a very useful service to the residents who otherwise had a lengthy walk to the village. The building for the new housing estates here commenced from 1958.

Lower Hanyards

Vivian Hughes found Lower Hanyards a picturesque source of subject matter for his paintings and nearly all his farm studies are of this site. He painted the

farm from many angles and when Arthur mounted the exhibition of his work in Cuffley he mistakenly labelled one of the Lower Hanyards pictures 'Upper Hanyards', (Appendix 3 : 1, p 239).

Years before there had been a court case between the Rural District Council and Lady Meux (1900-1901) over condemned cottages at Lower Hanyards Farm, the papers of which are in the County Archive (D/EL 5142/1-5):

"Cottages owned by Lady Meux at Lower Hanyards Farm and occupied by James Williams, E. Curtis, (perhaps a relative of the poacher Alfred, see p 19), *and Joseph Hopping. 'Nuisances at Northaw'. December 1900. Well at back of house from which all water used for domestic purposes is taken. There is a pump also and all waste water from this pump runs back into the well. Unfit for drinking purposes. Inspector of Nuisances, Inspector of Health, four dilapidated cottages, tenants reported they had a good supply of water from a*

Lower Hanyards Farm as it faced onto what became Station Road in an undated watercolour by
Vivian Hughes from the 1920s, (Catalogue 3).
He depicts the farmhouse and barns with characteristic detail and sets the elms into the background
to create one of his most appealing studies of old Cuffley sites.

*spring. Analysis later, found to be impure, liable to
serious contamination and unsafe for domestic
purposes. Well 13 feet deep".*

Albert Wombwell was the last owner of the farm
and it is on record that he bought the Great Wood in
April 1923 for £8,500.

The bulk of the 160 acres at Lower Hanyards were
on the opposite side of Station Road, facing the farm
buildings, and known to have been in use in 1786.
Obviously at that time the road would not have been
known as this. The title must have come with the
railway, around 1910. The 1916 Ordnance Survey
shows the whole length of the road as 'Cuffley Hill'.

Apparently established after Upper Hanyards, the
farm was always owned by whoever held the
Lordship of Northaw Manor and after the Enclosure
Award of 1806 a further 104 acres took the land
beyond the present day playing fields. It was
managed by a succession of tenant farmers,
including a William Webb who is known in 1851 to

have employed six labourers there. He was followed
by the Littlechilds and, finally, Albert Wombwell.

It is curious to think that the attractive barns,
which so caught Vivian Hughes' eye, at one time
were used to house exotic animals and one barn
even became the village telephone exchange for a
time. Gerald Millington records:

'Albert Wombwell came from a famous family of
showmen. In 1800, George Wombwell was keeping
a cordwainer's shop (a shoemaker or one who works
in cordovan [Spanish] leather) in Soho. In 1804 he
exhibited two boa-constrictors in a nearby shop with
such success that he formed a menagerie which later
became the first great travelling zoo in England. His
son, and later his grandson, 'Buster' Wombwell,
continued the menagerie, but eventually sold out to
the Bostock family, circus owners, in about 1908, on
condition that the name Wombwell be retained in
the circus title. The Bostock and Wombwell Circus

(Continued on page 30)

Above: Lower Hanyards Farm (c.1921) by Vivian Hughes, (Catalogue 6), showing the two tracks to Tolmers Road from the Station exit.
Left: the same view used in *'A London Family between the Wars'*.
Top right: Vivian's watercolour of Tolmers Road and barn of Lower Hanyards Farm and, below, a photograph of the same scene. Note railway signal, Lamb's thatched cottage and 'Lanthorne' cafe in middle distance, (Catalogue 8).

The 'A1' Dairies
(POTTERS BAR) LTD.

Above: Old types of milk bottles featured in this illustration from an A1 Dairies advertisement delivered to villagers from what they then called 'Hanyards Model Farm', which was Upper Hanyards, at the junction of Hill Rise and Hanyards Lane.

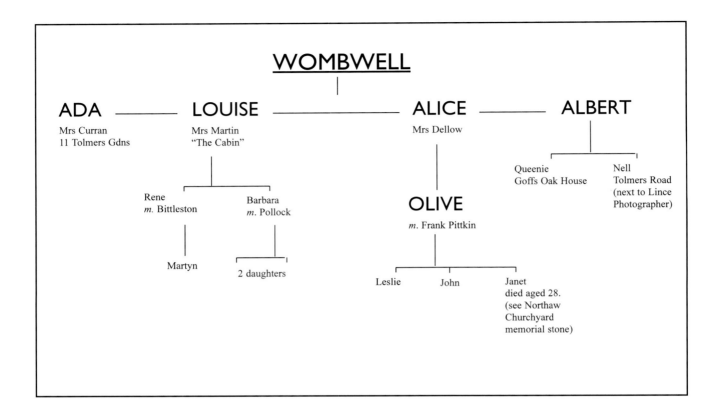

WOMBWELL

ADA — **LOUISE** —————— **ALICE** — **ALBERT**

Mrs Curran
11 Tolmers Gdns

Mrs Martin
"The Cabin"

Mrs Dellow

Rene
m. Bittleston

Barbara
m. Pollock

Queenie
Goffs Oak House

Nell
Tolmers Road
(next to Lince
Photographer)

OLIVE

m. Frank Pittkin

Martyn

2 daughters

Leslie   John   Janet
died aged 28.
(see Northaw
Churchyard
memorial stone)

The Wombwell's came to own Lower Hanyards, Hill Farm and the Great Wood. As well as being a famous Cuffley family, their name is firmly established in circus history and amongst showpeople generally. The farm had performing animals housed in the buildings before it was demolished in the 1930s. Descendants have kindly given us the above information. (See photo of Martyn Bittleston on page 256).

continued long after the First World War and had winter quarters for animals at Goffs Oak House. Many old Cuffley residents can remember seeing or hearing the different varieties of animals (camels, elephants, lions and circus horses) which were exercised on Lower Cuffley Farm. The Farm was eventually demolished in the 1930s to make way for Tolmers Gardens, and the Cuffley Hotel was built on the farmyard pond.'

Brickwall Farm

Part of the old brick wall after which Brickwall farm was named can be seen in a photograph of the junction of Plough Hill with Station Road, facing south towards Northaw Road East. It included a built-in post box where Vivian made a drawing of the Cabin, the last surviving barn here. The rest of the farm and outbuildings burnt down in 1900. The Cabin became the centre for the community entertainments in Cuffley until it was replaced by

the Cuffley Hall, Library and Health Centre in 1973. The Cabin, railway station and shops had created a nucleus of activity away from the original village green and its well pump at the top of Plough Hill.

Ownership by the Buckeridge family, recorded in the Parish as early as 1674, shows that the farm was certainly here in 1753. It was probably managed by tenants and was one of the smallest farms in the parish with fields located on the present site of St Andrews Church and beyond, along the west side of Northaw Road.

Castle Farm

Once described as a Keeper's Lodge to Enfield Chase, (possibly linked with the Keeper's Lodge on the edge of Home Wood), Castle Farm was hidden behind the bend on The Ridgeway where it joins the East Ridgeway and enjoyed commanding views over the valley. Something of a folly in appearance, it was castellated on one side with mock battlements

The Cabin in 1918 (*above, left*): the last structure of Brickwall Farm not burnt down in 1900. In 1756 it was recorded as being farmed by the Buckeridge family, who were also described as having lived in the Parish during the 17th C. The Wombwells converted the Cabin to become a village hall, with living accommodation, and Albert Wombwell moved to Lower Hanyards Farm in 1915 when his sister, Mrs Martin, came to live there. Initially, Mrs Martin lived in two army huts shown in a contemporary photograph of the Cabin. She is shown seated with her two daughters. *Right*, a 1967 bill from Wells Farm, (named after the well and its medicinal waters) when it operated as a garden centre in Northaw Road East.

and had two turrets, one on either side of the house. Recorded from the mid 19th century, all these buildings were cleared in the 1960s to be replaced by Cuffley Hills Farm. The site is now occupied by a modern house, Ridgemount, slightly nearer the road than the original location of Castle Farm.

Wells Farm
An attractive, simple mid-19th century farm house very like Colesdale and Thornton's Farms, Wells was known for its unusual staddles on the barns. Staddles were stilts to protect grain stores from rats and mice that could not climb round the top section and the familiar types are mushroom-shaped stones. Here they were cast iron. In an article *'Staddle, stilt or mushroom'* in The Hertfordshire Countryside in 1968, Pat Klijn noted: 'At Wells Farm, Cuffley, the single storey barn stands on the more unusual iron supports. These are possibly replacements for old crumbled stones. The barn has been standing since

the farmhouse was built in 1851 and is still used as a store and for the annual turkey plucking'.

It was demolished in 1978 and a new house with stable was built following a hundred years of various ownerships and a one-time merger with Colesdale Farm. Gower Morgan ran a garden centre and poultry farm from here after World War 2.

Brook Farm (*'Cuffley Farm', 'Pantiles'*)
Described in detail thanks to Gareth Thomas' research in Clark (2001), Cuffley School has a photograph of children visiting the farm on a project with their teacher, Mrs Brenda Brown, who also took the group picture, outside the front door in the 1990s. The Thomas family has lived and worked here since 1941 and in recent years the farm has taken over the fields of Burnt Farm to the south, as far as the Middlesex border. Notes on the wildlife were also given with the above reference and include the increase in fox, badger and muntjac deer

Brenda Brown's picture of a class from Cuffley School visiting Brook Farm. The farm,
named after the Cuffley Brook, featured in Clark, 2001, (see bibliography) and Alan Burn,
a teacher at Cuffley Camp, recorded the crops and field names in 1966. He listed 189 acres
under cultivation, 17 acres of permanent pasture and 2 acres of buildings.

populations in the last few decades whilst hare numbers have diminished. Rabbit damage to crops has again become significant because their numbers have increased as resistance to myxomatosis has grown. The pastures around the farmyard where the Cuffley Brook still flows much as it always has, without pipes or artificial banks, are particularly attractive. An old name for the farm was *'Pantiles'*. This probably came from the type of roof tile used on the building which has an S-shaped cross-section, laid so that the downward curve of one tile overlaps the upward curve of the adjoining tile.

Colesdale Farm

The farm is remembered as a place where crocuses smothered the garden in the 1940s and it was popular to have teas on fine afternoons in the summer there. It is also well known as the venue for the Point-to-Point race meetings. During the Second World War years gleanings from the stubble was made available as local chicken food for villagers to give to their hens. This field is now used for the summer car boot sales.

Hill Farm

This striking farm complex once stood on the original village green and featured a large pond by the road. The earliest photograph we have, of about 1900, (overleaf) shows flint and brick construction and this was later clad in part by the weather boarding to match the barns. It narrowly missed destruction from the falling airship in 1916. Soldiers were billeted there during the operation to clear up the airship wreckage. Every scrap of food and milk was used up in refreshments, the Grays recall, for the flocks of visitors and troops. The farm was demolished less than twenty years later when Kingsmead was built here in the 1930s and from his writings we know that Vivian Hughes regretted the loss of the old timbered barn in particular, (p 11).

In 1966 Brook Farm's fields and crops were called:
'Home', 'Five Acre', 'Sixteen Acre' and 'Second', *ryegrass*; 'Brook', *kale*; 'Meadway', 'Hill', 'Seventeen Acre' and 'The Roughs', *4 year grass ley*; 'Stallion', 'Chalk Pit', 'Home Paddock' and 'Meadow', *permanent pasture*; 'Wood', 'Woodland Way' and 'Pylon', *winter wheat*; 'The Paddocks', *ryegrass clover*; 'Ten Acre', *5 year ley*; 'Eight Acre', *winter oats*; 'Twelve Acre' and 'The Common', *spring barley*.

Nellie Wharf (page 205) worked for the Grays at the farm in 1915. She was one of 19 children, 4 of whom grew to adult life and most worked on Sopers and other local farms. Nellie was the only member of the family who learnt to read and write.

Sopers Farm

Cathale Priory was said to have stood near Sopers Farm, with the lake to the east, known as 'Fishponds'. Cottages from Sopers Farm were occupied for many years by the Richardson family in the 1940s. These were situated in the fields on the left of the railway as it leaves Cuffley in the direction of London. The path takes a sharp bend where the semi-detached cottages housed the grandparents and unmarried children on one side and another son, who also worked on the farm, and his large family, next door. There was no road to the houses and all the family had to reach the village via the path under the railway bridge and alongside the

Playing Fields or along the edges of the fields to link up with Station Road where Sopers Road now exists. Many of the children attended Cuffley School in the second world war. During the 1950s Mrs Richardson, the grandmother of the family, helped as a cleaner over the shop known as Novelties. She was a remarkably strong character, never miserable, fond of flower-covered hats, was lavish with furniture polish and enjoyed a chat. Her usual greeting was to do with the weather such as 'misty old morn', but then it probably was when you lived in the middle of a damp field. When the cottages were demolished the family was moved to Northaw from where one day, when the buses were cancelled, Mrs Richardson walked through the snow drifts to keep her appointment with the furniture polish.

Thorntons Farm (*'Brickkiln'*)

Thorntons Farm is situated at the foot of Vineyards
(Continued on page 38)

33

Hill Farm about 1900 when it was farmed by John Elsom. His son, Vic Elsom was born here and went
on to run The Sun Inn at Northaw where Barbara Stanbrook tells us you could have tea for 1/3 or 1/6
with a boiled egg. The Grays rented the farm from the Wombwells during WW1, (*see p 30*). The mighty
elm, probably *Ulmus carpinifolia*, next to Hill Farm and the village pump, May 1970, by Trevor James.

Prior to the Elsoms, Sam Peacock farmed at Hill Farm, which faced the Plough Public House on the original Cuffley village green. Under John Elsom the land was managed with the fields of Hanyards Farm. The buildings became the site office for the bungalow development to the rear prior to demolition in the 1930s.
Below: Betty Lanham very kindly had her painting of The Plough, Church, Hill Farm barn and distant Home Wood copied for us from her home in Somerset. We have no information on the artist, F W Fitch, but the trees suggest that the meet of the hunt took place on a wet November or December morning *in* about 1912 or 1913. Betty tells us that the painting was originally in the collection of the late Brian Deer (or Dia).

Hill Farm in about 1916, from the rear, facing the Plough Public House, in a watercolour by A W Head, via John Higgs, who tells us that the screen outside The Plough was the backdrop to a coconut shy, left over after a Bank Holiday. (See also Molly Hughes, p 164, in her book '*A London Family between the Wars*', 1940). The two children standing are the right age and size for Joan and Jack Gray, (p 67), who lived in the farm at that time.

Colesdale Farm, pictured by Trevor James in September 1967. (See also p 146). The original house was built around 1825 for John Whaley and subsequent farmers included Benjamin Baugh, Charles Claridge, Robert Morgan, James Troake and Ken Dallyn.

Park farm photographed in March 1977 by Trevor James. It was demolished in 1980.

Nyn Manor Farm with the Ridgeway and Cuffley in the background, January 1975, by Trevor James.

Nyn Manor Farm entrance and cottages in 1966: with a clotted cream sign. In his youth, Graham Rust (p 145) worked at this farm during one summer holiday.

Thorntons farm viewed from the footpath to Cuffley by Trevor James in January 1975, showing the ancient Frame Oak on the centre right of the picture. Such major oaks were named on early maps and include this old tree, the Cucumber Oak and Dog Kennel Oak in the Parish as well as the adjoining Goff's Oak, on Dury & Andrews' map of 1766, (see p 197).

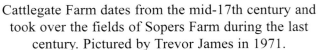

Cattlegate Farm dates from the mid-17th century and took over the fields of Sopers Farm during the last century. Pictured by Trevor James in 1971.

The 'special' daffodil recorded by Thorntons Farm: the double *Narcissus*, 'Vincent Sion', or 'Van Sion' (see text below left).

Road on the left hand side on the way to Northaw. Two name changes are worthy of note here because 'Thorntons' replaced the title of 'Brickkiln' Farm when it was named after an occupier, Henry Thornton, who farmed here in 1851, and Vineyards Road used to be called Handpost Hill. It was here, in 1923, in her 'Notes on Northaw and District' that Mrs Wilson-Fox (p 154) told of a field of 'Vincent Sion' daffodils past Thorntons Farm. This double trumpet daffodil came to England from Florence in about 1620 and it is possible that there were gardens or pleasure grounds here at the entrance to a path leading to the spa in the days when people travelled to Cuffley to take the waters. (A Sion colony also survives near Marden House in Tewin). Across the road was Lime Kiln Farm. A document transferring farm, kilns and paddock from the Hon Robert Arthur Talbot Gascoyne, Marquess of Salisbury, to John Pearson Kidston for £63.2s.5d. and a further 9 acres for £9.2s.2d, is dated 11 April 1867.

Thorntons Farm is of particular note for its forward thinking in wildlife conservation in the 1960s. At a time when badgers elsewhere were frequently gassed along with foxes and rabbits, the Tate Brothers were always careful to see that the occupants of their active badger sett survived the local persecutions of what is now a fully protected species. Chris Tate looked after an orphan badger cub before returning it, healthy and recovered from a bite wound, to the setts.

He allowed regular monitoring of the sett entrances on the land and a tenant at the farm, Tom Clarke, confirmed flints from the nearby Dell to be hand tools of what they then termed 'Forest Folk'. These early tribes lived at the site as hunter-gatherers or partly as early farming people, about six or eight thousand years ago. The badgers still flourish in the sand here and continued to be well cared for after the Tate family retired to Norfolk. Beyond the farm, the Dell has largely lost its original value as an old

The first colour photograph of a badger at Thorntons Farm in 1962 unexpectedly revealed the badger to be backing out of the sett entrance rolling a ball of clay between its front claws. This seemed to be part of the grooming process and clay lumps with badger hairs were later found around the spoil during daytime visits to the sett. Clay mixes with the sand in the huge mounds of excavated soil outside the earths and this entrance to the sett complex still exists today. The sett is thought to be well over a hundred years old. The Tate family kindly gave permission for the watching and photography at the time. An injured cub was looked after by Chris Tate and returned to the colony after Miss Freak, the Potters Bar vet, successfully treated a wound.

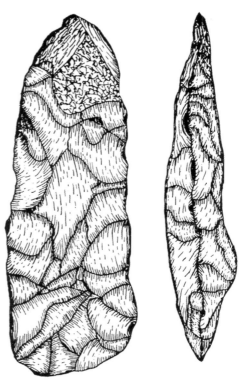

Tom Clarke, who lived on the farm in the 1960s, confirmed that flint hand tools found in the Dell were from early settlements in the valley. This drawing of two views of one of the hand tools found at Thorntons Farm is taken from one of John Lee's excellent papers, 1977 & 1983 (see p 245).

site and habitat for wildlife. Restoration is needed. **Cattlegate Farm, Nyn Manor Farm, Hook Farm, Park Farm, Upper Barvin and Lower Barvin, White's Farm** and **William's Farm** are all old farm sites either on the southern Parish border or on the Northaw village side.

Park Farm was recorded as early as 1756, but was allowed to become derelict and was demolished in 1980. In its heyday it had taken over the Lower Barvin farm land and by 1851 was the largest farm in the Parish. By the 1880s Sam Peacock farmed here before moving to Hanyards Farm.

Upper Barvin is thought to be built on a mediaeval site. Nyn Manor Farm was formed when 142 acres of land on Nyn Park House Farm were united with the 195 acres of Lodgehill Farm. The latter had been occupied by the Wackett family in the 18th century, (M & H, 83).

There were ten people listed as farmers or with farming connections in *Kelly's Directory* for 1929:

Herbert Blowes, who was farm baliff to George Painter Esq of Wells Farm, telephone Cuffley 34;
Samuel Dallyn, farmer, Park Farm, Potter Bar 267;
Ralph Gibbons, poultry farmer;
Alex MacMillan, farmer, Nyn Manor, Cuffley 49;
John Moore, farmer, Upper Hanyards Farm;
Alfred Tredgold, poultry farmer;
Jasper Troak, farmer, Colesdale Farm, Cuffley 52;
David Williams, farmer, Cattlegate Farm, (where the family still farms. Their cousins Ivor & Vaughan continue to farm at Tewin);
Albert Wombwell, farmer, Lower Hanyards, Cuffley 14.

Jack Gray (see page 67) has told us that when his parents rented Hill Farm, which stood opposite The Plough public house, their landlord was Mr Wombwell. They then rented the cottage where Molly Hughes later joined them with her young family. Both the Grays and the Hughes later built houses in East Ridgeway.

Vivian Hughes' Castle Farm watercolour, (Catalogue 43), from about 1923 shows Northaw Church in the distance over the fields and one of the decorative tops to the farm house's end towers. The west side was castellated and in 1851 the building was described as having a moat.

Two farmers here early in the last century were Isaac Hurt and Edward Littlechild.

Cuffley Hills Farm (seen from the fields, below, February 1969) replaced the building in the early 1960s, to the deep regret of the Cuffley artist Graham Rust, amongst others, (see p 145).

The Point-to-Point races at Colesdale Farm in the Northaw Fields have a long tradition which continues today. This is from a Hertfordshire Federation of Women's Institutes postcard sent in 1975. When a horse landed amongst spectators at a jump in the 1960s the picture made a double page spread in the Sunday Pictorial. Regular car-boot sales (*below*) on Northaw Common, also at Colesdale Farm, are a popular summer event now. (The site of the King's Well is on the hill behind, to the left of the water works roof in the distance).

The Great Wood viewed looking westward from the New Park Farm fields below Newgate Street where Milbrook Golf Course has been constructed. The wildlife interest in the wood stems largely from its origin as wood-pasture. The flora reflects it having been a former heath rather than an ancient, coppiced wood.

Chapter Three

Northaw Great Wood

Farming and wildlife are inextricably linked and both have flourished in the Parish despite the growth in road traffic and developments in housing. Hedgerows have been lost in places, but more have survived than in many parts of the county. The Parish and country towards Broxbourne has always been very well wooded, too.

Wildlife thus has a stronghold across the north and north-west boundaries of the Parish where only the Ridgeway (built as a toll road in 1811) divides the Great Wood from the well-wooded estate of Nyn. The countryside here is still the jewel in the crown as far as our natural history is concerned, although the Cuffley Brook (p 54) is a link to the attractive field and woodland habitats around Brook Farm and

the Theobalds estate on the south-east borders. Whilst Nyn remains a private estate, the Great Wood has welcomed visitors to its car park since 1938, following the acquisition of the wood by Hertfordshire County Council (north to the Cuffley Brook Parish boundary), in 1937. Much of this area is leased to Welwyn & Hatfield District Council, but HCC, (see p 257), very perceptively established a highly successful School Camp on the south-east boundary with Carbone Hill. Most of the school population of Hertfordshire has visited this camp at some stage in their education and the whole woodland attracts thousands of visitors each year.

You can still sense in this Country Park something of the 'trackless waste' that formerly covered the major part of the Parishes of Hatfield and Northaw. The wood was left and largely re-planted as the originally wooded part of Northaw Common. Whilst 'Northaw' is derived from 'North Haga' after 948, ('North Enclosure'), 'Cuffley' or 'Kuffele' as it was

Until the last century the wood was much more open, without the dense habitats of largely unmanaged trees it later became. Many insects typical of wood-pasture have been recorded here. Birds like the redstarts that were present in summer regularly up to recent times also reflect this origin.

known from 1228 until it became Coffley and then Cuffley by the 17th century, appears to be derived from someone called Kuffa. 'Leah' referred to a clearing in a wood and 'Cuffa's Lea' or, finally, 'Cuffley', was therefore originally just 'a clearing in the woods', within the once very extensive Enfield Chace.

Early records show that in 1550 the Great Wood included 10,000 oak and beech trees to a value of £350, (equivalent to perhaps £3.5m now). We can, however, see from the map detail that by 1766 Great Wood and Nyn were part of a vast forest pasture habitat rather than the dense canopy woodland we know today. In contrast it showed nearby Wormley Woods as thick with mature trees, but our Parish would have resembled the New Forest's attractive mixture of open grazed areas and woods we see in modern Hampshire.

The district is still well wooded, especially on the north-east side, towards Broxbourne. Poor quality

soil of heavy clay and, in places, boulders, was known to ruin the early types of plough which meant that any fields created were restricted to rough pasture. Only in modern times has the use of much more powerful equipment made arable working (with fertilizers and sprays) possible and economic. Most of the woodland has, however, survived this revolution in agriculture.

A thatched cottage stood up to the 1930s at the cross-roads from Cuffley which link The Ridgeway with Newgate Street via Carbone Hill to the north, and Northaw Village via Handpost Hill, to the west. At the Queenswood end, in front of Vine Cottage, once stood a similar cottage. At junctions, both might have been for toll collections.

Houses were built opposite the wood on the Nyn side of the road in the late 1930s, but were initially very hard to sell during fuel shortages in World War II. The wood lines the road opposite the houses and is particularly attractive with trees either side along

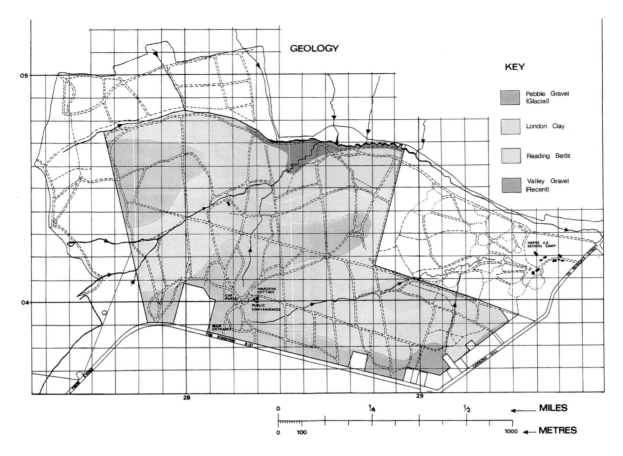

The Great Wood Country Park Management Plan of 1973 showing the geology and location
of the School Camp. Generations of children have walked to the village from here to shop
in Cuffley for postcards and souvenirs before leaving for home after stays at the Camp.

the 'switchbacks' where the road was constructed
following the hill contours with repeated
undulations, (see picture, p 234).

The modern visitor to the Great Wood car park is
first greeted by the dense introduced rhododendron
bushes, which now penetrate into the trees. They are
full of colour early in the year and provide cover for
deer, but are invasive, harbour oak 'black spot' and
efforts have been made to restrict their spread.

Diagrams by Graham Horsley and Peter Chance
for the Northaw Great Wood book, (1966) show the
tree types. In this book the wild life was described
in detail by members of the *British Naturalists'
Association*, enthusiastically encouraged by the
editor, Bryan Sage. It was published by HCC and
sold out rapidly. A reprint was made and copies are
occasionally found in local bookshops. Bryan had
made regular visits to the wood during the 1950s
and had already published *A History of the Birds of
Hertfordshire* (1957).

It was one of the first natural history studies of an
individual wood of its kind and Bryan has kindly
given us permission to reproduce material. New
information on the wildlife present is always needed
and all visitors are encouraged to record what they
find. If you are not familiar with the different types
of trees, for example, it is easy to start to identify
them. There are excellent field guides for all levels
of interest and they help observers to list the other
plants and animals they may see, too.

As you gain confidence and compile records these
can be vital in the conservation of these subjects.
Observers send information to the *Hertfordshire
Natural History Society* County Recorders and the
information is then made centrally available at The
Biological Records Centre at County Hall. The
Society publishes authorative papers on the wild life
of the County in its *Hertfordshire Naturalist*,
organises meetings and includes specialist groups
for birds, dragonflies, moths, and mammals.

The jacket design for the 1966 book on Northaw Great Wood which was compiled by members of the Hertfordshire & North Middlesex Branch of the British Naturalists' Association. It featured an owl with pheasant, muntjac and badger footprints.

Wild flowers and fungi are of immediate appeal and the woodland species make good photographic subjects. Mushrooms and toadstools may not, however, be removed from the Great Wood even if you are certain they are edible and wish to cook them. The code in Countryside Parks is to leave what you find for those who follow to enjoy.

The footpaths are well defined and if you get lost in dense fog, the slope down to the Cuffley Brook will always guide you out of the wood. The water runs down hill, west to east, between meandering banks with often very deep gullies where the soil has been worn away over the centuries. As an alternative to following the stream out, if you keep your back to the stream and continue to climb the hill, you will come out onto the Ridgeway or find yourself back in the car park.

The wood is recognised for its wildlife interest and is listed as a *Site of Special Scientific Interest* (a 'triple S I' as the term is abbreviated by *English*

Nature.) It covers over 217 hectares (537 acres) and has field study accommodation within the School Camp area. There is no public access to this without permission, nor to the Gascoyne Cecil estate land on the Hatfield Parish side of the Brook, where good forestry management is replacing the fir plantation with broad-leaved species. The lack of ancient oaks in the main wood is explained by the sales of them in 1874, (4,100) and 1877, (when 3000 mature trees and saplings were sold). Conifers were planted in Broombarns and ash trees in the Coldharbour plantation after 1918.

A major loss since the book was written has been the mature elm, which did so much to embellish the countryside and villages of Hertfordshire as well as provide habitats for insects, birds and bats in particular. Although it has always been a type of tree of the hedgerows and borders rather than dense woodland, suckers still grow where tall trees once stood in the wood. They become diseased at about

'*On the way to Newgate street*' by Vivian Hughes shows a glimpse of the more open Great Wood in 1939, also reflected in Frank Mead's 1930s study here of Major George Smith-Bosanquet's Hounds (by kind permission of Jim Meads).

Whilst the tree growth has increased in the woods, Carbone Hill, in 2002, has changed little from when Vivian stood here to draw the view (*left*) towards the Great Wood.

10 years of age due to fungal infection introduced by elm bark beetles. It was called 'Dutch' elm disease because the first link with the beetle and infection was made in Holland: the actual fungus was introduced from Canada about 40 years ago.

The School Camp badger sett has also been lost and part of the Parish disappeared as the edge of the SSSI was bulldozed in the 1970s. The course of the stream as it approached Postern Bridge was altered with this apparently unauthorized boundary change and the road now floods through the spinney during heavy rain where once the Brook drained the field to the bridge. Part of a new golf course has been allowed to replace this attractive wooded slope and the days when children would watch at the badger sett here are now just a memory.

Footprints of the muntjac deer are familiar throughout the wood and larger spoor may be found when the fallow, and more rarely, roe deer, visit from the Hatfield side. Muntjac colonised the Parish

in the 1950s as they spread across Hertfordshire from the Duke of Bedford's estate. The escape of the deer he introduced to the park at Woburn have resulted in Chinese water-deer also being seen in the county.

The most conspicuous changes in the bird life since the account of the wood was written in the 1960s have been the losses of the redstarts, hawfinches, nightingales, barn owls and tree sparrows. On the positive side, sparrow-hawks have returned and the collared doves, now familiar on the perimeter of the wood, were unknown in Britain at that time.

Amongst the butterflies, speckled wood had disappeared by the 1960s, but has recovered dramatically in recent times and is once again familiar in the wood. Wall browns were widespread then, but are never seen in the county now, let alone in the parish. Natural fluctuations in populations of animals have to be taken into account when

Trevor James' photograph of the School Camp in Northaw Great Wood suggests sparse facilities in 1970. Many ancient pollarded hornbeams feature here along the Cuffley Brook and along paths, (*left*, 1963; *above* 2001). Pollarding involved cropping wood from a height on the tree above deer or cattle browsing whilst coppicing saw the trees cut to near ground level. Young growth could be harvested at intervals and the trees provided continuous supplies of sustainable wood for hundreds of years. Hornbeams thus reach great ages through constant management and are for all intents and purposes 'immortal'. The name probably derives from their very hard wood branches which, when fallen, resemble scattered deer antlers or 'horns' - *Baum*: Anglo-Saxon for tree.

assessing how permanent a loss may be, but we have lost more species than we have gained.

Lichens, mosses, liverworts, amphibians, reptiles, beetles, snails, slugs and woodlice were also described in the Great Wood book. Many of the insects, including ants, bees, wasps, moths and flies were not covered, but observations have been made of them since then. Your own records may extend this knowledge greatly and will be welcomed by the Natural History Society Recorders, (see p 257). Conservation can only be successful when information about sites is available centrally. In a parish so near to Greater London almost anywhere is threatened with urban development. Details of how to join the *Hertfordshire Natural History Society*, (Trevor James chairs the Recorders Committee), *Hertfordshire & Middlesex Wildlife Trust*, *The British Naturalists Association* and the nearest wildlife group, *Cheshunt Natural History Society*, are kept in libraries and on the internet.

Field meetings allow members to learn from each other as they look for and identify types of plants or animals, (or their tracks and signs), along the way. Indoor meetings bring speakers to talk about their specialist subjects and conferences concentrate on several aspects of a single theme.

The Biological Records Centre processes and maps the information sent in from different organisations and individuals to help with planning applications and conservation policy generally in the county.

(When one of the authors first met Trevor James, on 5 May 1962, he was bird watching in the Northaw Fields. They both attended the same school via Cuffley station. Trevor recorded in his diary that he was counting whitethroats at the time: 4 singing males in the Dell and 4 in the Northaw Fields. He also saw a cuckoo and a common partridge before walking to Sopers viaduct where he recorded a reed bunting, two more partridges and a single mallard on 'Great Lake' - the lake in Theobalds Park).

Oak trees in Northaw Great Wood in 1999
by Trevor James. The oaks were left as
'standards' and cropped at much longer
intervals than the hornbeams

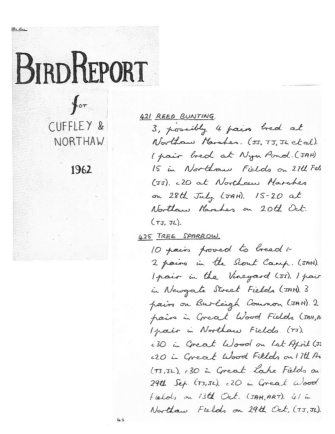

The second *Cuffley Bird Report* from 1962.
The reports covered a five year period and
were edited by Trevor James from local
recorders' material (see text).

Chapter Four

Wildlife recording

Information on the wildlife of the Parish has long
been published in the Transactions of the
Hertfordshire Natural History Society with flora and
fauna that reflect a rich variety of habitats. These
records and studies now appear as the *Hertfordshire
Naturalist*. Increasingly Northaw Great Wood
featured in Hayward and, later, Sage's annual bird
reports in the 1950s. Valuable detail came by way of
the 'Cuffley Bird Reports' in the 1960s. These have
nesting records and estimates of numbers that had
not been attempted before. Molly Hughes (1940)
had published a few notes on the birds and
mammals seen in her garden and the woods, but for
five years, between 1961 and 1965, Cuffley had its
own annual summary of the birds recorded in the
Parish. It was largely the work of a schoolboy,

Trevor James, who attended Hertford Grammar
School, now Richard Hale School. Trevor had
grown up in King James Avenue and his parents
were well known in the *Cuffley Horticultural
Society*.

When the final report was in preparation, Trevor
recognised that many of the group of watchers who
contributed records were dispersing, largely to
Higher Education, and commented: 'Lastly it
remains to be mentioned that this is almost certain
to be the last report for the district, and completes a
five year study period beginning in 1961. Much
information has been obtained in these years and
perhaps more will be forthcoming at a later date.'

The reports are a unique snapshot of the status of
the village wildlife at a time when bird watching
was not the popular pastime it has become. An
interest in conservation was only just beginning to
be stirred by books such as *Silent Spring* by Rachel
Carson (1961).

Eric Hosking's classic study of a Hawfinch at the nest with young from the Great Wood book, (1966) by kind permission of David Hosking and the editor of the book. Chapters were written by Bryan Sage and members of the *British Naturalists' Association*.

Amazingly, Trevor wrote out in long hand each copy of the first 3 reports and even produced a coloured map of the survey area in the first issue. He listed the contributors as P. Chance, M. Clark, A. Gladwin, A. Harris, G. Hart, M. Honnor (who occasionally still travels from Barnet to help out in the Cuffley Chemist shop), G. Horsley, A. Hudson, J. Jack, V. Jeffrey, I. James, J. Lines, D. Monk, B. Sage, R. Sinden, A. Tanner and Mr Woodbridge, who ran Cuffley Building Supplies.

The group made a special effort to distinguish how many individual owls were present and went to different parts of the parish to listen for the various species calling at night. Trevor was able to give a table of types and numbers by combining the times and results from each recorder. What stands out today is the number of owls, especially barn owls, which are now so rare in the county. In 1963 the survey recorded on 1 April: 28 tawny owls, 2 little owls, 5 barn owls (and a long-eared owl in July).

The commoner species were not neglected and special reports were made on moorhen and gull numbers. Alan Hudson analysed 41 nests of blackbirds and 22 of song thrushes in 1962. The blackbirds laid 95 eggs in total, hatched an average of 1.07 nestlings and reared an average of 1.03 fledglings. The song thrushes hatched 1.59 and reared an average of 0.88 fledglings. The pressures on the birds was described vividly: 44 blackbird eggs stolen by human predators; 24 song thrush eggs stolen by humans; 25 nests were deserted after one or more eggs were taken, (5 of these were song thrush); 18 had their contents 'sucked after damage by predators other than human'; (10 of these were song thrush). There had been a cold spring and clutch sizes were generally low. Nest height, species of trees or shrubs used and the colour of eggs were additional aspects of the report. It is illegal to take bird eggs and this is no longer the threat it used to be, apart from a minority of persistent egg collectors

Below: Fly agaric fungi in October rain. Described as 'under the birch, frequent' in the Northaw Great Wood book by the authors of the *Toadstools and other fungi* chapter, R G and P H White. The wood is a favourite site for autumn 'fungus forays' and this is just one of over 300 species recorded in the checklist for the wood. The species, *Amanita muscaria*, is one of the best known of all types but is both poisonous and hallucinogenic.

Above: a study of bracken in winter taken in Northaw Great Wood in 1960. 'Much of the undergrowth in the drier and better drained parts of the wood consists of bracken and bramble. The bracken is dense and almost completely prevents other plants from growing with it. In the spring, however, before the bracken has grown up there are large patches of bluebells and wood anenomes', wrote Eileen Aspden in the Northaw Great Wood book *Wild Flowers* chapter, (1966).

who threaten the rarer raptors nationally in particular. However, the increase in magpies due to the road casualties our vehicles leave, and the popularity of cats has replaced the direct persecution of birds by humans with the indirect, but vast, losses of fledglings and adults by crow species and pets.

Modern surveys show a marked decline in the song thrush numbers in particular and because common species were not neglected in the reports, we can judge the scale of such changes in bird populations. Who would have thought, for example, in the 1960s that the common house sparrow would disappear from many localities over the following forty years?

Although the reduction in the numbers of birds is significant, more dramatic is the disappearance of whole species in such a brief period of history: barn owl, wryneck, redstart, nightingale, hawfinch and tree sparrow are no longer recorded here and there are signficant reductions in many other unusual types. The lapwings that were described as

'breeding and in large numbers' in 1962 are now unknown as breeding birds, just occasional winter visitors. Their nests were so abundant 60 years ago that their eggs were collected as a food supplement rather like quail eggs are sold today, to be hard-boiled and then easily peeled for consumption with salads. In the 1960 reports flocks of 60, 45, 120, and 75 were regularly recorded.

As many as 70 tree sparrows were recorded in one flock (1964) and 18 hawfinches (1965). A total of 19 redstarts were seen in Northaw Great Wood (1964) and fluctuations in singing nightingales were typically from 2 in 1962 up to 7 in 1965. Sparrow-hawks were unknown to the young bird watchers of the day because they had already disappeared due to persistent chemicals in the food chain. Thanks to legislation on chemicals, these raptors have since recovered and the first appearances of individual collared doves were also noted in the Bird Report. Woodland management in the 1930s saw wide

Oak-with-hornbeam woods feature bluebells in Hertfordshire. Twelve tawny owls were recorded calling in April 1963 in the Cuffley Bird Report, edited by Trevor James.

The old beech (*left*) in Home Wood, 1961, had a stock dove nest, then a tawny owl nest in its hollow trunk the following year.
Trevor James is shown in January 1988 with his parents Joe and Ivy who were very active in Cuffley's Horticulture and Art Club circles.

clearings created which allowed light into sites. Many species of bird and butterfly, for example, need fallen trees or woodland harvesting by owners to create low shrub layers for food, shelter and breeding. The traditional cropping of wood by coppicing which left standard oaks can look devastating to the uninitiated. As a result there is great opposition to any felling in the woods, yet the trees re-grow and some coppice stools elsewhere can be thousands of years old. Here we have pollarded hornbeams of some 300 years. It is essential for the maintenance of our wild life that these activities continue, yet subsidies to landowners and conservation payments in general are rarely made conditional on such activities.

Without the insect life, the shrub layers for the protection of their nesting sites and flowers which re-appear constantly as woodland is managed, the birds disappear, too. In the middle of Great Wood in summer there are very few birds to be seen and this

is now a typical pattern repeated throughout the countryside. Dense, unmanaged woodland, global warming and the introduction of a prolific woodland predator of eggs, the grey squirrel, has brought many changes. Thanks to biological recording, like the *Cuffley Bird Report*, we have an accurate record of what has happened.

Trevor now lives with his family in Ashwell and works with the National Biodiversity Network Trust, based at Monks Wood. He helped to found the Natural History Unit in North Herts Museums before managing the *Biological Records Centre* in County Hall, Hertford for 11 years. He is a past President of the *Hertfordshire Natural History Society* and serves on its management committee. He has chaired the important Recorders Committee for the Society for over a decade. It was through his worthy band of recorders in the 1960s that we have a true picture of the bird life at that time to compare with today.

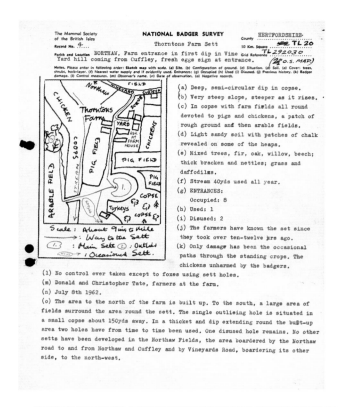

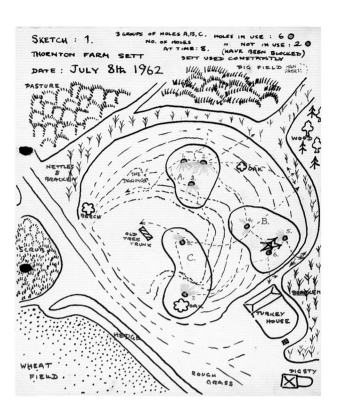

Record sheets from the first national survey of badger setts showed that Thorntons Farm (*top,* 8 July 1962), as well as the Northaw Great Wood, had particularly fine examples of these complex systems of tunnels and spoil heaps where the species makes its homes. Research for the Great Wood book included small mammal live trapping along the footpath which led into the School Camp from Carbone Hill. Here wood mice, *Apodemus sylvaticus*, our most common wild mammal, are released after measurements in 1962.

Yellow-necked mice *Apodemus flavicolis* are the close relative of the wood mouse that is more adept at tree climbing and much less common. Old woodland like the Great Wood is where most of our records for Hertfordshire have come from. *Above, right:* Bank voles *Clethrionomys glareolus* were found in even larger numbers than wood mice in the School Camp habitats in 1962 where 74 were caught, examined and released in one sample.

Right: Blackberry *Rubus fruticosus* that both human visitors and wildlife, such as those shown on this page, enjoy in the late summer.

After more than sixty hours of evening watching over several weeks the first pictures of badgers and foxes in the School Camp badger sett were obtained in 1961 and these two studies were made on 15 June, left, and 30 April, right, 1965. The foxes often bred in parts of the badger sett.

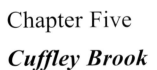

Left: a winter 1965 study of the Cuffley Brook
in Great Wood during snow.
Muntjac *Muntiacus reevesi, above,* were
established in Woburn Park in 1901 and are
now present throughout Hertfordshire. This is a
buck with a new set of the annually cast antlers
growing in velvet in July 1977.

Chapter Five

Cuffley Brook

Spring is one of the best times to follow the course
of the Cuffley Brook, when there is still a good flow
of water and cover has not obscured its route too
much. We investigated the source of the stream,
shown on the 1822 Ordnance Survey as rising at the
high north-west point of Great Wood.

This is also one of the highest points in the parish.
On later maps a slightly curved boundary ditch lines
the fields here. It runs along an attractive established
hedgerow with old field oaks dotted along its length.

To the west of Kentish Lane the ditch drains
towards Brookmans Park. The stream is on the
watershed between the Mymmshall Brook and the
River Lea: because it stands on the summit of the
hill here, the water can drain either towards

Brookmans Park or, on the Great Wood side, flow
eastwards to feed the Brook as it commences its
long journey to the Thames and the sea via the Lea
Valley. It is only in the Great Wood that the deep
banks and cuttings show a steep fall, indicating it to
be a very ancient water-way along this lower valley
in the trees, and its route is entirely natural, not
straightened in its course as in some later sections.

At the start of our walk a muntjac buck noisily
emerged from cover and ran off with its short tail up
in characteristic fashion. Hornbeams have fallen
across the banks in places, but there is little else to
obstruct the route alongside the stream for the
walker. The water gathers momentum as it drops in
height towards Carbone Hill. The folds in the hills
are very striking and what the Brook lacks in width
of water it makes up in the steep slopes, small
waterfalls and attractive 'S' bends.

Following the Brook on the north side is the 17thC
New Park wall which is easily overlooked because it

Hertfordshire Pudding Stone is exposed where the Cuffley Brook flows past swallow holes in the Great Wood. It is a local feature of the geology where the London Clay gives way to Reading Beds in this part of the wood. So named because they resemble a raisin pudding, they are of various sizes and are an extremely hard conglomerate rock of water worn flint pebbles bonded together with a siliceous material.

The North American Grey squirrel *Sciurus carolinensis* was released at several sites over a hundred years ago and replaced the native red squirrel, *S. vulgaris* in Cuffley in the 1940s. There are a number of tree nesting birds which seem to have declined as a result of these squirrels and the Great Wood book records how four young squirrels were found in the old stock dove and tawny owl nest site in the old beech (see picture, p 51).

now only shows as a mound of soil. The stones and flints which form this wall are largely hidden underground. The Parish boundary is the stream.

Although the hornbeams are the most dominant trees here, oaks and occasional beech also feature and the managed plantations of Broombarns and Coldharbour woods, part of the Hatfield Estate, face you across the stream. The bird life is limited to singing blackbirds, robins, chaffinches, blue and great tits in the main, but parties of long-tailed tits appear in the developing foliage and occasional nuthatches call out.

Badger, fox, muntjac and dog tracks often show in the mud and this is also one of the sections of wood where you are likely to put up a brown hare. It is always a surprise to see this mammal, which we associate with the open fields, living in dense woodland, but they have been known to enter the School Camp and the main Country Park woods on this side for at least forty years. They are more

typically seen feeding and courting out in the long, sloping Newgate Street fields above Great Wood, although in much reduced numbers than formerly.

The stream soon meanders into the group of pits known as the Swallow Holes where it drains into the chalk and can sometimes flood the area at times of very heavy rainfall. Swallow holes, where the soil seems to be 'swallowed up' by the ground, (hence the name), have appeared without warning in the Northaw Fields and can be a hazard to farm machinery. A special feature of the Great Wood holes was the exposed Hertfordshire Pudding Stone which once decorated the banks. These fascinating conglomerates appear to have been been dug out and stolen in recent years and this has considerably diminished the geological interest in the area.

Although Cuffley's main drains in the roads now take away the bulk of the surface water after rain, the Brook is still an important channel for field drainage. The hills, which are such an attractive

(Continued on page 60)

Various views of the Cuffley Brook, top picture by kind permission of Trevor James from May 1980, an 'S' bend pictured during the walk described in the text and the green tinge of spring growth in a new year. In places there is erosion into deep gullies.

There are in the region of 300 plant species recorded in the Great Wood, Home Wood and the route of the Cuffley Brook towards Theobalds. Greater Stitchwort *Stellaria holostea* and, *right,* Jack by the Hedge (or Garlic Mustard) *Alliaria petiolata* are two of the most common spring flowers along the banks of paths, roads and streams.

Below: Patricia Klijn pauses beside the Brook during a visit to the Scout Camp Outdoor Pursuit Centre during the dry summer conditions of 2003. The large 'tank trap' concrete blocks here and a pill box nearby were built early in the Second World War as part of defensive plans in the event of an invasion.

Above: wild Ramsons, (Wild Garlic) *Allium ursinum* growing on the bank of the Cuffley Brook to the rear of the bungalows in Brookside Crescent. In very wet years the stream can flood into the back gardens here.

Left: In the Home Wood, the stream Carbone Bottom feeds into the Brook past the Tolmers Road entrance, by the Scout Camp.

Opposite: The stream in flood at Brook Farm, Cuffley; part of the deep cutting after the bridge which carries the Brook under Cuffley Hill towards Theobalds; Gareth Thomas who, with his father David, helped with information about the farm for a special study in the *Mammals, Amphibians & Reptiles of Hertfordshire* (see pages 228-233 in that book) published by *The Hertfordshire Natural History Society* in 2001.

The aqueduct in Flash Lane on the edge of White Webbs where a loop in the New River
once flowed. There is an information board here to explain the history of the restored site
and its remarkable metal structure, (see text).

feature of the village, provide a steep drop in levels until the flow has left the parish. Most of these field drains have no names, but the linking ditch in Great Wood is called Grimes Brook and then Grimes Bottom before it enters Cuffley Brook in the School Camp. ('Grime' is Anglo Saxon for 'Devil').

Across Carbone Hill, in the Scout Camp area below Tolmers Park, a stream from Newgate Street meets the Brook and adds to its flow. Further drainage comes from Carbone Bottom in Home Wood as the stream emerges from the wood to flow behind the houses and divert into a culvert beneath the railway near Burleigh Farm. An outstanding colony of ramsons (wild garlic) features below Brookside Crescent where the gardens of the houses back onto the stream and John Parkes recorded winter floods on video. (It also occurs earlier, at the entrance to Home Wood, near Postern Bridge).

Brook Farm (pp 31-33) took on the name of the stream during the last century although it is still shown as 'Cuffley Farm' in the 1916 Ordnance Survey, for example. The water meadow to the east of the farmyard looks particularly natural as it flows without artificial banks towards the little bridge at Cuffley Hill.

To really appreciate how attractive and significant a little river the Brook becomes, it is well worth leaving the parish via Crews Hill and visiting Flash Lane on the edge of White Webbs where the long lost loop to the New River once passed over the Brook on an aqueduct. This has recently been restored to show the metal structure to the route of the waterway here and we found that there is an excellent modern display board to explain the repairs and clearance work carried out at the bridge. The 1822 map illustrates that the New River was still in use below the lake at Chasewood House, which is fed by Cuffley Brook. Although the New River loop was eventually cut off, if you visit Myddelton House you can still see two fine,

The Brook after winter rains have filled the water with soil and as it flows under the bridge housing the aqueduct. It continues to White Webbs Park and Myddelton Gardens as part of the Thames catchment area in the Lea Valley.

decorative cast iron bridges in the gardens. The long sweep of grass along the east flower borders follows the original line of the canal. Below the garden here the Cuffley Brook meets Turkey Brook and continues as Maiden's Brook.

Thus, to see Cuffley Brook at its best, we recommend a spring walk down the hill to the restored aqueduct at Flash Lane, where you can follow what has become a small river after winter rains, winding through trees and water meadows to White Webbs Park. After the golf course here, the Brook ends its connection with Cuffley at Myddelton Gardens.

If you walk to the left of the aqueduct, below the lake, you can find an original branch of Cuffley Brook which still collects some water in wet weather. Because the course of the stream was diverted to feed the lake and cascade over a weir back to the main route, we are left with this rather forlorn ditch parallel with the lake.

The Brook flows more naturally into the old lake at Theobalds, next to the site of Sopers Farm (p 33), upstream. The restored lake became known to the group of bird watchers in the 1960s as 'Great Lake'.

In Theobalds, grass snakes are still to be seen in the Brook's slow moving summer pools and, (like sightings of wildlife such as water shrews, water voles, bird life and dragonflies), all records made along the stream's length are welcomed for the county surveys. Sticklebacks survive in the tributary stream from Colesdale Farm to the Cuffley Brook which regularly produced great diving beetles and amphibians, including great crested newts.

A hidden, subterranean 'Cuffley Brook' filtered its water for the 'King's Well'. Although the site of 'King's Well' is marked on the Ordnance Survey maps and was a significant 'tourist' spot for at least three hundred years, there is nothing left to show its position except the location on the maps. As we will see in Alice Wilson Fox's account (p 228), James I

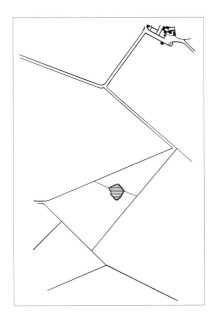 

Location of the original King's Well showing how ownership of the small pocket of land round the well was retained with access on both sides, 1822. Also shown is the route from East Ridgeway past the site where Castle Farm was built and (*top*) the cluster of Hill Farm buildings and cottages. These were on the original Cuffley Green with its pump. A village pond is illustrated where The Plough public house was later built. *Right:* Trevor James pictured the outflow of Cuffley Brook from the dam which created 'Great Lake' (near Soper's Road) and the plan, facing page, shows the extent of the 9 mile long brick wall constructed round the Palace at Theobalds. The railway and Sports Field is shown for clarity. Footings of the wall exist in the Playing Fields. Standing sections of the wall can be seen in the grounds of Capel Manor, the farmyard at Wood Green and possibly part of the old venison shed there. The site of the Palace adjoins Cedars Park in Theobalds Lane.

(1566-1625), probably visited the well on regular occasions to take the waters and is remembered in the nearby road names Kingswell Ride and King James Avenue. All traces of the well, and what must have been a significant gathering point for visitors, has gone. The 'spa' was probably destroyed as such when the Common was inclosed in 1806, but a pond remained here until about 40 years ago.

The 1822 map shows a clear roadway down past Castle Farm which would have taken visitors to the well and other routes would have also linked the original Wells Farm and Cuffley Hill to the site before the popularity of 'taking the waters' waned generally.

The ground rises steeply here and fine views of the Northaw Fields can be enjoyed from the top of Kingswell Ride. We can now only guess at what the site consisted of in its heyday. Before the Inclosure, the main road across the Common continued after Station Road straight up the hill, past the well, to

Northaw where it came into the village at School Lane. There is some suggestion that the well is of Roman origin and the Roman Road foundations parallel with Station Road head in this direction.

The persistent removal of anything of historic merit in Cuffley seems to have been a long tradition. It is amazing that such an important ancient monument, always recorded on old maps as such, should have been totally obliterated and it is somewhat surprising that Alice Wilson Fox only castigates a past owner of Castle Farm for the destruction of trees. The King's Well field shape is very odd and literally points exactly to the junction of the roads below, (see diagram).

The visitors she describes: Pitt (1759-1806) and Samuel Johnson (1709-1784), both suffered from ill health, (described in Geoffrey Treasure's entries in *Who's Who in Early and Late Hanoverian Britain* 1997). In her biography of King James, (1974) Antonia Fraser notes that Buckingham and his

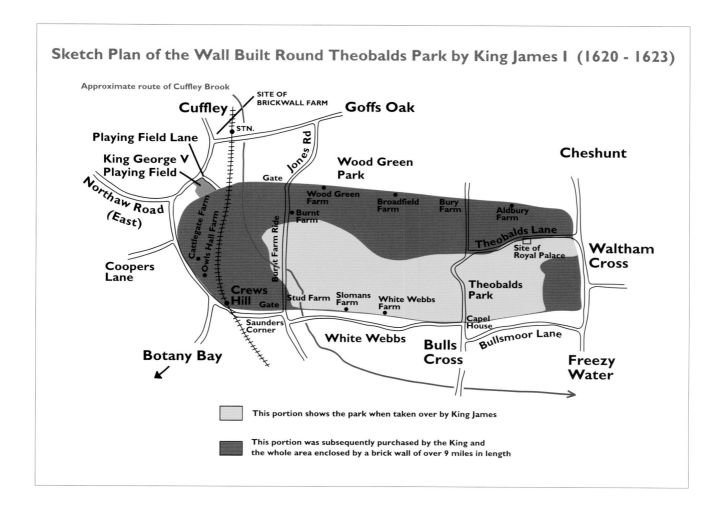

Sketch Plan of the Wall Built Round Theobalds Park by King James I (1620 - 1623)

Approximate route of Cuffley Brook

SITE OF BRICKWALL FARM

Cuffley   STN.   **Goffs Oak**

Playing Field Lane

King George V Playing Field   Gate   Jones Rd   **Wood Green Park**   **Cheshunt**

Northaw Road (East)   Wood Green Farm   Broadfield Farm   Bury Farm   Aldbury Farm

Cattlegate Farm   • Burnt Farm   Owls Hall Ride

Burnt Farm Ride   Theobalds Lane

Site of Royal Palace   **Waltham Cross**

Coopers Lane

Crews Hill   Gate   Stud Farm   Slomans Farm   White Webbs Farm   **Theobalds Park**

Saunders Corner   Capel House   Bullsmoor Lane

Botany Bay   **White Webbs**   **Bulls Cross**   **Freezy Water**

This portion shows the park when taken over by King James

This portion was subsequently purchased by the King and the whole area enclosed by a brick wall of over 9 miles in length

---

mother, distraught that the royal physicians were failing so signally in their treatments, tried some 'country' remedies, of the type which would now be described as homeopathic.

The charities that were formed in the 17thC (now amalgamated) included Mrs Rachel Bradgate (1671) and Babington Staveley (1686) who both came to live in Northaw to take the waters regularly. The Countess of Warwick, who was the widow of the builder of Nyn, left charities to benefit the Parish of Northaw (1604) and, as Gerald Millington pointed out:

'These charities signify extremes of wealth and poverty at that time in the Parish, which were created by two factors - The Kings Well and the Common. The wealthy would never have come to Northaw if James I and his grandson Charles II, had not popularised the King's Well. Apart from the notabilities, such as Dr Johnson and George II, who came in later years, many wealthy gout sufferers

built themselves mansions in Coopers Lane and elsewhere. By 1850 the Well had long since fallen into disuse and today the site is speculative, but it is certainly in the valley between Northaw and Cuffley - that is on the (former) Common'.

Cussans (1870-1873) describes the nature of the well in his entry for Northaw. (He uses the word 'chalybeate' with reference to any spring water containing or impregnated with iron salts). He describes the site we have now been able to pinpoint in our diagram:

'In a valley at Lower Cuffley, about half a mile east of the village, is a chalybeate spring, which, at the time when the Royal Court was held at the neighbouring Palace of Theobalds, was much resorted to; but it suffered the fate of similar places, and its medicinal qualities lost their virtues as soon as the spring ceased to be fashionable. The low wall which inclosed it has long since gone, and the spring itself, by sub-soil draining around it, can now with

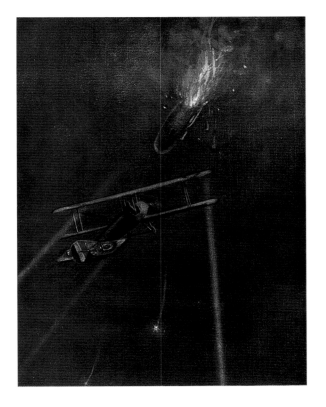

One of the most remarkable exhibits at the 1966 exhibition about the airship was a souvenir crepe paper doyley that had been kept folded in a drawer for fifty years.
Cuffley became so well known from the incident that the name even appeared in a Times crossword.

Above, left: the W. Avis painting 'Lieutenant W L Robinson brings down a Zeppelin at Cuffley, near Enfield' from Hutchinson's *'Story of the British Nation'* Vol 4, (1924), which noted that between December 1914 and June 1918 there were 51 airship and 57 aeroplane attacks on Britain in which 4,820 civilians were killed or injured. The 1966 exhibition explained that it was not a Zeppelin, but a Schutte-Lanz (SL 11) airship of wood and wire rather than aluminium struts. Peter Amesbury very kindly provided pictures of SL 11 and the crew.

difficulty be traced. The water contained a large quantity of iron, and a favourite diversion of the inhabitants was to induce strangers to make tea with it. Though perfectly colourless, as soon as the boiling water was poured on the tea, the iron combined with the tannin, and formed ink - as much to the astonishment of the tea-makers, as to the delight of the practical jokers.'

Cussans' reference to a wall surrounding the well site suggests that there may still be fragments of the foundations to this wall below ground, unless deep ploughing has dispersed all traces in the two hundred or so years since it was present there.

The suggestion has also been made that the stones or bricks may have been used to build Castle Farm. Let us hope that permission might one day be given for excavations to confirm its structure and precise position. Perhaps it might be brought back into operation.

Chapter Six

The Cuffley 'Zeppelin'

In addition to its fame for its waters, Cuffley is remembered for its part in the history of the First World War. An enormous amount has already been written about the dramatic events at Cuffley in the early hours of 3 September 1916 and we have restricted ourselves to a few original observations and accounts here. Aerial attacks on the British Isles began on 19 January 1915 and the first airship to be shot down over British soil was on top of Plough Hill, between two farms: Hill Farm, which stood opposite The Plough public house and Castle Farm, (later Cuffley Hill Farm) that stood at the end of East Ridgeway. Cuffley thus became a part of the international history of the First World War.

You only have to look in the accounts of the period

The Sphere published the superb work of Fortunino Matania RI (1881-1963) and his draughtsmanship in studies of people and horses became one of the most familiar images of combat. He visited the site of the fallen airship from his north London studio to record witness accounts, St Andrew's Church, The Plough, the wreckage and the hedge accurately; (p222-223, 9/9/16 and 279-280 23/9/16 issues of *The Sphere*).

such as the *Times History of the War* (Volume 10, pp 181-200, 1917), and *The Great War*, edited by H W Wilson for Amalgamated Press (Volume 8, pp 219-232, 1917), to find descriptions of Cuffley included at length. In fact there is usually at least a passing reference to the fall of the airship at the village in most of the books about the conflict.

Examination of the newspapers and periodicals of the time will also show the great depth of interest in the event and many aspects of the village are illustrated in newspapers such as *The Daily Mirror* and *The Daily Sketch* as well as the journals of the day, including *The Sphere* and *The Illustrated London News*.

For further, detailed reference, the interested reader should also see the two most authoritative books on the subject, both by Raymond Rimell: *The Airship VC* (1989) and *Zeppelin!* (1984). Ray is a top technical illustrator and also produced a poster on the occasion when William Leefe Robinson's VC

was sold as a 'Medal for life'. The sale proceeds went to a charity created by the pilot's niece, Gia Libin, in aid of childhood leukaemia.

Molly Hughes learnt of Cuffley because her three sons, Vivian, Barnholt and Arthur, cycled out from Barnet to see where the airship had fallen to earth. Across the world Cuffley came to be known for its association with the air battle of that night. For the first time civilians in England were being bombed from the air as part of the battles ostensibly being fought abroad. Crowds flocked to the scene and Ray Rimell describes in *Zeppelin!* how trains at Cuffley station took a thousand people back to London only to deliver a further thousand to the village by return. It was a scene repeated continually for several days. The country roads became choked with vehicles.

There was also a large crowd at the burial of the German crew and anger that they were given a military funeral: on a recent raid, by Zeppelin L 16, bombs had been dropped on Essendon, a village just

Vivian Hughes' 1920s watercolour of the land behind East Ridgeway and Plough Hill, (Catalogue 28), shows the hedge on which the airship fell. The hedge was at the bottom of the garden of *Tintern*, next to the memorial to Leefe Robinson, and Herbert Gray said that the gap in his hedge took years to recover.

to the north of Cuffley, where two frightened girls ran out of their cottage to hide in their garden only to be cut down by a bomb. Ray explains:

'Their father, the village blacksmith, had been the first on the scene and found that both his daughters had suffered horrifying injuries. Shrapnel had killed 26 year-old Frances Mary Louis Bamford outright, and 12 year-old Eleanor Grace had received a dozen wounds on her left side, her leg so severely shattered that it had to be amputated. Despite the efforts of the local doctor, the unfortunate youngster succumbed to her injuries the next morning'.

Raids had regularly caused death and destruction to the civilian population. For example, one formation of airships had killed as many as 71 people with 128 injured and thousands of pounds worth of damage on a single night (13 October 1915). What made feelings run even higher was that the funeral of the two sisters had taken place at Essendon on the same day as that of the German airship crew from SL 11 at nearby Potters Bar.

An exhibition and memorial service was held in 1966 on the 50th anniversary of the dramatic events. It is not surprising that a grateful country made a hero of the lone airman, William Leefe Robinson, who, at the end of his flying time in a fragile biplane, had shot down the Shutte-Lanz airship. At the 1966 service the crew of the airship who died in the inferno were also remembered and messages of appreciation for this were received from Germany. War can leave many bitter memories, but the spirit of a united, modern Europe and friendship between our countries so that we can avoid future conflicts has always been the theme of subsequent exhibitions and memorial ceremonies.

Peter Amesbury generously provided some of the rarer pictures and information for the exhibition from his collection. The Commander of SL 11, Hauptmann Wilhelm Schramm, had commanded several craft after joining the German Army Airship

The 4 September 1916 *Daily News* photograph and caption showing Jack and Joan Gray, who lived at Hill Farm, opposite the site where the airship fell, sitting on the rolled up wire wreckage of SL 11. This is described in *Jack's War,* 2002, (ISBN 1 84019 162 7), see text below.

Division. He took command of Zeppelin LZ 93 in February 1916 and then took over SL 11 during the summer: Peter has the only authenticated picture of the airship in flight in daytime over Germany, in August 1916. It had been photographed by Wilhelm's older brother Otto and had a crew of sixteen on board.

There were many related items contributed for show in the exhibition and these were put on display inside the newly built St Andrew's Church at the head of Station Road in Cuffley. This was felt to be particularly apt because the old church had featured in pictures of the wreckage, including perhaps the most dramatic contemporary painting by a very gifted illustrator of the day, Fortunino Matania. His paintings, featured in *The Sphere* and *The Illustrated London News* as well as elsewhere, were amongst the finest depictions of wartime events. He was able to portray soldiers and the contemporary machinery of war equally well. At this time the periodicals still

employed many reporter-artists as well as photographers. Hill Farm stood immediately behind The Plough in the right side of the painting and the two young children living there recalled the event vividly. During research for memorabilia to put in the display in 1966, a picture of these children, Joan and Jack Gray, was traced at Colindale Newspaper Museum. In his recent book *Jack's War*, (2002), Jack Gray, the little boy in the picture with his sister, records:

'I was at the tender age of three and was sat on the heap of wire by a photographer for the *Daily News* to feature with my sister Joan (aged 5) in the Monday 4 September editions of the paper. My mother was furious to see the picture and refused to have a copy kept in the house. We lived in Hill Farm on the ridge where the burning dirigible crashed to earth. As it passed over our roof to land in the field opposite bullets fell down the chimney and exploded in the fireplace. Our parents had taken us downstairs

(Continued on page 72)

CLEARING UP THE MESS AT CUFFLEY: REMARKABLE

Picking up valuable pieces. Many people who had found relics delivered them to the authorities yesterday.

Waiting to get home from Cuffley. The little local trains have never had such demands placed upon them.

The Zeppelin sailing over a London suburb.

OFFICERS WHO HAVE FALLEN.

Lieut. T. Newman Hall, Oxford and Bucks Light Infantry.

Victor Charles Douglas, youngest son of Bishop Boyd Carpenter.

Lieut. N. Shaw-Stewart, of the Rifle Brigade.—(Langfier.)

TO BRING THE GENERAL GOOD LUCK.

A British staff officer who has picked up an old horseshoe on the western front presents it to the general.—(Official photograph.)

Like Derby Day. The road to Cuffley.

Trying to get a glimpse of the wreckage.

The little country church where the remains of the c

To-day we are able to publish two remarkable photographs. One shows the raiding Zeppelin sailing through night over the houses of peaceful citizens and the other the just retribution which overtook her. There was

The Daily Mirror centre page spread from 5 September 1916. The coil of wire on which Jack and Joan

OGRAPH OF THE AIRSHIP CRASHING TO THE GROUND

Nose-diving to death in a blaze of ruby flame.

Rolling up the Zepp like a carpet. This tangled mass was an airship as recently as Saturday afternoon last.

R.F.C. men clearing away the debris. Crowds watched them collect the wreckage and place it in lorries.

...day were almost as big as on Sunday.

...after being extricated from the jumbled wreck.

...at rush to Cuffley yesterday, but the sight-seers had but a poor reward for their journey. All that was to ...was a scorched and blackened patch in a hayfield and a motor-lorry full of the wreckage.

An elderly lady, who was staying near the spot where the Zeppelin fell, with her daughter. She had gone there for a "rest cure."

THREE MEN WHO ARE MISSING.

Lce.-Cpl. T. S. Glasson. Write 57, Oswald-street, Carlisle.

Pte. H. E. Brum. Write 40, Chaucer-road, London, W.

S. M. Thompson. Write Home Farm, Hasketon, near Woodbridge.

A HUN SHELL WHICH DIDN'T GO OFF.

A German "dud" lying on the top of our trenches at Thiepval. "Dud" means a shell which does not explode.—(Official photograph.)

were pictured (*previous page*) is shown with St Andrew's Church in background, *top right*.

Nil desperandum!   Any use, mother?

The jurymen going to view the bodies before the inquest.

Cuffley was again the Mecca of thousands yesterday, children bringing sugar bags, buckets and all sorts of utensils to carry away any souvenirs. Many brought garden implements to get a better scrape, but it was labour in vain.—(*Daily Mirror* photographs.)

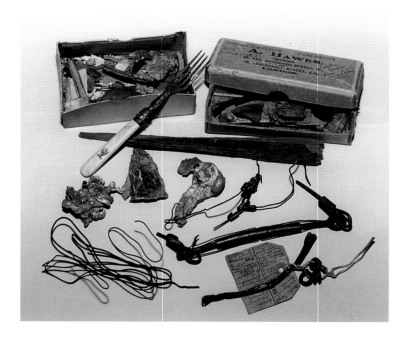

Left: The Daily Mirror (6 September 1916) showed people searching for souvenir parts of the fallen airship and the jury for the inquest held in the original St Andrew's Church. It described the occasion as 'The Strangest Inquest Ever Held. Coroner's Jury Inquire Into Fate of Zeppelin's Nameless Crew. The inquest on the crew recovered from the ruins of the Zeppelin brought down in the early hours of Sunday morning at Cuffley took place yesterday within 100 yards of the spot where all that was left of the airship was represented by a mass of twisted wire'. It went on to describe another event at the nearby village of Essendon where the two daughters of the village blacksmith had been killed by one of the airship's bombs. It was the funeral of Frances Mary Louis Bamford and Eleanor Grace who had been found by their father with terrible, fatal injuries from the bomb.

The crew were: Wilhelm Schramm, Hauptmann; Jokob Baumann, Obermaschinist; Hans Gettel, Leutnant; Rudolf Goltz, Vizefeldwebel; Karl Hassenmuller, Feldwebel-Leutnant; Bernhard Jeziorski, Gefreiter; Fritz Jourdan, Untermaschinist; Karl Kachele, Untermaschinist; Fritz Kopischke, Obersteuermann, Friedrich Modinger, Obermaschinist; Reinhold Porath, Obermaschinist; Rudolf Sendzick, Obersteuermann; Heinrich Schlichting, Unteroffizier; Anton Tristram, Unteroffizier; Wilhelm Vohdin, Oberleutnant; Hans Winkler, Unter maschinist.

Left: souvenir fragments of SL 11 are distinctive due to the wood and wire construction. These are typical pieces picked up and were given by Arthur Hughes. He and his brothers cycled out to Cuffley from Barnet and collected them before they came to live in the village. They were preserved carefully by Molly Hughes in a cigar box.

IN MEMORY of the Zeppelin crews brought down at Potters Bar and Cuffley, the German Ambassador laid a wreath on their graves at Potters Bar.
13 MAR 1933

William Leefe Robinson salutes as he leaves Windsor Castle on 9 September 1916. He had received the quickest investiture of the VC ever, from King George V.
(Picture kindly given by Ruth Leefe Irwin).
Below: Joachim von Ribbentrop (1893-1945) was German ambassador in London 1936-38 and visited the graves of airship crews at Potters Bar. Although this *Daily Express* cutting (kindly copied from their files in Fleet Street in 1966) was about the visit of another ambassador, Jack Gray recalls vividly directing traffic at Potters Bar crossroads when he was in the Territorial Army to allow Ribbentrop's car through just before he went off duty and he joined the crowd at the graves in Mutton Lane. He asked one of the staff why they gave the Nazi salute and was told 'We are watched everywhere we go'. Just such a salute is being given on the extreme right of this March 1933 picture, too, just a month after the Reichstag fire.

Herbert Gray's photograph of the newly dedicated Leefe Robinson Memorial next to his home, *Tintern*, on East Ridgeway, 9 June 1921.

Paid for by readers of the *Daily Express* on land given by Mrs J M Kidston of Nyn, the memorial has had its original RAF wings replaced after theft.

to the kitchen for safety and I always say that I came closer to being hit by German bullets when hiding under the kitchen table at home as a three year old in the First World War than I did on active service in France and around Britain throughout the whole of the Second World War. The caption to the picture read: *"Two babies that escaped the baby killers, although they lived within 50 yards from where the Zeppelin fell".*

My mother commented that the airship "may not have taken your lives, but it certainly looks to have taken your wits". Colindale Newspaper Museum kindly copied the picture for us. Fifty years on I was at last able to see what we looked like'.

Jack's father Herbert Gray said that the hedge at the bottom of their garden where the airship had fallen was so badly seared by the heat of the fire that it took many years to recover from the damage. The family had built a house, *Tintern*, in East Ridgeway above the site in 1921 and the *Daily Express*

Memorial to Leefe Robinson was unveiled here on 9 June 1921. (It features behind several pictures of the Leefe Robinson Memorial).

One of their neighbours near Hill Farm on Plough Hill during the war was Harry Shepherd who described the scene:

'I ran out into the yard. I saw the thing on fire up there in the heavens, white flames shooting out of the top of it. We stood there looking at it - heard it cracking - saw the stuff at the bottom of it doubling under. All the twisted metalwork collapsing, smouldering at absolutely white heat. The flames ran up the side of it until the whole thing was in flames: incandescent. It was coming down above the cottages - the girders folding in, a train of fire behind it, pieces of flame flying off, the sparks showering back from it. Like the tail of a big comet. It turned off slantwise - it was going to miss us. We heard it come down on the ground with a crunch - strangest sound I ever heard, that. And over behind

Lieut. W. L. Robinson, V.C.

The caption to this 1916 postcard reads: 'Lieut W L Robinson VC cheered by his fellow airmen after destroying the Zeppelin, 3 September 1916.' It was from Suttons Farm, near Hornchurch in Essex, that he had flown at night in his BE2c 2693 biplane to shoot down SL 11.

the Plough we could see the fire shooting up'.

Staying with the Shepherds on Plough Hill was Sam Lambert and he had a similar experience with the bullets as Jack had in Hill Farm. Ray Rimmell quotes from his account in *The Airship VC* (1989), part of which reads: 'When we got over the field we could still hear the crack, crack, crack of the cartridges exploding in the fire. This must have kept up for about twenty minutes. The thing I was thinking was that there wasn't much of a wreck there for an airship - only about twenty-five square yards of it. I had a great fear at the back of my mind that it might be one of our smaller airships after all. Then we found the propeller...'

Various pieces of wreckage were lent, given or sold to us for the 1966 exhibition and they were a reminder that the thousands of visitors to the village in September 1916 must have combed the surroundings for the slightest piece of charred wood and metal. Aluminium struts from the tangled

wreckage of the Zeppelin LZ 31 that fell partly across an old oak tree at Potters Bar were sometimes contributed as Cuffley items, but the differences in the construction between the two craft allows for their parts to be distinguished.

The memorial services and exhibitions have brought together many old colleagues including Air Vice Marshall Frederick Sowrey, (son of Frederick Sowrey, the famous 'Zeppelin pilot' who shot down L 32 at Great Burstead, Hornchurch, Essex, on its thirteenth flight); Wing Commander R S Stammers (who was stationed with the airmen at Suttons Farm airfield); Squadron Leader H E Hervey, (who was a prisoner of war in Germany with William Leefe Robinson); Gia Libin, (William's niece); 'Cat's Eyes' Cunningham, (the Second World War pilot who continued in peace time as a test pilot for de Havilland), and many more. The closest living relative to Leefe Robinson to visit us was his sister Ruth Leefe Irwin: a very special guest.

THE "ROBINSON" TOUCH
an impression by an eyewitness - 20 miles away.

Airship brought down in flames at Cuffley, Herts, by
FLIGHT-LIEUT. W. L. ROBINSON, V.C., Sept. 3rd, 1916.
Sanctioned by Censor, Press Bureau, Sept. 22nd, 1916.

Left and facing, lower: Cuffley airship postcards, both published in the weeks after the event, 1916. The gap in the hedge behind the main wreckage shows clearly. Of the many published, these are scarce and reflect the view thousands of people in North London had of the event.
Below: The sketch map published in *The Sphere* of 9 September 1916 showing the location of the fallen airship across the field hedge.

Facing page: the contrasting portraits of William Leefe Robinson given by Ruth Leefe Irwin after her visit to his memorial in 1966. They show how weak he became after two years as a prisoner-of-war in Germany. Due to a number of escape attempts he was transferred to the prison camp at Clausthal in the spring of 1918 where he was victimised by the notorious Camp Commandant Karl Niemeyer. The final portrait was shortly after repatriation in December 1918 and he died later that same month from influenza, on 31 December 1918. He had been in prison with Squadron Leader H E Hervey, who continued hot-air ballooning into his 90s and produced beautiful miniatures of wildlife subjects. One of the authors was able to visit Mr & Mrs Hervey for Sunday lunch and see his studio in 1967. He visited Cuffley and William's grave which is at Harrow Weald in All Saints Churchyard, opposite the restaurant named after him, the *Leefe Robinson*.

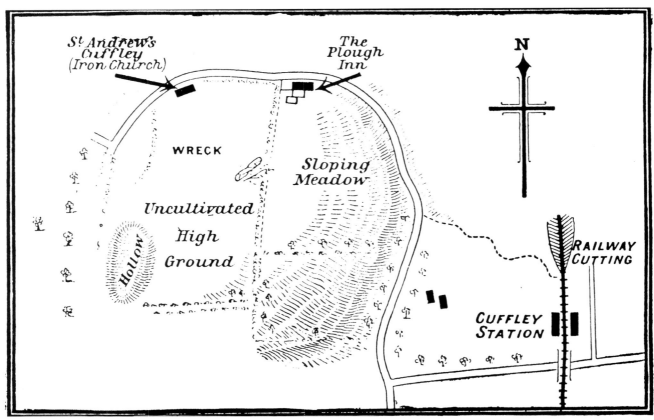

As communication moves increasingly into electronic forms we wanted to celebrate the great age of the postal services: *above left* is the rare Edward VIII pillar box at the corner of Acorn Lane in Tolmers Road. Only a few were completed before the King abdicated (1936) in advance of his Coronation.

Chapter Seven

Communications

It was way back in 1896 that the Parish Council was notified that the Postmaster General was about to erect a box for posting letters in the outlying hamlet of Cuffley. Two years later it was noted that 'very little use was being made of this facility'. This would have been the box in the wall of Brickwall farm. Bearing in mind the nature of the community at the time, which consisted mainly of farmers and workers on the land, it is not surprising that few had time or perhaps the ability to write letters.

However, as time went on Cuffley acquired more and more letter and pillar boxes and it has proved an interesting exercise to take a closer look at some of the examples in Cuffley and Northaw today. The area can boast boxes bearing a range of ciphers and it was pure co-incidence that many of the

photographs were taken at the end of May 2001 and show sealed up boxes from a recent postal dispute. There are examples of George V, George VI, the comparatively rare Edward VIII and several EIIR boxes in the villages. The plain, bold GR surmounted by a crown and the words Post Office underneath are on the pillar box at the end of The Meadway in Cuffley denoting a George V box. Formerly a post box had been near the bus stop where you wait to go up the hill to Goffs Oak by the station, which did seem a more useful place. Now a special little spot has been concreted over for the box and our photograph features the side of the Cuffley Motor Company.

The Edward VIII box stands in Tolmers Road at the junction with Acorn Lane. It was formerly on the opposite side of the road in the grass outside Molly Hughes' cottage at the corner of Oak Lane. It is listed at that spot by W Branch Johnson in his *Industrial Archaeology of Hertfordshire*: 'Cuffley,

There is another Edward VIII box in Hertford Museum. The Post Office Queen Elizabeth II Station Road box, *left, on facing page,* the East Ridgeway George VI box, *above,* and the George V Cuffley Motor Co Meadway box were all photographed during a postal strike in 2001 and have had their slots closed.

junction of Tolmers Road and Oak Lane' with the grid reference TL 302031. Post boxes, however, clearly have a habit of moving about and it is more sensible to place them where people pass on a pavement or more often draw up in their cars to post their letters. It was recorded in 1987 that nearly 150 Edward VIII pillar boxes 'are still in existence' but seventeen or more years later that figure may well be different.

For George VI boxes we need to look on the East Ridgeway and for the one tucked away at the junction of Brookside Crescent with Homewood Avenue. The ciphers do not always face the road and walking about usually ensures you spot something not seen from a car.

There is one example of a letter box in Well Road, (turn left at the end of the Ridgeway switchbacks and the box is on the right). It is a small EIIR box on a post, but it provides a useful facility for nearby houses as well as for passing motorists.

It is said that post boxes are less used nowadays with the increase of e-mail and fax facilities. It may well prove to be useful in times to come to record the cheerful red boxes in use because they are such a part of the village scene.

The first telephonist in Cuffley was Olive Pittkin, (nee Dellow), a niece of Mrs Martin. The telephone 'exchange' was housed in the Cabin, Cuffley and at first there were 40 subscribers to the service.

Olive remembers living in the hut by the Cabin as a child and in 1924 one of her duties was to run the telephone exchange. Louise Martin, (p 30), Albert Wombwell's sister, ran the Cabin as a shop, meeting place, and, increasingly, the centre for all village entertainments, meetings, concerts and dances.

Olive's mother was Alice Dellow, (nee Wombwell), who with her sister, Ada, (later Mrs Curran), continued to live in Cuffley after they married. In later years Alice was in Tolmers Road and helped in the kitchen at Cuffley School. Ada

The Queen Elizabeth II pillar box at the corner of Tolmers Avenue in Tolmers Road, *left,* and one of the small types of Queen Elizabeth II boxes near Queenswood. The slots are all filled for the 2001 postal strike. They show 6.15pm amd 6.00pm final collection times.

lived in Tolmers Gardens and was well known as an expert in crochet shawls and blankets. Descendants of the Wombwell family of circus fame, Albert Wombwell had moved to Lower Hanyards farm and the barn became the home of his sister Mrs Martin and her children. Rene and Barbara, her two daughters, also stayed in Cuffley, Rene becoming Mrs Bittleston and Barbara Mrs Pollock. Albert's children were Queenie and Nell; Queenie later living at Goffs Oak House. Nell lived next door to Lince the photographer in Tolmers Road.

Mrs Olive Pittkin for some time lived opposite the old Wheelwright's Arms in Goffs Oak. Her son John recalls how the lions from Fossett's Circus were housed at Goffs Oak House and he would hear them roaring as he lay in bed as a child. The circus tradition was flourishing. It was not unusual to see elephants parading through Cuffley, out for exercise. For a short time, after being bombed-out in the Second World War, the Pittkin family lodged with

the Fenshoms at 27 Plough Hill and the two Olives became good friends.

The telephone gave some difficulty to Molly Hughes when she set off to the village to use the facility to ring the London University with a query on an exam paper. Having paid sixpence for the call it did not occur to Molly that an exchange was needed as well as the number of the University: 7000. It was only later that her son Arthur pointed out the exchange on the University headed paper. Trouble with technology is, therefore, nothing new as people today grapple with computers, e-mail and the internet. The telephone was giving problems then too.

Molly also mentions visits to other houses to hear 'the wireless'. The Neills were known as the first people on the Ridgeway to possess a television, (certainly pre-war), and it came into its own for the Victory Parade in flickering black and white, watched, of course, in the pitch dark.

The Queen Elizabeth II pillar box in the Ridgeway service road (with the Great Wood in the background) displays a 6.00pm final collection time and the King George VI box, (*right*), outside the old post office and stores in Northaw, shows 6.30pm.

Today the Cuffley telephone exchange occupies a corner site on the bend at the top of Station Road as you turn left towards Northaw. The increase in the number of subscribers saw the number patterns changed and the Sidney Morris coal office, with its memorable 'Cuffley 2000' faded into the history books.

At one point a special section in the telephone book was devoted to Cuffley subscribers. It was provided in an orange Waltham Cross edition and at the back 'Cuffley Telephone Subscribers' ran to some seven pages with nearly two pages of advertisements.

Such directories are a valuable way to track down old residents, house names and movements of families. So often the telephone book is neglected and a treasure trove of information for those interested in local and family history is missed. Goffs Oak, Northaw and Newgate Street numbers were also listed in this section which indicates that

Cuffley in the late 1940s was still quite small.

Telephone boxes have also undergone changes from being cream painted, with red doors, depicted on some of the old postcards, (next to Blaxlands) to today's grey versions with phone card facility and open sides. In between, the more familiar red kiosks with button A and button B prevailed and conjure up memories of people far away being 'put through'.

Today, the mobile phone threatens the telephone box just as television threatened live theatre and CDs threatened vinyl. Yet all these survive in a mixture of collections and photographs, memories and museums, as well as thriving dramatic groups and music societies. Cuffley copes pretty well with progress, but now and again it is useful to stop and assess the changes taking place: an 87 went in front of our telephone numbers and, with the code 01707, would mean Cuffley. At the moment it does anyway.

The importance of the railway to Cuffley has continued since the opening of the line on 4 April,

TELEPHONE EXCHANGE, PLOUGH HILL, CUFFLEY

The Telephone Exchange and oak trees at the junction between Station Road, Plough Hill
and Northaw Road East. The Exchange was built in 1937 and this W F Edwards postcard
dates from about 1966.

1910. Many will recall days when you could send 'luggage in advance', collect your box of day old chicks from the booking office or sit comfortably by the coal fire in the waiting room.

As Vivian recalled, (p 15) there was an early poster produced by the railway to promote Cuffley as a destination that bore the design of a shepherd in a smock and the invitation, *'Come to Cuffley'*. Cuffley did become a place to visit to collect blackberries or have a picnic. It was said that the station was sited 'in the middle of a field', as indeed it was.

The Sopers Farm viaduct was a major civil engineering project between Cuffley and Crews Hill. The eleven arch brick construction still carries the line and there is a fine view of the surrounding countryside from the train. On the left is a game wood and farmland lies to the right as you travel towards London. The Northaw Brook passes under the viaduct to join up with the Cuffley Brook just further east.

The first passenger on the train from Enfield to Cuffley is said to have been the landlord of the Wheatsheaf on Windmill Hill, Enfield. The Great Northern Railway Company, as it was then, could see the potential for further residential development at Cuffley.

Since then the line has undergone several name changes as the steam trains of the LNER (London North Eastern Railway) gave way to Great Northern Electrics, British Rail (Eastern) and the present WAGN (West Anglia Great Northern). Timetables over the years reflect these changes with different logos and designs quite apart from the actual train times and frequency of the service. The first stage of the electrification of the line was completed in November 1976. On the first anniversary of the event Mrs Frances Orman of Cuffley sent a birthday card to the Kings Cross Divisional Manager saying how delighted she was with the service. Mrs Orman was a clerk at the Bank of England and declared

Vivian Hughes' watercolour of the stationmaster's new house with a train leaving Cuffley Station, September 1922, (Catalogue 16). It was painted in the fields where Theobalds Road was built. Overleaf is the same view about ten years earlier and shows the Goffs Oak windmill, on the horizon, to the left, still with its sails fitted.

herself 'a very very satisfied Cuffley traveller'. This was duly reported in the regional magazine *Livewire*.

There have also been strike timetables and special services when the 'Hertford Loop' is used in emergencies such as the accidents at Hatfield and Potters Bar. A bus service often replaces the train during engineering works and when the loop is used for main line trains from the north there is no train service for commuters.

The most memorable days for Cuffley Station were when the crowds descended on the village to see the airship wreckage in 1916. But there are cub scouts being photographed with Tiny Webb as they go off on a trip, nostalgic photographs of sack trucks and memories of railway staff.

In 1918 the stationmaster was Francis Thomas Graves. In later years Mr Camm held the post and there was always a porter on duty, his room being on the 'up to Hertford' side of the platform. George was a porter for many years and the signalman was Tom Jackson.

Trains evoke passion, nostalgia for the steam age and impatience with modern delays. Cuffley relies on trains and the existence of the village owes much to this transport system.

Bus services invite many of the same feelings. On 23 August 1933 Central Buses began to run the route 205 from Waltham Cross to Cuffley. By 13 March 1935 this was extended, running on from Cuffley to Potters Bar bus garage. Single deck buses were operated by the one-man system and the service was hourly. This continued until October of 1941 when the route became the 242.

The 308 'green bus' to Hertford was introduced much later and continues today providing a useful rural route to the county town. More recently a bus runs to Enfield and supermarkets in nearby Cheshunt provide a free bus service to encourage shoppers who lack their own transport.

(Continued on page 94)

Two watercolour studies of Cuffley Station by Vivian Hughes. The top one, (Catalogue 14), is marked 'September 1920, looking north'. Note the 'Cuffley and Goff's Oak' sign and the cottages. The path from these cottages in the lower picture, (Catalogue 15), leads to the station. Vivian was near his home in Tolmers Road, looking south towards London from the back of Oak Lane.

The detail of platform construction and sleepers in Vivian's watercolour, (*opposite*), is exceptional. At about the time of Vivian's paintings this photograph (*above*) was taken, showing Lower Hanyards Farm in the background, as a train leaves for Hertford. In the mid 1950s Anthony Clark pictured one of the express trains (*inset*) that had been diverted through Cuffley and was waiting near the embankment shown in an old land sale plan of the area which also maps the Cuffley Brook and corner of the Spinney below Tolmers Road.

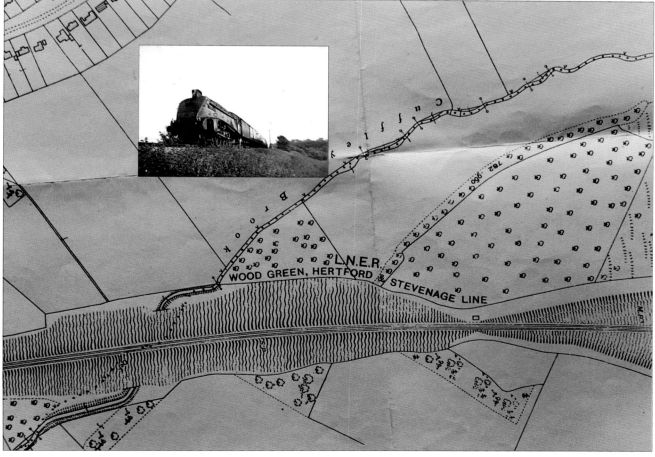

Two remarkable photographs taken on Cuffley Station which show Tiny Webb with cubs on an outing just before the war, in which she was killed by a bomb, and one taken during the war of a US Soldier who shared the name Cuffley. Melvin Bedford kindly lent the original picture of Tiny and we understand that she became Mrs Dench, later Jill Dench's mother. Mr Dench was a local builder. They lived on Plough Hill, next to Mr Gardiner, and Tiny baby-sat for Alan Gill and his sister Mary. The Denchs moved to Wormley Wood where Tiny was tragically killed protecting her baby Jill during a WW2 air raid.

Our picture of 'Hank', Henry Leroy Cuffley (1916-1985), *right,* was taken next to the waiting room window on Cuffley station in 1943. It was sent to us with other material (see pages 256-258) by David Cufley and he was descended from Charles Francis Cuffley who emigrated to America about 1874, aged 16, from Enfield. Whilst this branch of the Cuffley families use the double 'f' spelling, the majority of the Enfield line use the single 'f'.

By 1963, (*right*), the view towards London from Cuffley Station showed the maisonettes in Station Road. On the same early spring day, the diesel locomotive 7B40, pulls goods wagons, and the station wheelbarrows were also pictured, (on an Agfa Sillette 35mm camera and film processed at Hornsey College of Art in Bowes Road).

With Joan Upton, as Joan McRitchie was then, (see pages 169 to 173), Jack Gray must be one of the last surviving passengers to travel regularly to school from Cuffley Station before 1925. Jack, born in 1912, attended Merchant Taylor's School between 1924 and 1929. He had attended preparatory school in Holland House, Hove, prior to this. Vivian's youngest brother Arthur was Jack's close companion on the train, as well as at home where their families had come to share the cottage.

At 92 Jack still recalls an unhappy personal incident when he was playing with lead soldiers in Tolmers Road, just outside the cottage. A daylight raid of a group of bombers flew over. (From the records, this was probably the Gotha attack of 7 July 1917 when 24 aircraft flew together, killed 57 civilians, caused £2,100 damage, at the expense of 5 aircraft lost). Jack's mother rushed out and took him indoors at the noise of the raid.

It was not the sight of the aircraft that upset him as a five year old, he remembers: when he later returned to where he had been playing he found all his toys had disappeared!

Rodney Slatford (pages 136 and 144) has kindly copied a 1956 painting by Christine Morter of Station Road before the trees and hedge disappeared from the left side. Everybody was an actual person: on the right is Margery Briggs with Anne, and Richard is in the pram. The boy is Michael Clarkson with his mother Eileen. The man with the stick is Mr Wenn and the two black Scotty dogs are with Gladys Gibb. The green van was Thrussell's, the greengrocers. A 242 bus is below the railway bridge.

Two January 1965 views of Cuffley Station showing the name 'Cuffley' still in windows on the London bound side of the platforms and an unusual rear view of the same waiting room from the embankment. Both pictures by R A Yeomans via John Parkes with grateful thanks.

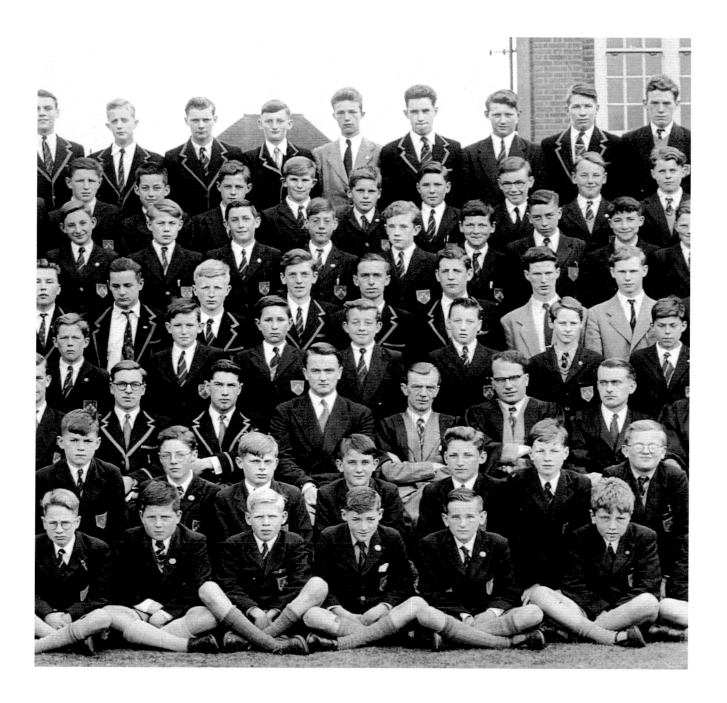

Before alternative schools were available locally, many pupils from Cuffley attended Hertford Grammar School via Cuffley and Hertford North stations. At this time the Ware Grammar School girls (see Patricia Klijn's poem, pages 252-253), travelled by coach. During the Suez crisis in 1956 when petrol supplies dried up the girls used the train, too, for a short time. Pupil numbers increased during the 1950s and 1960s when the travellers became known as the 'Cuffley Train Boys'.

Our detail is from a 1956 Hertford Grammar School photograph and features Donald Heath, an expert on all matters relating to the railways, (third from right, fourth row down). The picture also includes Robin Hasler, (top row, light jacket), Anthony Clark (top row, third from right) and Martin Harvey, (next row down, far left). Richard Hodder, (fourth from left, third row down) is Captain of the Old Boy's Golf Club and the member of staff, seated extreme right, third row up, is Richard Gander - the long standing and very helpful historian of the School.

Special thanks for help to Michael Creasey, (fourth in from the right, second row up), who also established the high standard of printing of the Old Boy's Journals.

Two views by kind permission of Trevor James show (top) a diesel train to Hertford 'in the valley of Cuffley, 1971'; Cuffley, in Trevor's words, as a 'Shanty town', with its little units for the coal office, Lulworth Florists, the public toilets and bus stop by the station, 1967!

The station underpass in 1971, also by kind
permission of Trevor James.
The culvert on the route to the site of Sopers Farm
under the railway from the Playing Fields, (right), and
the view of an electric train heading south towards
London across the picturesque eleven-arched viaduct
were pictured in the 1990s.
The reedmace in the foreground (below) grow in the
stream which drains into the Cuffley Brook below
Theobalds from the Northaw Fields, known as
Northaw Brook.

Above: a miscellany of Cuffley ephemera and images associated with the station and transport generally.
Facing page, top: a Daimler owned by Alfred Neill in the 1940s when car ownership was very scarce in the village. *Top, right:* A study, about 1961, by Anthony Clark of his jeep (with yellow 5 gallon 'jerry' can of spare petrol strapped at the rear) as he waits for Ron Offlow to have his Ford filled with BP petrol at Cuffley Motor Company. (The bungalows to the rear were demolished to make way for more flats in Station Road). One of the Festival of Britain events in Cuffley in 1951 was the 'best kept car' competition, won by Bernard Clark, centre, who is holding the spot light prize as he is congratulated by W J 'James' Paine. He drove the green open-top Singer Nine, registration number CCH 776 and the runner up, Mr Dicks, from the post office, (second left) drove the Austin, LXU 640. Also shown are Mr and Mrs Arthur Treadwell and Mr and Mrs Frank Bennett. Chair of the Parish Council, County Alderman C Gordon Maynard JP, after whom Maynard Place in Cuffley and the Maynard Gallery in Welwyn Garden City are named, is second from right.

Our look at the history of transport in Cuffley ends with a view of the entrance to the station on the east side from about when it opened in 1910, and a 1963 picture of 'Uncle Benny' who sold papers for Wackett's in the subway. The hand-coloured postcard (via David Dent) is reproduced by kind permission of John Higgs.

Although the railway and the station have been central to the development of the community and well used by most of the people of Cuffley, cars are now the usual way to get about. Motorists were few in the early years, (Cuffley Motors opened in 1937), but the Ridgeway residents soon acquired wheels and today the household without at least one car is unusual. Cars are perhaps also beginning to record the history of a family as outings are remembered in particular vehicles. Old vehicle registration numbers are rarely forgotten.

Chapter Eight

Cuffley & Northaw Organisations & Societies

In common with many villages and communities, organisations and groups are the backbone of Cuffley and Northaw society. A sense of belonging to the area stems from spending time with like-minded people and sharing interests and enthusiasms through study, sport, charitable work, art or horticulture.

The Women's Institute at Northaw, which was founded in 1917 by Miss LeBlanc and Miss Poland, was Hertfordshire's first Women's Institute. This was a clear indication that the district wished to develop beyond the bounds of home and church. One of the earliest activities for the institute was

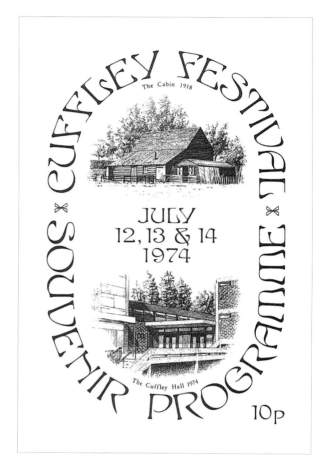

Festival of Britain 1951 and Cuffley Festival 1974 Programmes. The 1951 week of events included the Best Kept Car (previous page) which would have been pictured by R W Aspden, listed as official photographer.

caring for the wounded and convalescent of the First World War. It was many years later that a second institute was set up at Northaw meeting in the evenings to cater for women at work or busy with young children in the daytime. This is called the Tolmers Women's Institute and continues as a flourishing organisation today.

The importance of village halls to bring people together in a community perhaps goes without saying and Cuffley's Women's Institute met initially in the old 'Cabin' hall. The monthly Wednesday afternoon meetings became a valuable time for many residents interested in handicrafts, speakers, competitions and debates on national issues. The institute is still going strong and until recently the weekly morning market was an opportunity for Cuffley members to sell cakes, crafts and local produce.

The churches had similar groups: Northaw's Mother's Union with the beautiful banner which hangs in St Thomas of Canterbury Church; the Ladies' Night, run for many years at Cuffley Free Church with a programme of walks, talks and outings in the county; and St Andrew's Cuffley Wives with speakers, film shows and demonstrations. Many recall these groups with affection covering a wide variety of interests from Danish Embroidery to a trip on the river in a narrow boat at Broxbourne.

With the importance of village halls in mind it is worth recalling that discussions were going on regarding the building of a village hall at Northaw at many meetings of the Parish Council in 1919.

Amongst those serving on the committee for the proposed village hall were Mr Wombwell, Mr E J Searchfield, Mrs Wilson Fox and Miss Poland. Initially Miss Poland had opposed the idea, but when she was outvoted she thought baths should be included in the proposed hall. The Comrades of the First World War felt a corrugated iron hut should be

Cuffley Victory Centre: the Cabin in September 1974 shortly before it was replaced by the new Hall, Library and Surgery complex. Picture by kind permission of Trevor James. The old Brickwall Farm barn was originally adapted for accommodation, (right) and a foyer added, but the distinct roof shape survived.

built instead of using bricks and mortar. In the end a 72' x 32' secondhand YWCA hut was up for auction at Richborough, near Sandwich, in Kent and £412 was paid for the hut, (which had been expected to reach £600). The hut is illustrated on page 235.

There was a final minute on the subject:

'Mr J E Beaumont of 205 High Holborn undertook to arrange transport and the hut was now on rail. December 18th 1919'.

Cuffley Homemakers, ten years old in 2002, provides a morning group meeting with speakers ranging through subjects such as *Enfield Wildlife Rescue and Ambulance Service*, *The Work of the Citizen's Advice Bureau*, *Women in Roman Times* and *Inside Hatfield House*.

The men of Cuffley and Northaw were able to use the Kidston Institute, join the Men's Fireside, belong to the Cuffley and District Round Table No. 797 or, later on, the Cuffley 41 Club. The Men's Fireside was started by Arnold Cope and held meetings in

member's homes with speakers from all walks of life amid much pipe smoke and cups of tea.

For many years the Northaw and Cuffley Ratepayer's Association produced a handbook listing local societies and organisations, the sixth post war edition coming out in 1962. The Association was founded in 1930 and immediately set to work to avoid the villages being incorporated in the Cheshunt Urban District Council. From such beginnings Cuffley School was built in Theobalds Road in 1938 as a result of estimating the growth of the village in 1932. All local amenities interested the group: from polling stations, telephone kiosks, pillar boxes, lighting and footpaths to bus and train services and the cesspools on The Ridgeway.

The Ratepayers inaugurated The Northaw and Cuffley District Nursing Association. Road stewards collected a quarterly subscription from members. This was contributed to Hertfordshire County Nursing Association who in turn provided a District

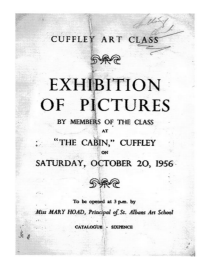

CUFFLEY ART CLASS

EXHIBITION OF PICTURES

BY MEMBERS OF THE CLASS

AT

"THE CABIN," CUFFLEY

ON

SATURDAY, OCTOBER 20, 1956

To be opened at 3 p.m. by
Miss MARY HOAD, Principal of St. Albans Art School

CATALOGUE · SIXPENCE

CATALOGUE OF PICTURES

No.	Title	Artist	Price
1.	Miss Ramsden	M. C. Hart	
2.	Profile	D. F. Cheshire	
3.	A Sketch	M. A. Cheshire	N.F.S.
4.	Mr. Thomas	R. E. Matthews	
5.	Girl's Head	M. Ramsden	
6.	Michaelmas Daisies	Joan Wood	4 gns.
7.	Monday Night at Eight	T. Gordon Jones	
8.	Mary	K. Francis	£4 0 0
9.	Church Tower, Northaw	A. E. A. Gentle	3 gns.
10.	Compton Bay	M. Bowmaker	
11.	Still Life	Beryl Bedford	
12.	A Member of the Art Class	J. E. Leage	
13.	Cactus	G. F. Douglas	3 gns.
14.	Cottage at Northaw	Vida Slatford	
15.	Figure Drawing (1)	Brigid Wright	
16.	Hickling Broad	Christine Morter	5 gns.
17.	Quick Sketch	Yvonne Aspden	
18.	Mr. Thomas	E. Pitchford	
19.	Oil Sketch of D. Whyte, Esq.	Hilda Neville	2 gns.
20.	Seascape (after Vernon Ward)	D. Whyte	
21.	A Model Reclining	M. C. Hart	
22.	Flowers	D. F. Cheshire	
23.	Riverside	M. A. Cheshire	10 gns.
24.	St. Helens	R. E. Matthews	4 gns.
25.	Portrait of a Young Woman	M. Ramsden	
26.	Flower Piece	Joan Wood	4 gns.
27.	Low Tide, St. Ives	T. Gordon Jones	5 gns.
28.	Head Study	K. Francis	£4 0 0
29.	Late Daffodils	A. E. A. Gentle	3 gns.
30.	Mister Thomas	M. Bowmaker	
31.	Poppies	Beryl Bedford	
32.	Cornish Scene	J. E. Leage	
33.	Trixie	G. F. Douglas	N.F.S.
34.	Brunette	Vida Slatford	
35.	Figure Drawing (5)	Brigid Wright	
36.	State of Mind	Christine Morter	3 gns.
37.	Janet	Yvonne Aspden	
38.	Mr. Thomas	Yvonne Aspden	
39.	First Attempt, Still Life	Hilda Neville	3 gns.
40.	Northaw Church	D. Whyte	
41.	Janet Hilliard	M. C. Hart	
42.	My Sister	D. F. Cheshire	
43.	The Old Vicarage, Northaw	R. F. Matthews	5 gns.
44.	Sports Attire	M. Ramsden	
45.	Still Life	Joan Wood	2 gns.
46.	K. Morter, Esq.	T. Gordon Jones	2 gns.
47.	Flowers	K. Francis	£4 0 0
48.	Mr. Thomas	A. E. A. Gentle	3 gns.
49.	Sketch	M. Bowmaker	
50.	Maurice Cheshire, Esq.	Beryl Bedford	
51.	Portrait of Meryl	J. E. Leage	
52.	Sketch of Trixie	G. F. Douglas	N.F.S.
53.	Portrait	Vida Slatford	
54.	Figure Drawing (4)	Brigid Wright	
55.	Figure Drawing (3)	Brigid Wright	
56.	Northaw	Christine Morter	5 gns.
57.	Sid Thomas	Hilda Neville	By arrgt.
58.	Summer (1956), Sea	D. Whyte	
59.	A Portrait	M. C. Hart	
60.	A Sketch	D. F. Cheshire	
61.	Portrait	R. E. Matthews	
62.	W. S. Thomas, Esq.	Joan Wood	3 gns.
63.	Old Houses, Teignmouth	T. Gordon Jones	3 gns.
64.	Portrait I	K. Francis	£4 0 0
65.	Early Daffodils	A. E. A. Gentle	
66.	Portrait	M. Bowmaker	
67.	Nasturtiums	Beryl Bedford	
68.	Mr. Thomas	G. F. Douglas	By arrgt.
69.	Figure Drawing (2)	Brigid Wright	
70.	Cley Windmill	Christine Morter	5 gns.
71.	Dutch Scene (imaginary)	Hilda Neville	Sold
72.	Fellow Student	D. Whyte	
73.	Autumn	R. E. Matthews	7 gns.
74.	Janet	Joan Wood	3 gns.
75.	Portrait Study	T. Gordon Jones	2 gns.
76.	Kenneth Morter, Esq.	Beryl Bedford	
77.	Meryl	G. F. Douglas	By arrgt.
78.	Little Girl in Red	Christine Morter	2 gns.
79.	"The Sun," Northaw	D. Whyte	
80.	Mary	Joan Wood	4 gns.
81.	Model Resting	T. Gordon Jones	1 gn.
82.	Janet Hilliard	A. E. A. Gentle	3 gns.
83.	Portrait	M. Bowmaker	
84.	Sydney Thomas, Esq.	Beryl Bedford	
85.	Janet	G. F. Douglas	By arrgt.
86.	W. S. Thomas, Esq.	Christine Morter	N.F.S.
87.	The Estuary, Bantham	D. Whyte	
88.	Miss Ramsden	A. E. A. Gentle	3 gns.
89.	Mr. Thomas	Olive Brewer	
90.	Northaw Church	Olive Brewer	
91.	Tudor Cottage	Olive Brewer	
92.	Dutch Reproduction	Olive Brewer	N.F.S.

The Art Class Programme of 1956, showing cover and inside spread. Over 90 works were on display, including those by Hilda Waller, her husband T. Gordon Jones, Vida Slatford, David Whyte, (who lent many of the early pictures of Cuffley for use in the 1966 history and airship exhibition), Olive Brewer, Christine Morter, A E A Gentle and Brigid Wright. Mary Hoad, who opened the exhibition, ran the Foundation Art Course at St Albans which later led to BA degrees in many different specialisms. Students were funded to attend there with grants for travel costs, but the awkward bus routes across from Cuffley to St Albans by public transport meant that by the 1960s students could apply to travel by train to London Colleges, too.

Nurse, assistant nurses, maternity and midwifery care and even bought a freehold house for the District Nurse, (Miss E M Sivell) at 47 Theobalds Road for £1,311.5s. Another item of expense was the bicycle allowance of £5.00.

By 1975 the Ratepayer's booklet had abandoned advertising and the local telephone book. Much of the charm of the early editions was lost, along with those memories of now long forgotten shops and businesses. There was, however, a wonderful cover of line drawings of Northaw and Cuffley landmarks by Roy Coulthurst, (see p 106). On an earlier edition the cover was by Christine M Morter showing the pump at the top of Plough Hill with the backdrop of pine trees, the heart of old Cuffley, (see p 20).

The Northaw and Cuffley Resident's Association developed from the original Northaw group started in 1930. Cuffley was added when the association reassembled after the Second World War in 1945. The Association is still very active and concerns itself with planning applications, mis-use of land, the mobile library, preservation of woodland and local footpaths. There are monthly meetings held at Northaw Village Hall and at the annual meeting a speaker from the police, countryside management or planning authority keeps residents advised of local developments and proposals.

Outdoor interests are catered for by the Cheshunt Natural History Society, which meets in Goffs Oak. The society began in March 1968 at the home of John Killick at Cuffley. The Hertfordshire Natural History Society, Herts & Middlesex Wildlife Trust and the British Naturalists' Association also attract members who like to watch and study wildlife.

Walks in the area are organised by many groups, preservation of footpaths being of prime concern. Loss of a stile, re-routing of a track and the disappearance of hedgerows is of major importance in the preservation of a rural community. Currently Hywel Morris is collecting data on footpaths as the

(Continued on page 102)

The Festival of Britain 1951 Cuffley Carnival Queen, Doreen Bennett, was crowned in the Playing Fields on Saturday 24 June with Stella (*left*) and Christine Jones who much later attended the 1993 re-union in the new Hall and met Robert Marshall, (*lower picture*).

Robert had been their next-door neighbour in Hill Rise. He followed in his father's footsteps by becoming a policeman and moved to Devon. He is also seen (*facing page, on left*) with Michael Clark at Hanyards Farm (1954). The Home Wood shows up well in the background. Five years later the fields were built over. The twins (a day younger than Michael Clark, who was born at 44 Hill Rise) are daughters of Hilda and T Gordon Jones. Hilda kept her maiden name of Waller in her professional capacity as a painter, (see overleaf and other references in index).

Facing, top left:
one of the still life paintings, particularly of flowers, for which Hilda Waller became so well known. Hilda became an RA when her picture here, *right*, of lilies and cacti was exhibited in the Royal Academy of 1951.

Facing page, centre:
an informal group at 15 The Ridgeway, Cuffley, after the 23 June 1945 wedding of 'Laurence' A J Lawrence to Grace Waller (centre) at Northaw Church. Hilda is on the right with her twin daughters, Christine, front, and Stella, behind. Also, left to right, are Vi Lawrence and Cissie Pledger, (nee Lawrence). Picture via Vernonne Adams.

Facing page, bottom picture:
in a recent family photograph, Hilda is seated on the right. This picture was also kindly lent to us by Vernonne Adams, Grace Lawrence's daughter, who provided access to much of the material here. Vernonne is in the centre of the photograph, with Stella and Christine and their families on either side. (The family home in Victorian times, Paradise House, has been illustrated in Jack Edward's book, *North & West Cheshunt Past*, 1981, showing a 1928 study of the grand building, Park Lane Paradise, near Hammond Street. He noted: *'This was once the home of a Mr Waller, a London theatrical costumier'*).

This page, top left: Hilda's husband T Gordon Jones' house and garden watercolour and Grace's pastel study, *top right*, reflect the exceptional artistic nature of the family.

Coronation procession with rather modest decorations on the Cuffley Hotel in the background in June 1953. The railway bridge appears on the far right. Following the Salvation Army band is a server with Thomas Becket Northaw Church banner and choir in procession.

local footpath secretary for the Parish Council. Just occasionally Cuffley and Northaw have cropped up in published books of footpaths in the county including an old one published by the LNER railway.

By far the biggest group in Cuffley is the Horticultural Society. At the 26th Annual Show in 1968 there were 441 exhibits. Competition is always keen and numerous cups and trophies are presented. In 1969 the Summer Show was held in the garden of Mr J V James (an enthusiastic beekeeper) on the East Ridgeway and attracted a record number of over 300 entries. Nowadays there are three shows, monthly talks and slide shows and a programme of outings. Visits to gardens throughout the country are arranged.

Cuffley Floral Art Club was founded by Mrs Eve Travers in 1962 and at the seventh annual show in 1969 there were 75 entries. The event was attended by over 170 people. Members still enjoy talks,

demonstrations and taking part in Church Flower Festivals in the area.

Cuffley Winemakers was formed in 1960 with the objectives of encouraging the making of homemade wine and cooperating with other societies to discuss and exchange views on wine. In 1971 a report stated that the average cost of a bottle of homemade wine was 11p. The group is still growing with social events and plenty of wine and beermaking.

The Cuffley Art Class changed its name to the Cuffley Art Society at a committee meeting in 1969. The group had been asked to show paintings at Hatfield during Hatfield Civic Week. Since its inception the group has flourished with an annual October exhibition at Cuffley Hall. Among the early members of the society were T Gordon Jones (a watercolour of 'The Cabin' by him hangs in the Cuffley Hall) and his wife Hilda Waller RA. Flower paintings were her speciality and others in the group were Christine Morter, Maurice Hart, Vida Slatford,

The Cuffley Carnival Procession in the summer of 1974 as it leads out of the station car park, *top left*, passes the coal office (which has lost its Sidney Morris name from the front), *left*, and continues under the railway bridge, *above*, on the wet Saturday.

Edith Eastgate, Ivy James and Christine Groves.

Sport at both Northaw and Cuffley has always been a popular pastime. Cricket clubs in the villages ensure that summer weekends include the sound of ball on willow. References to cricket can be found elsewhere in the book, (see pages 150-153 with reference to Northaw Place School and the item on Walter 'Wally' Hammond on pages 156-158).

Originally the courts in the King George V Playing Field at Cuffley bore the name Northaw and Cuffley Lawn Tennis Club. Now there are floodlit hard court playing surfaces and a much more substantial pavilion for the players. Members take part in tournaments and social activities and one court is available for the public. A flourishing Bowls Club also has its home in the playing fields. Members visit many other clubs in the area and take part in matches. The green is well kept and another pavilion enables club members to store equipment and entertain visitors from other clubs. Indoor carpet

bowls is a more recent introduction at Cuffley Hall and has proved to be a very successful development.

Football is well represented in the playing fields where the Cuffley Football Club has its home. At one time the facilities for the home team showed a somewhat inadequate shelter for the players, (see next page). Youngsters are coached and the Cuffley team competes regularly with fixtures throughout the county. The team has gained the nickname over the years of 'the Zeps', a nice link with a bit of history.

Another football side was founded in 1951 called 'Oakley United' with team members Roger and Brian Thrussell, John Pittkin, John Fishpool, Derek Gower, Trevor Brown, Eric Duggan and Kevin Toomey among them. They competed in the East Herts 14-16 Youth League and comprised boys from Goffs Oak and Cuffley. (John Pittkin also recalls helping Ted Lewis, milkman with the A1 Dairies, to do the Hanyards Lane round. The horse would be

The King George V Playing Fields caters for all kinds of sporting events including tennis, cricket, bowls and soccer. The lavish facilities for the home football team (a few years ago) are illustrated. The Cuffley football team is known as 'The Zeps' and plays in the Hertfordshire Senior County League, Division 1.

allowed to gallop down an unmade Tolmers Avenue where there were no houses, only brambles).

Political groups have found their place in the villages. Cuffley's Young Conservatives in 1958/59 produced a magazine *The Cuffley Review*. As well as listing their activities, car rallies, talks, debates, visits and annual dinner/dance, the booklet listed the films on at The Ritz Cinema, Potters Bar, with a separate programme on Sundays.

The Northaw and Cuffley Labour Party is listed in the 1975 Ratepayer's booklet. At that time results in the local elections were listed as follows:

Conservative: 1047, Liberal: 421, Independent: 321 and Labour: 218.

The parish had always been considered a safe Conservative seat in the General Elections, but in 1966, when the village was still included as part of the Hertford constituency, the MP Lord Balniel experienced a very close run result. Our picture, (overleaf) was taken at a meeting in the old Cabin

building on Friday 11 March 1966. The meeting had been arranged before the announcement of the General Election and Lord Balniel is shown with the Chairman of the local Association, Frank Bennett, answering questions from the floor. Two present at the time recall that he was given a tough time by the audience.

The Labour Party, with Harold Wilson as Prime Minister, won (Thursday 31 March) and *The Times* (2 April) gave details of the Hertford result. *The Sunday Express* commented favourably on Robin Balniel's approach (3 April) and felt that he had won the seat by adopting the informal 'Robin' Balniel rather than 'Lord' in all publicity material.

The WEA or Workers Educational Association started a branch in Cuffley in 1968 with the slogan *'Widen your Horizons'*. That year classes in literature, natural history, archaeology and local history were on offer. Since then there have been classes each year offering all manner of subjects

The Bowls Club with its attractive, simple architecture and pristine green in the mid-1980s.
The Playing Fields are still surrounded by farmland with many fine trees.

including heraldry (a memorable course from Bert Longden, warden of Tolmers Scout Camp), family history and world religions. A very flourishing group with expert tutors has supplied intellectual stimulus to many over the years.

From that original literature class sprang the Book Group, still going strong and the nucleus of the Cuffley Writers Circle which was set up by Audrey Curson after a summer school with the WEA.

The Writers Circle is remembered for a series of celebrity lunches held in the Cuffley Hall for visiting writers. Guest speakers at the first 1985 event were the writers of *'Tenko'*, a very popular TV drama series at the time, Jill Hyem and Anne Valery.

In 1988 a visit from Monica Dickens, author of 'One Pair of Feet', 'One Pair of Hands', numerous novels and the children's book 'Follyfoot', saw her signing copies of her latest novel 'Dear Doctor Lily'. In 1991 the group welcomed Alan Plater, author of 'The Beiderbecke Affair', another

television series being screened at that time and based on his love of jazz music.

Early members of the group included Barry Appleton, originator of the TV series 'The Bill', Mary Rensten, who has written plays for radio, numerous articles and interviewed countless celebrities for magazines, and Anne Forsyth, children's author and wife of the local doctor.

Scouts, Ventures, Cubs and Beavers, Guides, Rangers and Brownies continue to have lively troops, companies and packs in both Northaw and Cuffley. It was Lionel Gill who started up scouting in Cuffley, getting the hut built on Plough Hill and leading the 1st Cuffley Scouts for 35 years until he retired from scouting in 1970.

The troop still enjoy a programme of camps, meetings and the opportunity for learning outdoor skills. Their history is documented on old films and in photographs of Scouts at local Tamashas, fetes

(Continued on page 108)

105

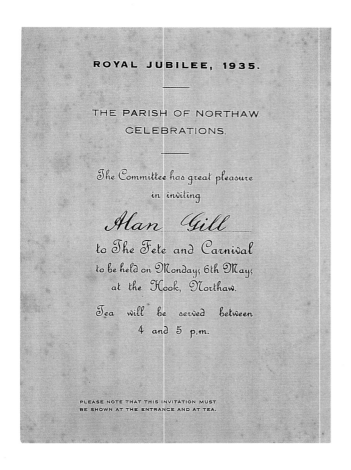

ROYAL JUBILEE, 1935.

THE PARISH OF NORTHAW
CELEBRATIONS.

*The Committee has great pleasure
in inviting*

Alan Gill

*to The Fete and Carnival
to be held on Monday, 6th May,
at the Hook, Northaw.*

*Tea will be served between
4 and 5 p.m.*

PLEASE NOTE THAT THIS INVITATION MUST
BE SHOWN AT THE ENTRANCE AND AT TEA.

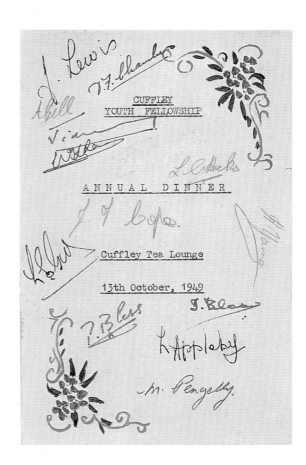

CUFFLEY
YOUTH FELLOWSHIP

ANNUAL DINNER

Cuffley Tea Lounge

13th October, 1949

Northaw & Cuffley
RATEPAYERS' ASSOCIATION

YOUR MEMBER OF PARLIAMENT
LORD BALNIEL
AT THE CABIN
ON
FRIDAY MARCH 11th.
AT 8·30p.m
COME EARLY

Alan Gill has kindly lent two items for reproduction here: his 1935 Royal Jubilee Fete and Carnival invitation, (when the whole Parish celebrated together at the Hook, Northaw), and his Cuffley Youth Fellowship signed menu from the Cuffley Tea Lounge in 1949: facing page. Below, on this page, is a 1974 car window sticker that was in use during the weeks prior to the event. Cecil Parkinson's Northaw old vicarage home is illustrated on the Ratepayers' Association Handbook cover (bottom, right line drawing by Roy Coulthurst) from 1975, facing page.

Above, Lord Balniel speaking at a meeting in the Cabin, Cuffley, on Friday 11 March 1966. The Chairman of the meeting, Mr Frank Bennett, is standing taking questions with fellow members of the local Conservative Association. The meeting had been arranged before the 1966 election had been announced, but went ahead as planned. Isobel White of the House of Commons Library has very kindly provided career details for Lord Balniel who became Minister of State for Defence, 1970-72 and Minister of State for Foreign & Commonwealth Affairs, 1972-74. He was the first Crown Estate Commissioner 1980-85. Lord Balniel lost his seat when the Labour Government was elected in 1974 and his son took over the title whilst he became the 29th Earl of Crawford and 12th Earl of Balcarres.

Please Support **CUFFLEY FESTIVAL** July 12th, 13th & 14th, 1974

Cuffley Writers Circle (WEA)
Invite you to
A Literary Luncheon
In Cuffley Hall
Maynards Place
on Wednesday
17th July 1985
12·30 for 1pm

FREE CAR PARK
£3·50 (incl wine)
BAR

SUMMER 85
CUFFLEY LITERARY LUNCHEON
meet guest speakers
TENKO
Script writers Jill Hyem & Anne Valery
ALSO MEET
THE WRITERS OF CUFFLEY

Cuffley Writers Circle
& Cuffley WEA
Invite you to
A Literary Luncheon
In Cuffley Hall
Maynards Place
on Wednesday
6th July 1988
12·30 for 1pm
BAR
FREE CAR PARK
Lunch wine coffee
£5·75 Inclusive

SUMMER 88
CUFFLEY LITERARY LUNCHEON
meet guest speaker: Writer
Monica Dickens
MBE
ALSO MEET
THE WRITERS OF CUFFLEY

Two examples of the attractively designed Cuffley Writers Circle invitations to literary lunches:
the script writers of Tenko, Jill Hyem and Anne Valery and Monica Dickens MBE. Alan Plater was another
guest speaker to the Circle.

and parades. John Parkes, now an honorary scouter, has been responsible for introducing the idea of Christmas Card deliveries locally by the Scouts in Cuffley since 1982. Each year a stamp is designed with an appropriate commemorative significance and the stamps themselves are a unique introduction to stamp collecting. A look at the subjects covered include the Cuffley Player's 60th Anniversary in 1993, The Cuffley Horticultural Society 1940 - 1995, numerous local landmarks and scouting related anniversaries. Ken Stroud was Group Scout leader for many years.

Guides in Cuffley are synonymous with the name of Nancy Marriner who started the 1st Cuffley Guides and served as the Captain of the company. Church parades, camps, weekly meetings (often in her wonderful garden on the East Ridgeway) inspired generations of girls as well as equipping them with useful skills in first aid, knots and outdoor cookery.

The later 1st Cuffley leaders for many years were Pam Bateman followed by Gwen Waddingham of Northaw. There were companies of 2nd Cuffley, St Andrews (Alison Wimms) and 3rd Cuffley Guides (Mary Gill) in later years. The movement has moved on to provide a more modern programme, but the principles of Scouting and Guiding remain the same.

Brownie packs provide the Guides of the future. For 18 years Mrs N Blackford ran the 1st Cuffley pack as Brown Owl, grappling with the inadequacies of the Old School Room. At one time there were three Brownie Packs in Cuffley. Leaders have included Mrs E Williams (2nd Cuffley, St Andrews) and Mrs Jean Roser (3rd Cuffley pack meeting at Cuffley Free Church).

Northaw has always maintained separate troops, companies and packs and a steady stream of recruits have kept the units thriving.

There have been many Queens Scouts and Guides over the years, the ultimate badge for young people.

Following the death of Lionel Gill, the Cuffley Scout Headquarters (opened in 1964) was named after him on Saturday 12 April, 1986. Ruth Gill unveils a picture of her husband Lionel on the occasion with Group Scout Leader Ken Stroud. H S 'Jum' Thomas, centre, was the former Group leader (retired 1984) and Don Munns, Chairman of the Scout Executive Committee is on the right.

Often the bearers would go on to help run units themselves for new children to experience and enjoy the world of scouts and guides.

Fundraisers galore abound in Cuffley and Northaw. Cancer charities, the NSPCC, the Red Cross, the Royal National Lifeboat Institution, the National Childbirth Trust, the Cat's Protection League, the four churches: St Thomas of Canterbury, St Martin de Porres, St Andrew's and The Cuffley Free Church all have their fundraising events and social activities.

There are groups for line dancing, a bridge club, darts teams and it can be seen that the villages of Northaw and Cuffley do their best to interest and educate the residents. There are many reasons that people need to take part in community activities and all the societies welcome fresh faces and new ideas: newcomers to the area and anyone who is perhaps alone for the first time are particularly welcome.

Perhaps the last organisation to mention, and there

must be many that have been omitted, should be the Leonard Cheshire Cuffley Care at Home Service. Staffed by dedicated carers, many Cuffley residents are able to remain in their own homes when no longer strong enough to look after themselves. So many people have enjoyed the cheerful service of these reliable and helpful people. The idea was developed in Cuffley by Gill Stephenson. The link with Leonard Cheshire was at a later date, and the service operates from their base in the Cuffley and Northaw Youth Centre.

They really are a tribute to 'organisations' in the area and provide a link for the elderly with the outside world when the older people are no longer able to go to their favourite meetings anymore.

Perhaps we can finish this look at the organisations by reminding ourselves of the great imagination shown by the planners of the Jubilee celebration on the 1 July 1897 which was held at Northaw.

(Continued on page 120)

The Cuffley Scout Headquarters   *Jennifer Cook*

The original 1st Cuffley Scout Hut, built in 1930. It was set amongst the trees at the foot of Plough Hill. It is shown here in 1964, just before demolition to make way for redevelopment as part of the St Andrew's Church site. *Below:* Jennifer Cook's illustration of the new Scout Headquarters which was featured on the 1989 Scout Christmas Stamp, (see page 115).

A sepia wash drawing of Scout Leader Lionel Gill by Graham Rust, 1970. Reproduced by
kind permission of the artist. (For further examples of Graham's work before and after he
moved away from Cuffley, see pages 146-150).

Post Card of Tolmers Scout Camp and Activity Centre, (Tolmers Road, EN6 4JS) and the entrance in 2000, showing the sign & badge. The postcard illustrates canoes where the Cuffley Brook has been diverted to make a small lake in the valley, created in memory of Bert Longden, a former warden of the Camp.

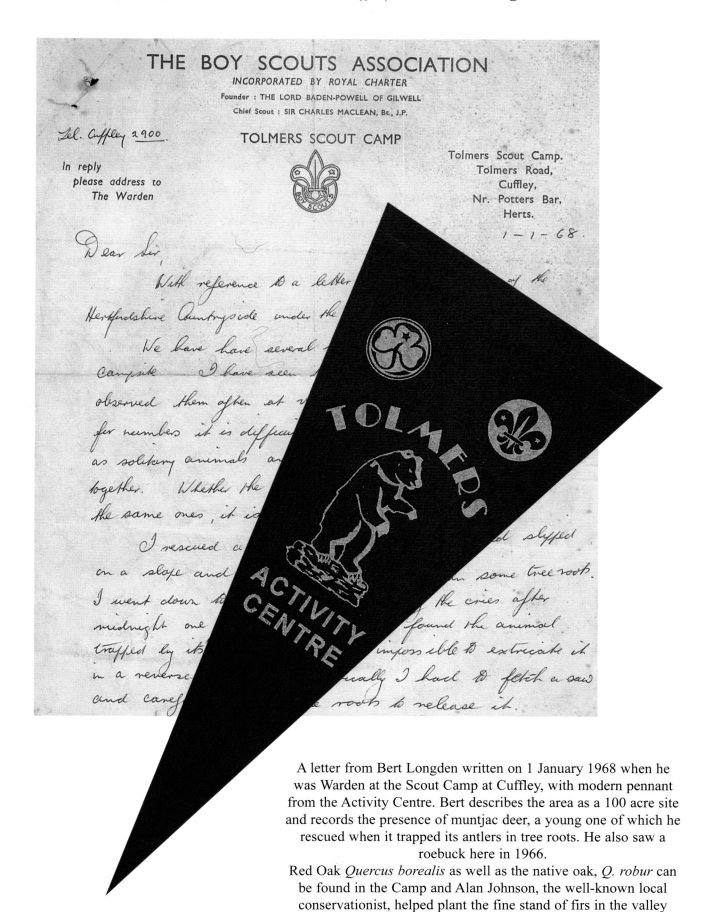

A letter from Bert Longden written on 1 January 1968 when he was Warden at the Scout Camp at Cuffley, with modern pennant from the Activity Centre. Bert describes the area as a 100 acre site and records the presence of muntjac deer, a young one of which he rescued when it trapped its antlers in tree roots. He also saw a roebuck here in 1966.

Red Oak *Quercus borealis* as well as the native oak, *Q. robur* can be found in the Camp and Alan Johnson, the well-known local conservationist, helped plant the fine stand of firs in the valley above the Brook, about fifty years ago.

John Parkes, an Honorary Scouter, who still organises the Scout Postal Service (see facing page). Lord Baden-Powell of Gilwell (1857-1941) founder of the Boy Scout Movement. His wife Olave went on to form the Girl Guides Association. John Parkes lives in Brookside Crescent and this view towards Cuffley from the Cuffley Camp site about 1946, shows the fields before the houses were built here. Tolmers Road houses and the hill rising up to Hanyards Farm are in the background. By kind permission of Alan Gill.

1st CUFFLEY SCOUTS

CHRISTMAS DELIVERY SERVICE 5p

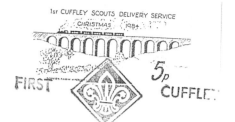

The 1952-1977 Queen Elizabeth II Jubilee tea and disco organised by the Guides at the Cuffley Youth Centre on Tuesday 7 June 1977, (*top*). District Commissioner Patricia Klijn is escorting Division Commissioner Mrs Charlton, (*top left*). Klaas Klijn, the friendly and helpful face for visitors to Novelties for many years, is facing the camera, (*top right*) and Pat Cheetham, who ran the Youth Centre at this time, and later managed Cuffley Hall, can be seen in a light jacket. His son, Brent is shown on page 237. The Guides procession for an earlier event turns into Station Road from Plough Hill, (by 'Photo-Art Studio 1 Station Road Cuffley').

The Guides' procession (*facing page, bottom picture*), is led by, right, Ruth Ogborn, Tessa Godfrey, Georgina Hardwick, Brenda Le Maitre, Jill Rawlings and Belinda Bath (looking towards the camera).

Right: The Presentation by Queen's Guide Tessa Godfrey to Nancy Marriner, remembered by so many (see text), on her retirement, inside the Old School Room on the site of what is now St Andrew's Church. Nancy's family had owned parts of Home Wood some of which became the Scout and Guide camp. Now known as the Tolmers Activity Centre, it was featured on national television when BBC Breakfast, (8.20am, 8 August 2003), showed Scouts seated outdoors at the site under a canopy, working on computers round the camp fire.

The First Cuffley Guides pictured in the Playing Fields Cuffley about 1951. In the picture above at Nancy Marriner's retirement, Lady Pryke and Mrs N Blackford are shown seated at the back of the classroom. (Jack Gray recalls attending this classroom for the first time with his sister Joan when it was the village school during the First World War. "We were too young to be in a lesson so they sat us on the stage pulling threads from material and told us it was for the war effort!")

Overleaf: Tolmers Activity Centre from the air. Reproduced by kind permission of the Centre.

Exterior and interior views of Cuffley Youth Centre.
The Leonard Cheshire Cuffley Care at Home Service now has offices in part of the building.
Below: a view from the sports field.

(Jubilee celebration on 1 July 1897): 'After the *Dinner to Parishioners over 50* (12.45), *the Cricket Match* (1pm), *the Steam Circus* (2.30pm), *the Tug of War (Farms versus Houses)* and the *Obstacle Race* (2.50pm), during the children's tea there would be three races for the parents:

Married women's race - *thread needle held by husband half way and return threaded.*

Grandfather's race - *light pipe half way.*

Husband's & Wive's race - *husband blindfolded to find wife at a given point and return together'.*

Chapter Nine
Cuffley's shops

Cuffley's shops are an interesting reflection of the changes and needs of the village over the years. The premises are a mixture of freehold and leasehold and the documentation of just some of these changes induces a wave of nostalgia and memories. The business history is the life blood of a small community and for a place the size of Cuffley there have always been numerous shops to support. The starting point was the rough list made for a talk by Patricia Klijn in the 1980s.

The shops in Cuffley as I remember them as a child during the 1940s included, at the top of Station Road, the post office, where sweets were kept in large glass jars. It was crowded, dark and small. Something about the size of the place prevented too

Cuffley Stores pictured in a contact print made from a glass negative in David Whyte's collection of old Cuffley images lent to the authors in 1965. This now houses Thurlow's Insurance Brokers.

The date of 1925 is given by Gerald Millington for the photograph and he recorded that the shop was built for Mrs Martin and leased to Blaxlands, the grocers, of Cheshunt. Blaxlands moved into a single storey shop next door before the Second World War, but this side was burnt out when a bomb fell in Station Road during the conflict. The building was reconstructed and for many years now has been an off-licence.

Over the next two pages we reproduce two enlargements made from the same glass plate negative in 1965 to show the detail in the windows.

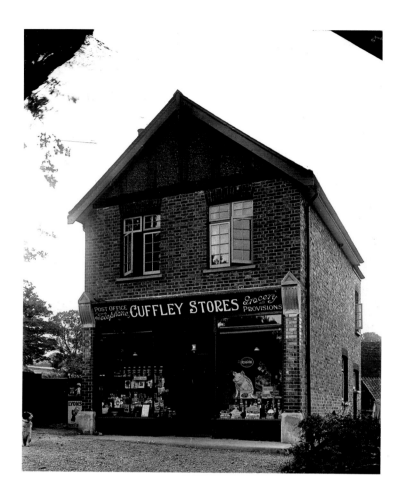

much lingering inside. But next door was a paradise. Blaxlands the grocers, with glass-sided tins of loose biscuits, rows of wooden shelves and assistants who trotted up and down to fetch the items on the shopping list. Cheese would be cut with a wire, ham and bacon was sliced and each purchase ended up neatly folded into a greaseproof paper parcel. The bill had to be paid at the cash desk - a large wooden cage with a glass front, rather like a railway ticket office, where presided Miss Millington, accurately adding up purchases and giving change. Blaxlands was fun.

The opposite side of the road also boasted a cash desk in Ripleys the butchers. Here meat was in short supply and the magic words 'offal' or 'liver' soon ensured a queue would form out onto the pavement. There was also a fresh fish shop at no. 16, presided over by a plump lady with dark hair tied back in a bun. Rovers the Bakers at no. 18 served light refreshments and handled vast quantities of bread,

rolls and cakes as well. The Eddowes family ran the shop for many years. An anecdote was told of a lady from the Ridgeway who came in for 'half a loaf as she only wanted it for breadcrumbs'.

The Tea Lounge was a more traditional cafe, usually busy with a 'good lunch' and numerous tea and cake customers. The shoe repairer was Mr Hand and his wife helped in the front shop. It was here that the rose hips we all collected had to be handed in to be sent off to make juice as part of the war effort. Mrs Hand was in fact a wonderful seamstress and embroideress and many years later (1961) gave us a pair of embroidered pillowcases for a wedding present. The pillowcases are still treasured. Although this was no. 22 Station Road, the telephone book of the time still used '3, Station Parade'. No 2 Station Parade was A K M Baynton & Co, and their advertisement proclaimed that they were 'the oldest established estate agents in Cuffley'. Houses and bungalows were shown for sale and wanted, rents

were collected, surveys and valuations could be obtained, but at that time few people were moving and families tended to remain in the same houses for many years.

There was always a chemist on the corner, trading for a lengthy period as C M Holmes Ltd, full of intriguing bottles and potions where Mr David Smith was the pharmacist. Theobalds Road, unmade then, was the way to Cuffley School and crossing the road here brought us to the second block of shops. W D Jones (Greengrocer) had the corner site, piled with vegetables and fruit in season. There were brass scales and Mrs Jones invariably wore gloves to handle the potatoes. The shop, with bare wooden floor, smelled of freshly boiled beetroots. These were a favourite item in the Cuffley School dinner menu and salads were always red with beetroot.

Then came Churchills, a hardware shop where Mr and Mrs Blunt sold everything remotely connected with pots, pans, brushes, polish, soap powder and

garden tools. (They must have also provided animal foodstuffs because we were able to get 'Karswood' there which had to be fed to our hens).

Next door was Mayfair, the confectioners, then run by Mr and Mrs Sutcliffe. Here, too, was a lending library where books could be borrowed for 2d a week - a bit like the Boots Booklovers Library. At the same time they were calling their address no 32 Station Road. Barclays Bank was for many years at no 34 and had a dark brown counter with bars behind which officiated the well dressed staff.

Mr Bowles ran 'Novelties' with a wonderful mixture of toys, stationery, books and haberdashery at no 36. There was a tea room at the back and a large display window crammed with merchandise.

The Perrys ran a drapery at no. 38 where aprons, stockings, tea cloths and such vied for space. A chair was provided for purchasers at the counter, but a gloomy atmosphere prevailed in the shop because a blind half covered the window.

Facing page and above: details from the 1925 glass plate negative of Cuffley Stores. The enamel advertising signs and product names are particularly attractive and many local people will remember when sweets were dispensed from the large glass jars, safely out of easy reach, on the top shelf. There are the familiar names such as Mackintosh's Toffees and Peek Frean Biscuits. Local View Postcards are also advertised.

In February 1997 Steve Wackett posed for us outside the long established family newsagents which is referred to in the text. Opposite: bills from the electrical shop. The name was changed by the owner in 1954 and both invoices feature one of the outline letterpress display typefaces that were fashionable at that time.

Wacketts has always been Wacketts and Ralph and his wife were always seeing to the needs of Cuffley newspaper readers with magazines, sweets and stationery. From here came our weekly 'Sunny Stories' price 2d and the Daily Sketch. In an advertisement for 1947 there was also a library at Wacketts. Ralph's father Sidney Wackett took on the shop at no 40 Station Road in 1929 when he gave up cycling from Cheshunt every day with the newspapers.

The end shop, no 42, was originally a dairy, but became 'Adele' the hairdressers. Little cubicles with curtains ensured that hair cuts were very private affairs between you and the lady with the scissors. For many years it was here that we went for a trim 'just above the ears'.

Where Lambs Close now stands there were glasshouses and a shop called Thrussells selling vegetables and fruit. Lambs Close takes its name from the butcher called Lamb who had a shop on the site where the maisonettes are now built. This shop was burnt down many years earlier.

Off under the bridge towards the bus stop and across the road were two important places 'The Kiosk' and the coal office, or more correctly, Sidney Morris, coal merchant. The Kiosk was run by Mr Len Duncombe, who lived on Plough Hill, serving teas, snacks and breakfasts for passing workers.

S. G. Morris was an important port of call where you climbed rickety wooden stairs to order or pay for the vital coal or anthracite. It had a lovely smell of coal sacks and dust. The station yard nearby provided the storage for coal and trucks. Different bill heads show the Cuffley telephone number: 'Cuffley 2000'. (The reference to the LNER railway had gone on the second version). The little hut appears in numerous pictures and is illustrated on pages 90, 103, 128, 129 and 130 of this book.

So to the last of the Cuffley shops, the Lulworth Florists, at that time run by the Warmerdam family.

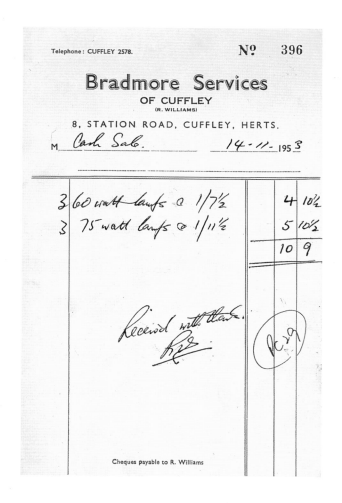

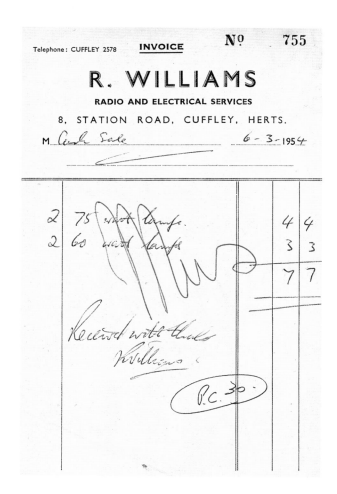

(They also had the glasshouses of Lulworth Nurseries at the top of Cuffley Hill).

Later on Cuffley gained more shops as the site was rebuilt at the top of Station Road to house the Cuffley Building Supplies, James R Rogers, estate agents, a new Ripleys grocers and R W Childs, a shop selling bicycles and toys.

At no 8 Bradmore Services from Brookmans Park opened an electricians run by Mr Ron Williams and his wife, Peggy. Shortly afterwards the name changed to R Williams who traded there from 1953 until his retirement in 1993. *'In those (early) days,'* wrote Mr Williams, *'we could re-charge your accumulator for 6d, or test all the valves in your radio for half a crown'*. In later years the Williams opened the first video library in Cuffley, which was passed on to the Wacketts in 1993. The other 'half' of the shop was occupied for many years by a dental practice under Mr Baird and later Mr Choksi which later moved up the road. The combined premises

now hold a veterinary practice, 'The Cuffley Hill Veterinary Surgery'. It is not on Cuffley Hill, but with all the other mixed up names for Station Road it is unlikely that Cuffley minds. And how much more convenient to take your animals down the road than traipse to Potters Bar or Cheshunt as before.

Maywyn at no 10 Station Road delighted many new residents of Cuffley who marvelled at the overflowing stocks of vests, childrens wear, wool and clothing. Over the years the owners were W & M Olphert, at 2 Station Road in 1947, offering wools, hosiery and fancy drapery. Then Mrs D Parr (1954) followed and latterly Mrs Tibbs. Curson and Poole took the premises on as estate agents and this trade continues now in the hands of Bairstow Eves.

It was many years after the construction of flats on the 'Cabin' side of Station Road that shops were built where the dry cleaners and the Indian restaurant now stand. W G Proctor had a furniture

(Continued on page 128)

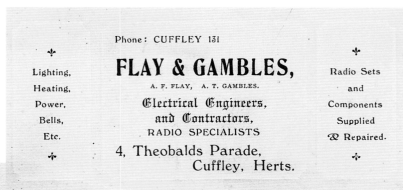

Phone: CUFFLEY 131

FLAY & GAMBLES,

A. F. FLAY, A. T. GAMBLES.

Electrical Engineers,
and Contractors,

RADIO SPECIALISTS

4, Theobalds Parade,
Cuffley, Herts.

Lighting,
Heating,
Power,
Bells,
Etc.

Radio Sets
and
Components
Supplied
& Repaired.

Telephone: CUFFLEY 2206.

"NOVELTIES"

(Proprietor - C. J. BOWLES)

**STATIONERY ▪ CHINA ▪ TOYS ▪ ETC.
ARTISTS' MATERIALS ▪ HABERDASHERY.**

HOME-MADE CAKES AND JAMS.

**TEA ROOMS:
36, STATION ROAD, CUFFLEY.**

(Opposite Cuffley Hotel).

194

Flay & Gambles,
with the telephone number
Cuffley 131, were the
previous occupants of
Novelties and used the
original address of
'Theobalds Parade' before
'Station Road' was
adopted.
The letterhead was from a
1940s print run.
Patricia (left) and her
mother, Olive Fenshom,
are pictured in the
entrance to their shop in
about 1950.

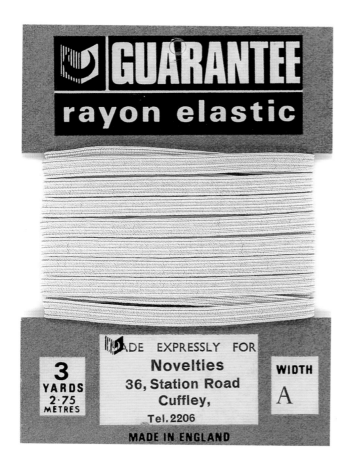

Rayon elastic 'made expressly for Novelties' came
with a guarantee in the 1950s.
A signwriter from about 1955 listed the main
attractions as a customer, oblivious to danger,
gazes at the toys.
A colour postcard from the 1980s shows the shop
when it became 'Parade', four shop fronts from
the left.

An edition of lithographs limited to 17 prints was made of the Sidney Morris coal office in December 1973. (See the bill on page 92). Facing page: an earlier view of this little office which also features elsewhere in several of our pictures in this book.

shop here for some time and then Joyce Ridgway ran a children's wear shop and school outfitters that subsequently became Leejoy, (still trading in Potters Bar). Tycon and Modernistic Supplies were two of the former names for the shop now the dry cleaners, Lady Valet.

Maynard Place has seen shops such as the Co-op remain since they were built, but trades have altered in some of the businesses on the walkway along to the new Cuffley Hall. The dress shops have seen several owners and Vivienne Laurence, Francesca, Ann Chambers, Sirocco and Maroulla Designs reflect some of these changes.

The Bread Shop still flourishes as Jimmy's Bakery & Patisserie, as do Hicks the greengrocers, now into another generation of the Hicks family. Ron Hicks has retired and the business continues with Graham at the helm, supplying schools and restaurants in the area as well as the shop trade.

In 1972 Richard Briggs opened Cuffley Travel at 4 Maynard Place, giving Cuffley a first taste of a travel agency. He has now moved on to serve his customers via e-mail and the internet and home visits. The Lush beauty shop replaced Cuffley Travel; Harwins electrical shop was replaced by a saddlery and is now a children's wear shop called 'Attitude'. The Parish Council have made offices of a former dry cleaners and a florist, Cut 'n' Dried, still carries a vital service for the village.

As Cuffley developed with the building of several new estates in the 1960s Frank Head took over two shops, numbers 18-20 Station Road, and turned Rovers the Bakers and the Tea Lounge into a small, but very successful, supermarket. He had previously had a round selling groceries from his van and had thus established a strong customer base. The shop subsequently changed hands several times through Wavy Line and Londis managers and is now back into smaller units carrying a variety of trades, including mobile phones and fishing tackle.

Alan Gill has kindly given us permission to use his picture of a Free Church outing with Mr Erlebach (far left), Doreen Bennett (fourth from left), Mary Gill (fifth from left), Alan Gill (third from right), Mrs Ruth Gill (second from right) and Mrs Erlebach (far right). The clock says 3.05 and it was taken in about 1946.

A similar experiment was tried up at the Village Walk, next to Cuffley Builders, where pet foods, secondhand furniture and a kitchen outfitters occupied some of the units. For a time there was a very comprehensive sportswear shop and outfitters shop here that had originated in Maynard Place. Later on this became Peachwoods beauty shop, health spa and boutique with toning tables (said the advertisement). Nowadays it is a dental practice.

James R Rogers halved his shop and his wife ran the Stallington Shop where much Wedgwood, Denby and Aynsley china, porcelain and pottery found its way into the homes of Cuffley. Nowadays this is a Ladbrokes betting shop. Cuffley Barbers occupies the slot that traded as a grocery for many years for Ripleys at no 12. Several greengrocers succeeded the grocer's shop, at one time B Thrussell of the family that had traded from the Lambs Close outlet; for eight years, 1987-1994, John and Sandra Stone were the popular owners. No. 14 still has a

flourishing butcher's shop as Seagrave's cater for the needs of Cuffley. Ripley's continued for years and it only changed hands when Steve Newman sold out to them.

The fish shop at no 16 Station Road enclosed the old shutter type open shop and continued as a traditional fish shop under Geoffrey Hodson for many years. He was the first person to supply Cuffley with fish and chips, which had long been opposed by some of the community, and stayed for many years with his family. The shop still has food connections and has now become the Oriental Star Chinese restaurant. The shoemenders, Hands', old shop at no 22, stayed under Mr Kew as such for several years until selling up to a hairdressers, Hair Boutique which is now Stephen Fine.

The corner chemist was David Smith, followed by Ian Wright, then Ian Cope and still continues as a vital village necessity under the name Salepick Ltd.

Jones the greengrocers sold out to Barclays Bank.

By the 1960s (this was taken in 1964) the Sidney Morris Coal office began to disappear under foliage from an elder. Lulworth Florists, in an almost identical building, can be seen on the right, adjoining Cuffley Motor Company. Typical advertisements for two of the shops and the Tea Lounge are also reproduced and a unique view of the Lanthorne Cafe, in 1967, taken from the forecourt of 54 Station Road, is shown opposite. Tolmers Road is in the background. The happy baby is Sarah Klijn.

Churchills sold to Mrs Price, the Faulkner family, and finally changed to become the Solicitors Property Centre under Leslie Dubow. It continued as an estate agent called Millennium Estates, now The Moloney Partnership. Mayfair sold on to Mr and Mrs Best (1950s) and then Mr and Mrs Brown and their cousin Miss Nightingale. The shop continued with their fine selections of sweets and ice creams, cigarettes, tobacco and greeting cards. It became the Busy Bee, an interior design shop, Debbie Edwards, then the Chase Window Company. The Cheshunt Building Society replaced Barclays Bank at no 34 and latterly, as that was taken over, it became the Bristol and West Building Society until 2004.

Mr and Mrs Fenshom became shopkeepers in 1949 when they took over Novelties at 36 Station Road. Originally the shop had been an electricians called Flay and Gambles, before Mr Bowles' tenancy. Generations of children remember Novelties for its toys, Matchbox models, Hornby train sets, Meccano and Waddington games. Dressing the window at night, balancing the little Britains farm and zoo animals on glass shelves, angling every item so that whichever way you looked the window was full of interest, was Mr Fenshom's job, as was all the paper work after his normal day's work in London. Mrs Olive Fenshom ran the shop with her sister Miss Knight and later with more assistants. In 1961 Mr and Mrs Fenshom were joined by their daughter and son in law, Patricia and Klaas Klijn who continued the shop selling stationery, toys and haberdashery. In 1968 they took on the bookshop formerly run by Mr W Shepherd in Potters Bar High Street and then from Newgate Street. The shop supplied schools and libraries which enabled it to survive with trade from outside the immediate village. The Book Room became a much appreciated amenity in Cuffley. Later on, in an attempt to restore the idea of the old tea rooms, and to satisfy a childhood dream of running a cafe, a Coffee Shop was added and the

shop diversified into gifts generally in the 1980s. The name change to Parade reflected the old address of Flay and Gambles 4, Theobalds Parade. The shop sold out to Favourite Fried Chicken in 2000. It is now called Dixy Chicken.

The drapers shop at no 38 became a launderette with the latest machines and tumble dryers and then The Birkbeck Cleaners, where for some years Mrs Elsie Duncombe, wife of Len at the Kiosk, served the customers. It was followed by B G Juniper, Opticians, with a dental practice above. This now occupies the whole building as D W Lester or Cuffley and Ware Dental Care, as the sign says.

Unchanging are the Wacketts at no 40. Now into the fourth generation of the same family, the service of providing Cuffley with its daily newspapers and magazines continues. The shop has variously sold wool and haberdashery, records for some years, and now continues with a video library, stationery and toys as well as racks of cards for every occasion.

Children can still choose sweets in little baskets and Stephen and his wife Glenda are joined by their son Paul. Sally, their daughter, still helps as does Stephen's sister Vivienne.

We are now back to the end of the road, to no 42, where many hairdressers including Martine, Rosalie, Paul Charles and possibly others carried on with the scissors and curlers. For some years a gentleman's barbers was established in a separate room at the side of the building. The shop now carries the Cuffley Pizza and Kebab Shop, reflecting the changing needs of the village and the Cuffley Village Arcade includes Sunkiss, a beauty parlour, Mumbai Brasserie and the Village Coffee Bar. The restaurant opposite is the Sonarbangla Tandoori.

Just before the railway bridge is the little shop with Curiona selling sculptures, Scooter Trooper dealing in motorised scooters and Vidicall, the security company. This little site has seen lots of changes. A millinery shop, antique dealers, shoe repairers and

Original fabric collage by Patricia Klijn inspired by the Novelties shop window, 1982.
Note the pint of milk and dog in the doorway. (See pages 126 and 127 for other views
of Novelties in Station Road).

lawn mower menders are just a few of those that are remembered. On the other side of the road The Lanthorne Cafe operated for some years from two cottages at the foot of Tolmers Road. These were demolished and maisonettes were built on the site between the Harvester and Tolmers Road.

Nothing now replaces the kiosk site or the coal office, but just further on by the bus stop where you wait to go to Goffs Oak and Cheshunt is the Bridge House building of Tilgear. Tools of every kind for the specialist and craftsperson are here in a modern building which looks more like offices. This was where the Lulworth Florists stood. The station has a coffee shop called 'Cafe 2 Go'.

Sopers Road has always been the industrial heart of the village. Although it is not a vast area, it has always featured important and very necessary trades converging there. For some time there was Mackintosh's Timber Yard, (see Diana Mackintosh's reference on page 141), now occupied by Sir

William Burnett. St James Tile Company made exclusive mosaics and tiles in a unique business. Several builders had units there and Jeffrey Chapman and R Dench both had stores and offices in Sopers Road. Victor Value operated a bacon and cheese packing factory from a cold store. This meant that the wrapping of these commodities had only moved down the road to keep up the tradition started at Blaxlands all those years earlier. Later this passed on to Tesco when they acquired the premises. Amicus, a computer outlet, operated from Sopers Road before transferring to a retail site in Potters Bar. A box factory ran for many years specialising in packaging and cardboard engineering and now Tams Packaging occupies large premises on the other side of the road, continuing the tradition. Many famous companies have had their packaging made in Cuffley.

Another big name in the annals of Cuffley business history is the firm of Everest. The firm has provided

Maynard Place off Station Road before the development of the Millennium Garden and showing the Hall entrance, Library, Clinic and Doctors' Surgery. The Place is named after Alderman Gordon Maynard (see page 92).

employment for numerous people over the years and to many the name is synonymous with Cuffley. For over 30 years the company has continued to supply doors, windows, soffits, guttering, conservatories and garage doors to its customers. Newer and more substantial buildings have replaced the earlier offices. Everest and Cuffley have become firm fixtures.

Cuffley Gate is the name given to an area occupied by numerous smaller businesses at the end of Sopers Road. Allan & Bertram, Anglian Dental Engineering, Airflow Environmental, Associated Roofing, Brooksby Engineering, Ben Barrett and Sons are only a few of the names with the Cuffley Gate address. Baines have their printing works at Barley House in Sopers Road.

The garages of Cuffley have expanded to cater for the ever increasing number of mobile Cuffley residents. Cuffley Motors has showrooms and workshops in Sopers Road as well as the more

prominent position on Station Road. It no longer sells petrol, but caters for the customers that need four-wheel drive vehicles as well as the repair service and MOTs.

Volvo have long enjoyed a dealership at Cuffley. Marshalswick Motors from St Albans occupied the site for many years. It is now under the name Evans Halshaw. To the rear of the building are numerous little motor related workshops. The garage is now called turbocentre.co.uk and is a Gulf petrol station. The showrooms sell Porsche, Audi, BMW and 4x4s.

Cuffley's industrial heart finishes abruptly at the end of Sopers Road as it joins the surrounding farmland. One year the village fete was held in the fields at the end of Sopers Road. There had been the annual procession of floats and there were races as well as all the usual stalls and sideshows. But this sort of activity belongs in the next chapter, that devoted to entertainments and village occasions and there have certainly been plenty of those.

133

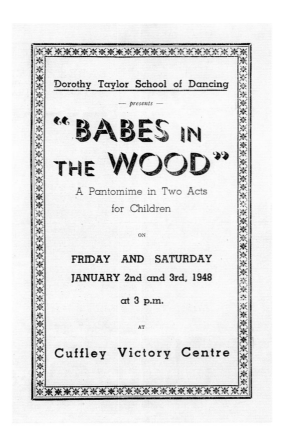

'Babes in the Wood' programme for the 1948 pantomime for children performed over two days.
Above, right: Mrs Katie Wiltshire as Mother Goose, with Patricia Fenshom, centre, and Marjorie Barrett as
'Broker's men', 'Debit and Credit', January 1953. The programme stated that 'proceeds are to be used to
entertain both the Young and Old during Coronation Week'.

Chapter Ten

Entertainment through the years in Cuffley

Pupils of Mrs Margaret Cope and Miss Dorothy Taylor gave 'a successful and entertaining show' said the *Hertfordshire Mercury* in April 1947: Children aged from 3 to 16 took part in a programme of tap dancing, ballet and musical comedy dancing with plays and sketches.

The children were all from Mrs Cope's elocution classes or the dancing classes run by Dorothy Taylor. Costumes were much admired, especially the soldiers in the dance routine who were dressed in blackout material as skirts and crepe paper tabard-like tops. The event took place at the Cuffley Victory Centre with Councillor Frederick Slatford as

compere, Mrs Vida Slatford as the perruquier and Mrs Margery Briggs at the piano.

The event was typical of numerous such events that took place in the Cabin over the years. In 1948 The Dorothy Taylor School of Dancing put on a pantomime 'Babes in the Wood', again an all children's performance, with printed programmes and the cast drawn from their weekly classes in the Old Schoolroom. In 1946 Dorothy Clark, (nee Taylor), had been widowed, leaving her with a baby son and two invalid parents. Making theatrical costumes and running dancing classes enabled her to support her family. Years later (1994) Dorothy Alys, as she is now known, is still a theatrical costumier from her home in Stevenage. Dorothy sang a most poignant song 'This is my Lovely Day' beautifully in her wedding dress on a windswept impromptu stage in the King George V Playing Fields for one occasion. Only later does the true significance of that act sink in.

A rare colour photograph of a typical Cabin production of Dick Wittington taken by John Carter and kindly copied to us for this book. John commented that it was his first attempt at photographing a production in colour and the camera had to be hand-held with a long exposure - hence the soft focus.
About 1960. Note the scenery and footlights.

Mrs Margaret (Lottie) Cope ran elocution classes from her Tolmers Road home, where each week the pupils had to learn and recite a variety of poetry. Occasionally they were entrants in poetry and drama festivals and the stage performances encouraged self confidence and enjoyment. It was Margaret's son Ian who later ran the chemist's shop in Cuffley.

Some names crop up frequently in chronicles of Cuffley entertainment. Margery Briggs' daughter Anne went on to open her own ballet school in Cuffley and it is still flourishing today. The Anne Briggs School of Dancing opened in 1954 and hundreds of would-be ballerinas have danced their way through her classes and on to the stages of the Cabin or Cuffley Hall and taken part in various examinations. Mrs Katie Clark Wiltshire, under the heading the 'K.T. Company' produced annual pantomimes, drama sketches, organised concerts and musical entertainments. The group was always well rehearsed in her Plough Hill home before taking to

the boards of the Cabin and enjoyment was the key to her success for both audience and cast alike. Never happier than when performing herself, Katie Wiltshire delighted in her role as pantomime dame in a lurid jumper and brightly coloured wig, clowning through the show with perfect timing. She inspired many would-be actresses and was always cheerful. Her daughter Kitty, (another 'K.T.') often took the role of principal boy in the pantomimes and carried on the enthusiastic company style. 'Mother Goose' in 1953, (also performed at Tolmers Hospital), 'Cinderella' in 1955, and 'Little Red Riding Hood' in 1956 carried on the tradition and the pantomime was given a repeat performance at Forty Hill.

Graham Rust took part in the 1956 show, Kitty was Prince Charming and Maureen Green was little Red Riding Hood. The Cabin was packed for matinee and evening performances and a huge tea was served by Mrs French, the caretaker's wife, between

135

Children from Mrs Margaret 'Lottie' Cope's elocution classes and Dorothy Taylors dancing pupils take part in a concert at the Cabin. Note the black-out material used for curtains and the soldiers' skirts. (Picture stamp on reverse of 'J T Lince, Press & Commercial Photographer, 36 Tolmers Road, Cuffley'). Included are Roger Wilkes, Patricia Fenshom, Maureen Chapman, Sandra Piedot, Janet Hilliard and Astra Eddowes.

the shows. There was no hint of stage fright as all tucked in readily to the brightly coloured pink and yellow cakes.

Rose Hilliard, who was often billed as singing at concerts and entertainments, helped behind the scenes and her daughter Janet Hilliard was part of the comic duo in several of the pantomimes. Janet recalls carrying her costume on a hanger in the snow from Burleigh Way to the Cabin. 'There were no cars then', she says. 'Cinderella' in 1955 saw Rose as the Baroness and Janet Hilliard and Patricia Fenshom as the Ugly Sisters. Years before this show Janet and Patricia had dressed up as 'Bisto Kids' at a village function and carried off a prize, (overleaf).

Mary Stuart's School of Dancing provided the dancers for some of the shows and Ralph Wackett provided the box office facility from his shop in Station Road. Mrs Culpin, (Mary Stuart), ran dancing classes for years in the village from the Cabin. Ballet and tap classes were equally well

attended. Cuffley has always enjoyed dancing, from Vida Slatford's Scottish Dancing classes to today's Line Dancers and the continuing Anne Briggs School.

'The late Mrs Martin's 29th Concert in aid of The Hertfordshire Fund for the Blind' read a programme in 1953. Lots of the same names crop up in this particular year, but with gaps for war years, the concerts had always been an opportunity for Cuffley to show its charitable heart. Nowadays many events are held in aid of a charity and the Old Time music halls chaired by Sid Perkins raised funds for many organisations under their name 'The Charitees'.

The Patron of the 'Cuffley Operatic Society' is Rodney Slatford, a familiar BBC Radio 3 voice from Manchester, (p 144). Started up in 1975, many wonderful shows have graced the stage of the new Cuffley Hall using all the facilities the larger stage offered. Old favourites like 'Salad Days', 'Fiddler on the Roof', 'The Merry Widow' and 'Oliver' have

'Little Red Riding Hood' in the Cabin from about 1952, including Graham Rust (see page 145) on the extreme left. The group also includes Patricia Fenshom, Sally Mumford, Pat Raven, Maureen Green, Kitty Wiltshire, Avril Sare, Alec Gibb, Janet Hilliard, Elizabeth Hall, Susan and Jackie Barrett.

all attracted full houses and been very professional entertainments. Margaret Briggs, wife of Richard, who ran Cuffley Travel and started the Cuffley Business Association, has starred in many productions, memorably as Anna in the 'The King and I', swishing and singing beautifully in her crinoline skirt. Her son, Paul Briggs, takes part too, and also joined the West End cast of 'Oliver' for a season. The shows use a professional orchestra and draw on cast members from the 'Wood Green Operatic Society', where some performers have acted for both companies.

No chapter on the story of entertainment in Cuffley can be complete without 'The Cuffley Players' being featured. Started in 1934, the Society came into being from the idea of the then vicar, Rev. Lionel Sparks. The first production was 'Crazy Cruise'. After a break in the war years, the Players formed again in 1947 with a performance of an original pantomime 'Forty Winks for the Princess'. The

company *'continued as an integral part of the village life'*, said an entry in the 6th Post War Edition of the Northaw and Cuffley Ratepayer's Association Handbook.

The idea of the original Players was to perform plays written by a member of their own circle, thus creating drama which would have its first production on the Cuffley stage. Grappling with the vagaries of the old Cabin platform and lack of backstage facilities was always a challenge, but sets and scenery have been stunning and worthy of West End settings.

For years Geoffrey Orme was the playwright and the assistant producer was his wife Evelyn. He gave up a career in insurance to become a full-time writer after his war service. It was a prodigious output, with new plays twice a year for the Cuffley Players, as well as his other work as a scriptwriter for a film company. He also wrote plays for the radio. The Cuffley Players always wore evening dress to usher

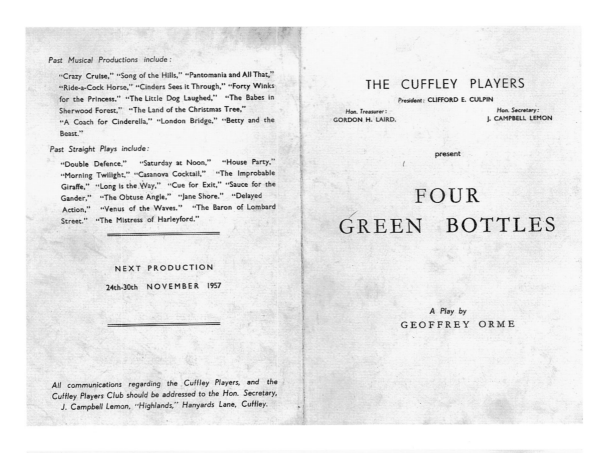

Past Musical Productions include :

"Crazy Cruise," "Song of the Hills," "Pantomania and All That,"
"Ride-a-Cock Horse," "Cinders Sees it Through," "Forty Winks
for the Princess," "The Little Dog Laughed," "The Babes in
Sherwood Forest," "The Land of the Christmas Tree,"
"A Coach for Cinderella," "London Bridge," "Betty and the
Beast."

Past Straight Plays include :

"Double Defence," "Saturday at Noon," "House Party,"
"Morning Twilight," "Casanova Cocktail," "The Improbable
Giraffe," "Long is the Way," "Cue for Exit," "Sauce for the
Gander," "The Obtuse Angle," "Jane Shore," "Delayed
Action," "Venus of the Waves," "The Baron of Lombard
Street," "The Mistress of Harleyford."

NEXT PRODUCTION

24th-30th NOVEMBER 1957

*All communications regarding the Cuffley Players, and the
Cuffley Players Club should be addressed to the Hon. Secretary,
J. Campbell Lemon, "Highlands," Hanyards Lane, Cuffley.*

THE CUFFLEY PLAYERS

President: CLIFFORD E. CULPIN

Hon. Treasurer:
GORDON H. LAIRD.

Hon. Secretary:
J. CAMPBELL LEMON

present

FOUR
GREEN BOTTLES

A Play by
GEOFFREY ORME

CHARACTERS

(In order of appearance)

STELLA RAINE	Brenda Lemaitre
HENRY FORSYTH	Warner Hall
HUBERT LOXLEY	Jack Hemmings
DICK MEDLICOT	Stephen Hall
MARY PETERS	Lynda Stone
BERNARD MEDLICOT	Geoffrey Orme
CAROL DANE	Mary Lewis
GERALDINE WENDOVER	Pat Parrot
MRS. DANE	Winifred Wilkes
INSPECTOR HAWK	David Whyte
EILEEN MOODIE	Violet Beetch
JOE MAYNARD	Philip Wilkes
JENNIFER MASON	Sylvia Meakin
MERVYN WHITTAKER	Ronald Offlow
DORIS CROXLEY	Barbara Spencer

Production by Geoffrey Orme.

The action takes place near Victoria Station, London

ACT 1.   Mr Loxley's Chemist Shop.

Scene 1.   Morning.
Scene 2.   Afternoon.

ACT 2.   Police Station

Scene 1.   Early Evening.
Scene 2.   Late Evening.

ACT 3.   The same

Scene 3.   Later that Night.

Stage Manager : KEN JOHNS
Assistant Stage Manager : GERALD BRANDOM
Property Master : IAN NEWMAN
Lighting : JACK LEMON
Equipment : STRAND ELECTRIC
Sound Equipment : J. R. WHITE
Scenery Designed by ERNEST WRIGHT and executed by
Members of the Company
Wardrobe Supervision : VIDA SLATFORD
Hall Manager : CLIFF CULPIN
Publicity : GERALD BRANDOM

THE PLAYERS WISH TO THANK ALL THOSE WHO HAVE ASSISTED
SO GENEROUSLY AS PROGRAMME SELLERS, HALL STEWARDS,
AND IN VARIOUS OTHER CAPACITIES.

Both sides of the same 1956 Cuffley Players programme. Hon Secretary Jack Lemon was a near neighbour of 'Geoff' Orme (see text opposite) and the Lemon's house in Hanyards Lane was later replaced by two new properties at the same site. It can can be partly seen in the background of the picture on page 259.

The *Bisto Kids* fancy dress performers Janet Hilliard (*left*) and Patricia Fenshom. The costumes were hired from the actual Bisto Company because they had found there was such a demand for performances that it was worthwhile organising their own service to performers. In the right side of the background of the picture is the Spiritualist Meeting Hall, next to the Cabin.
Freddie Shepherd starred (*right*) with Winifred Wilkes (*left*) and Violet Beech (in nurse's uniform) in the Cuffley Players' production of 'Venus of the Waves'. Geoffrey Orme is in the pith helmet. John Higgs holds the archive of programmes and has many pictures from memorable performances of this very creative group.

you to your seats, (and still do) and such a sense of occasion was created worthy of any first night. Annual membership of the Cuffley Players Club used to cost five shillings and with that you received a ticket for each of the two main productions during the year.

Geoffrey Orme lived in Hanyards Lane in a house designed by Clifford Culpin called 'Dalarna'. Starring in many of his earlier plays was Freddie Shepherd, another Hanyards Lane resident. Freddie was equally at home in comedy roles or as the romantic lead, often opposite Maureen Fry, who still attends the Cuffley Player's productions. 'Venus of the Waves' was a typical such play in 1955, with Freddie as a cockney comic, (Corporal Bender) and Maureen as the Venus of the title. Two of the girls in the harem were Maureen Best and Patricia Fenshom, recognisable as shopkeeper's daughters from the sweetshop, Mayfair, and the toyshop, Novelties. Costumes were hired from Charles H Fox and the

cast felt as near professional as possible.

Not to be forgotten are pantomimes put on over the years at the Cuffley Free Church, produced and written by Pat Roser, or those produced by the members of the Northaw and Cuffley Youth Centre, usually staged at Northaw Village Hall. All have given hours of fun to the actors and audiences as well as aiding the funds for the organisations themselves.

When Cuffley acquired a grand piano for more serious classical music, (following a heated debate on its purchase at a meeting in the temporary Cabin), the village was able to attend and enjoy a continuing series of classical concerts. The Cuffley Concert Club was set up by Reg Platt and celebrated artists were engaged to perform on Sunday evenings in the new hall. It has meant new opportunities for residents to hear live classical music without travelling to London or elsewhere.

Organ recitals have taken place in St Andrew's

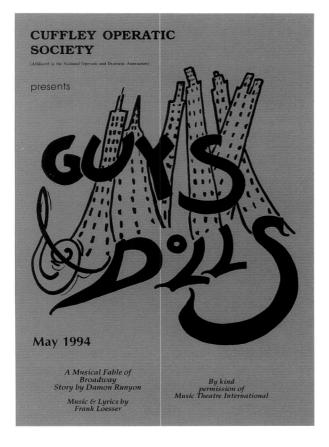

Two of the excellent productions put on by the Cuffley Operatic Society. Rodney Slatford (page 144) is the Patron of the Society. Margaret Briggs continues to be a leading singer with the Group. Her husband Richard and his sister Anne Briggs are very well known Cuffley people for their work in travel and dance.

Church with many famous names like Carlo Curley playing for the Cuffley audiences.

Both Women's Institutes at Northaw and Cuffley have always had lively drama groups performing not only for the entertainment of their own members but for charitable and other fundraising events.

Cuffley Players ticket for their Millennium performance *'Murder in Play'*.

Chapter Eleven

People

The Parish has links with many people who have made a name for themselves in various walks of life and become known nationally. Research has also thrown up some surprises and we have selected more recent names, followed by entries which have been listed alphabetically. We would be pleased to know of people we have unintentionally missed out.

Sir Cameron Mackintosh

During the preparation of this book we quickly accumulated a folder of press cuttings about the brilliant theatre impresario, Sir Cameron Mackintosh, who we knew had grown up in Cuffley. It was, however, his mother, Diana Mackintosh who kindly provided us with the most helpful insight into

During the preparation of this book Sir Cameron Mackintosh's mother Diana (*left*) sent us this delightful family picture of Cameron with her in the early 1970s. Diana also described aspects of their life in Cuffley to us in letters including the one quoted (see text below).

his formative years and has allowed us to reproduce her letter in full:

'Cameron has asked me to answer your letter as he is on his way to New York. I am his mother, so I am sure I can help you.

Firstly, the house on the Ridgeway you mentioned belonged to my brother-in-law, Bill Mackintosh - we lived in Vineyards Road, in a house called Willow Mead, and that is where all the children were brought up, and where Cameron had his first Puppet Theatre. The barn in the back of the garden was turned into a miniature theatre and Cameron wrote the scripts at the age of eight, and his brother Robert pulled the strings! Cameron went to a prep school in Cricklade and afterwards to Prior Park College in Bath. John McCarthy, who was held hostage in Beirut for five years, was a close friend.

You also mentioned the house of Walter Hammond on the Ridgeway. Just by coincidence we viewed the house with the intention of buying it, but in the end

we decided on Willow Mead because it had wonderful views, a large garden and a tennis court, which was more suitable for the boys.

We lived there until 1973. I remember well the Novelties Toy Shop. It was on the way to my husband's Timber Yard by the railway station.'

Cameron's entry in *Who's Who* catalogues his amazing success story and hard work in the theatre, following a visit to Julian Slade's *Salad Days* with his mother and aunt at the age of ten. He has produced over 400 productions world-wide and his London productions include **Godspell** (1975), **Oliver!** (1977 & 1994), **My Fair Lady** (1979 & 2001), **Oklahoma!** (1980 & 2000), **Cats** (1981), **Les Miserables** (1985), **Phantom of the Opera** (1986), **Miss Saigon** (1989) and **Carousel** (1993).

Cameron was knighted in 1996 and our press cuttings speak of him *'saving the musical for Britain'* as well as listing some of his good works in funding many charitable projects. *'Mackintosh*

Cameron, (*left*) with his brothers Robert and Nicholas performing in the 1960s at their home in Vineyards Road, Cuffley (*facing page*). 'I've always loved musicals,' he has said, 'ever since my aunt took me to see Salad Days when I was ten'. *Right: Les Miserables* programme from 1985, by kind permission.

displays few signs of ego or empty affectation,' said a Sunday Times profile, (31 December 1995) and added: *'Everybody agrees he is a very nice man; nobody has a bad word to say.'*

Amongst all the references to his creative drive and hard work it is his eye for detail that is suggested as one of the clues to his success. Thankfully, having been 'stage-struck' at such an early age, he was able to develop this creative genius producing puppet shows with his brothers in the barn at the end of the garden in Cuffley.

John McCarthy

Diana mentioned John McCarthy in her letter. He also grew up in Cuffley and moved with his parents to Broxted in Essex in the 1970s. Our newspapers from 9 August 1991 show how John's release from captivity as a hostage in Lebanon was front-page news after 1,939 days of agonising imprisonment.

We have found John's subsequent books about his

life are valuable records of the effects of such cruel treatment and his recent *A Ghost Upon Your Path* reflects on his search for his family history in Ireland as he comes to terms with the loss of his mother when he was still a hostage. The personal tragedy of not being able to see her or share her last years is one of the most poignant personal concerns he wrestles with on the beautiful County Kerry coast, but he always writes with gentle humour and insight so that serious themes are woven into his narrative and make his style of writing very digestible. It is a book which you regret has to end: it has so much descriptive appeal, laced as it is with perceptive critical analysis of modern life.

His other books are *Some Other Rainbow* (with Jill Morrell, who led the campaign for John's release), *Island Race* (with Sandi Toksvig, well known for entertaining us on *Call my Bluff* and *I'm Sorry I Haven't a Clue*), and *Between Extremes* (with Brian Keenan, his indefatigable fellow hostage).

Sir Cameron Mackintosh's Cuffley home, above, left, where he put on performances for the family which 'consisted of my two brothers and myself doing puppet shows'.

John McCarthy's childhood home on the Ridgeway, above, right. His experiences as a hostage have now featured in the film *Blind Flight* which went on general release in April 2004. John still visits Hertfordshire: (*right*). He is shown presenting awards at his old school, Haileybury College in the *Hertfordshire Mercury*, 19 November 2004.

With John is the Haileybury College student Nikki Wrangle who had won the 2004 Employer's Award.

Trevor Bentham and **Rodney Slatford** were both born a few years before Cameron and John, but have also become very successful in the Arts. Trevor shared an air raid shelter in Hill Rise as a baby with one of the authors between 1943 and 1945 and although he later moved away, their parents regularly kept in touch and he visited Joan Clark, two doors away from his old home, in 1995. Trevor always loved the theatre and became a stage manager and screenwriter. He met Nigel, later Sir Nigel Hawthorne, during the production of *Privates on Parade*. In his autobiography, Sir Nigel describes how he only came to really enjoy life after he met Trevor. They later lived both in North Hertfordshire, near Baldock, and in East Hertfordshire, near Ware.

Rodney attended Guildhouse School near his home in Carbone Hill and Bishop's Stortford College thereafter. He not only succeeded as a leading double-bass player, but became a familiar voice on Radio 3 through his introductions to concerts in

Manchester. He set up a company Yorke Edition which specialises in everything connected with the double-bass instrument. There is an excellent web site e-mail info@yorkedition.co.uk and Rodney has homes in both Manchester and Norfolk.

Other well known contemporary artists have made brief appearances in our Parish including the fine stage and film actor **Albert Finney**, who appeared in *Night Must Fall* (1964), directed by Karel Reisz (filmed at Vine Cottage, then the Vicarage) when Max Bryant lived there. Susan Hampshire starred with Mona Washbourne and Sheila Hancock, all of whom were charming to visiting locals who the Vicar allowed to watch the production. Michael Clark wrote a long description of the filming at the time in his journal which included:

'The Vicar introduced me to A.F. and he was as polite and charming as the Vicar said he would be. (He had brought his parents down to watch the filming earlier in the week). After shaking hands we

Trevor Bentham (see previous page) on a visit to his old friend Joan Clark who lived in Hill Rise, Cuffley. Trevor's mother and Joan would together resort to the air raid shelter with their children in World War 2.

Rodney Slatford in a *Hertfordshire Mercury* feature from 1975 and during a presentation by Her Majesty Queen Elizabeth II in 1998 at the Royal Northern College of Music in Manchester, (*centre*). Details of Rodney's work can be found on his Yorke Editions website and he is Patron of Cuffley Operatic Society. The *Mercury* feature describes his mother Vida's energetic work with many of Cuffley's societies. She was also a School Governor and Chair of the Parish Council. Grace Lawrence lent us a copy of Vida's wartime memories (see pages 249 to 251). His father, who died in 1952, was the first Chair of the Appeals Committee for the Cabin which eventually led to the building of Cuffley Hall.

talked about the murder scenes in the film. One scene, he told me, had a body thrown into some water, but no actual murder is shown. The "death" we were about to witness was the closest to seeing the event. I commented that the film was hardly a musical and he laughed, saying: "It is just a happy little comedy!" He took the pig's head from a bag for the final rehearsal and amused us all by talking to it as if it was a person. There was no sign of artistic temperament and as 'Danny' rose in the undergrowth to attack the head, the 'gardener' as they called one of the crew, dropped the foliage he had cut earlier so that the camera zoomed in on AF. A bottle of blood was added to the gory scene. When he was done, he leaned back on his haunches and breathed deeply, head raised. After three hours of preparation, about 40 seconds of film was in the can.'

Rev Max Bryant had previously performed the wedding of Maurice Norman at Northaw Church,

one of the famous 1961 Tottenham Hotspur team that achieved 'the double' that year when Danny Blanchflower was captain. He hosted the entire team in the village and it was one of his proudest moments when he showed his servers from St Andrew's Church all the signatures of the team at a servers' breakfast. We can also boast **Peter Simpson** of Arsenal, who still lives in Cuffley, and **David Beckham** has been known to call in for food in Station Road where his son Brooklyn has been to the dentist and David's sister-in-law Louise Adams has had a dress shop. **Mary Bourne**, from Hill Rise, who studied at the University of Hertfordshire's School of Art in St Albans, takes part in the annual Open Studios events from her home near Hertford Heath and **Sam Morley** wrote several books about golf and his life in commerce from his Ridgeway home: *Start Off Smashed*, *In Search of Eastern Promise*, *Victory in 'Site'*, *If It Wasn't For Golf* and *By Yon Bonnie Links*.

Albert Finney (see page 137) in a 1964 poster for Karel Reisz's film made in the Parish. The play by Emlyn Williams was first made into a film in 1937 and described as an 'unconvincing but memorable Hollywood expansion of an effective British chiller'. The story is of a bland young bellboy, really a psychopath, who attaches himself to the household of a rich old lady.

W. Gordon Smith produced an 'interview with a camera' of Albert Finney in 1964 for *Scottish Field* from which this picture amongst eight studies of the actor in conversation is taken. Although *Night Must Fall* was not liked by the critics, we were able to witness one of our finest actors ever, (recently seen as Churchill), working in our Vicarage and surrounding woodland. Oddly enough, forty years on, the same woods were the scene of a real murder investigation.

Graham Rust

Graham kindly drove up from his home in Suffolk to meet us on a dark January day in Cuffley. His superb work as a painter, book illustrator and mural artist has been acknowledged widely in Britain, Europe, The Middle East and America.

The Painted Ceiling is the title of just one of his many books and his biblical scenes, cherubs, clouds, birds and magnificent skies recorded in the book show the great skill of this artist who is particularly admired for his intrepid work on high wall paintings and ceilings.

As a child Graham attended Cuffley School and then St Dominic's Convent at Newgate Street before going on to Hertford Grammar School (now called the Richard Hale School).

Memories are precious and during his visit to us Graham did not wish to return to see his old homes in Kingsmead and Sutherland Avenue. Instead we set off to Northaw Parish Church to see the murals

inside the church. The churchyard contained memorial stones to relations of Graham's mother.

Graham Redgrave-Rust, to use his full name, (as depicted on his book-plate), was concerned that 'no old buildings have been preserved in Cuffley'. He remembers vividly as a child being deeply upset by the demolition of Castle Farm. Other memories included seeing a grass snake by the viaduct (they survive in the Parish) and the freedom of life in a village where you could wander safely through woods and bracken.

The image of a snake recurs as one of his designs in a book he wrote in collaboration with his two sisters: *Needlepoint Designs*. A childhood pet was a tortoise which inspired a chart which could be used for a doorstop or cushion.

The major works of this remarkable artist include the spectacular murals and ceilings at Ragley Hall in Warwickshire. His fifteen years of work there, mainly Michelangelo-like on scaffolding, have been

Colesdale Farm, Cuffley, in an atmospheric etching by Graham Rust in 1959, previously unpublished. Graham, now based in Suffolk, points out that the drawing was reversed in printing. Pictures in this section have been reproduced by kind permission.

described as *'one of the great pieces of decoration this century'*. (*Tatler* June 1983)

Graham's work for charity includes donating watercolours and drawings in aid of *Sightsavers* (formerly the Royal Commonwealth Society for the Blind).

As well as the major projects over the years there have been numerous paintings of houses, animals, trompe l'oeil effects, flowers, fruit and vegetables. His highly realistic paintings are in great demand and his style often incorporates borders of shells and scrolls in a rococo manner. He has produced designs for elaborate dog kennels, worked for *Moet et Chandon*, created wine labels, book-plates and even a butterfly tiara.

His meticulous detail is achieved by making many preliminary sketches before the final piece is drawn or painted. Graham will also look in hedgerows and gardens to include only the correct species in his work. When he was commissioned to paint the

Queen reviewing troops, Graham visited Buckingham Palace where the Queen's dresser showed him the actual clothes the Queen had worn on the day because he had not been able to get close enough for accurate sketches.

A set of ceramic plates were made for the *Queen Elizabeth Foundation for the Disabled* and depicted famous country houses and includes one of Hatfield House. Margaret Thatcher commissioned a *'Chequers'* plate and plates depicting ginger roots and bananas also find their way into his *The Fine Art of Dining*.

Cuffley can be justly proud of Graham. One curious fact emerged as we looked through *The Painted Ceiling*. Graham worked on a series of painted rooms for an apartment in Beirut in the Lebanon. Another boy who spent part of his childhood years in Cuffley was, as we have seen, John McCarthy, who was imprisoned in totally contrasting circumstances in the same city. Both,

Graham Rust on scaffolding at Ragley Hall, Warwickshire, (see text). A master of trompe l'oeil, (painting to give a convincing illusion of reality, from the French, literally: 'deception of the eye'), the figures and architecture are all painted on the upper level of Ragley's staircase. Graham is internationally renowned for his murals and ceiling paintings, found in houses in North America as well as in Europe.

too, now live in Suffolk.

Graham's published work includes:
Decorative Designs (1996) Cassell (out of print).
The Painted House (1998) Cassell (also available in paperback).
Needlepoint Designs (1998) Ward Lock (Cassell).
The Painted Ceiling (2001) Constable.

He has also illustrated ***The Secret Garden,*** ***Little Lord Fauntleroy*** and ***A Little Princess*** all by Frances Hodgson Burnett; ***Recipes from a Chateau in Champagne*** McDouall & Bush; ***Some Flowers*** by Vita Sackville West and ***The Fine Art of Dining***.

Ronnie Aldrich (1916 - 1993)
Born in Erith, Kent, Ronnie Aldrich was a well known bandleader during the 1950s and 1960s. For much of this time he was living on The Ridgeway, Cuffley, in a delightful home, now much altered and modernised.

He was a gifted pianist, studying intensively and spending a period at the Guildhall School of Music in London. During the Second World War he arranged for the RAF Dance Orchestra and afterwards remained with the band which was relaunched as the Squadronaires. He became leader and conductor of this most successful of British big bands until it broke up in 1964.

Ronnie Aldrich recorded over thirty albums, (which often featured his 'twin pianos'), worked on numerous radio programmes and directed specially formed orchestras.

He was later employed as a musical director for Thames Television (including the Benny Hill Show). He would often be seen in the village shops in Cuffley, but few realised the great talent of this unassuming pianist. His list of works includes:
• ***All Time Hits Of Jazz*** (Ace Of Clubs 1960)•
Melody And Percussion For Two Pianos (1961)•
Ronnie Aldrich And His Two Pianos (1961)• ***Love Story*** (1971)• ***For The One You Love*** (Decca 1980)•

A further example of Graham Rust's superb trompe l'oeil painting at Ragley Hall,
reproduced from his book *The Painted House* (1988). The tall flower at the top of the
design is a rare cultivar called the Ragley Penstemon.

Study of a Parrot tulip by Graham Rust. One of Graham's botanical paintings, published in
Decorative Designs, (1996) by Cassell.

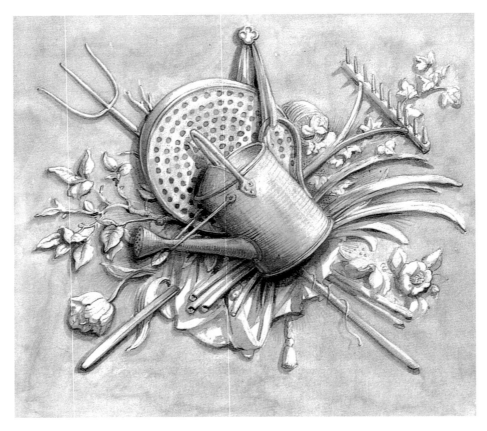

Chimney board decoration by Graham Rust from 1988 and reproduced by Cassell in
Decorative Designs (1996), now out of print. For a list of books which illustrate Graham's
extensive range and quantity of work, see the text on page 141.

One Fine Day (Decca 1981)• *Night Birds* (MFP
1982)• *Tender Love ... Tender Moments* (Contour
1982)• *The Unforgettable Sound Of Ronnie
Aldrich and His 2 Pianos* (Decca 1984)• *Sea
Dreams* (MFP 1984)• *Silver Bells* (Audio Fidelity
1984)• *28 Great Piano Classics* (Horatio Nelson
1985)• *Soft And Wicked* (Jasmine 1985)• *The
Aldrich Feeling* (Decca 1986)• *All-Time Piano Hits*
(Decca 1986)• *Focus On Ronnie Aldrich* (Decca
1986)• *For All Seasons* (MFP 1987)• *Two Pianos
In Hollywood* (London 1988)• *An Hour Of Ronnie
Aldrich* (Hour Of Pleasure/EMI 1988) • *Melody and
Percussion for Two Pianos*;

London Phase 4 (as in the following): SP-44007 •
Ronnie Aldrich and His Two Pianos, London SP-
44018 • *The Magnificent Pianos of Ronnie
Aldrich*, SP-44029 • *The Romantic Pianos of
Ronnie Aldrich*, SP-44042• *Christmas with Ronnie
Aldrich*, SP-44051 • *Magic Moods of Ronnie
Aldrich*, SP-44062 • *That Aldrich Feeling*, SP-

44070 • *All Time Piano Hits*, SP-44081 • *Two
Pianos in Hollywood*, SP-44092 • *Two Pianos
Today!* SP-44100 • *For Young Lovers*, SP-44108 •
This Way 'In,' SP-44116• *Its Happening Now*, SP-
44127 • *Destination Love,* SP-44135 • *Here Come
the Hits!* SP-44143 • *Invitation To Love,* SP-44176
• *Come to Where the Love Is*, SP-44190 • *Soft And
Wicked*, SP-44195 • *Top of the World,* SP-44203 •
The Way We Were, SP-44209 • *In the Gentle
Hours*, SP-44221 • *Love*, SP-44253 •
Reflections, SP-44264 • *Close to You*, London H-
17156 • *Soft & Wicked*, London H-17195 • *One
Fine Day*, Amberjack 90281.

Clement Attlee (1883 - 1967)
A family friend of the Attlees, the Rev F J Hall, ran
the preparatory school at Northaw Place in
Hertfordshire. It was here at the age of nine in 1892
that Clement Attlee joined his elder brother Tom at
the school where the Rev Hall was assisted by the
Rev Poland, B M Humble and Alan Clover. These

A recent photograph of what was once Ronnie Aldrich's House on the Ridgeway, Cuffley and a Squadronaires cover sleeve from one of his numerous LPs, (see list starting on page 141). Klaas Klijn recalls Ronnie coming into the Novelties shop regularly for soft pencils because he used so many annotating his scores.

three had little training as teachers and Attlee wrote in his autobiography 'were not qualified to give other than fairly elementary instruction.' But it was here that the boys were to be prepared for entrance to Haileybury College at Hertford Heath. Religious studies played a large part in the education of the boys, (between thirty to forty at that time); classical studies were poor, whilst geography and history mainly consisted of learning lists of facts. The 'real religion' at Northaw, wrote Attlee, was cricket. Hall and Poland ensured that cricket was played most summer afternoons and a 'paper cricket' game in the evenings. Indeed, the school produced 'plenty of good cricketers' noted Attlee.

The days spent at Northaw Place were remembered as a happy time. Mrs Hall was very competent in taking care of the boys, assisted by a kindly Scots matron, Mrs Ross. He wrote of cosy evenings in the gas-lit schoolroom, Mrs Hall at the piano in the beautiful drawing room and skating on the pond in

the hard winter of 1895. In summer, Dodson the gardener might give you an apple and on walks through the lanes to visit Mrs Kidston, *'an opulent neighbour'*: there would be an apple or orange for each boy.

Attlee's earlier education at home in his father's library and with a private governess, Miss Hutchinson, who had formerly taught Winston Churchill before she joined the Attlees, ensured the bright little boy survived without too much educational pressure at Northaw Place. Hilton Young, later Minister for Health in the Ramsey Macdonald government, was head boy at Northaw when Clement joined the school. William Jowitt was put in Attlee's care when he arrived. He later became Lord Chancellor in the Labour government and a distinguished lawyer.

So Clement Attlee inherited a governess from Winston Churchill and also his job as Prime Minister when he won the post-Second World War

Clement Attlee was a schoolboy in the Parish at
Northaw Place and went on to attend Haileybury
College and then Oxford.
He is seen here at eighteen in a photograph
published with kind permission in Francis
Beckett's *Clement Attlee* (1997)
Cohen, London.

Clement Attlee, painted by Derek Fowler in the 1950s,
(in the dining hall at Haileybury College, Hertford
Heath, by kind permission of the College and with the
help of Margaret Ball and Fiona Bedford).

election! He had spent four happy years at Northaw,
doing quite well in his work, but never being much
good at the game of cricket. In 1896 he moved
across Hertfordshire to Haileybury College, then
Oxford, and a political career that took him to the
top job.

Edward John Burra (29/3/1905 - 24/10/1976)
Born at the home of his maternal grandmother,
Edward Burra was a frail child who suffered from
arthritis and, later on, the pernicious anaemia that
ended his days in formal education. School, where
Edward was sent as a boarder at the age of nine, was
intended to prepare him for life as a scholar at Eton.
The preparatory school was Northaw Place in
Hertfordshire. Thus it was during the First World
War years, 1914 to 1918, that he was a pupil there.

Never good at spelling, (a trait that continued with
him for the rest of his life judging by the numerous
letters he penned to friends and relations), the early

letters home include all sorts of schoolboyish
comments. On 18 October 1914 he asked for *'my
tortch with a new battery in it....please when you
send the tortch send a cake with it.'* A year later on
the 17 October he writes to his father *'We heard the
Zepps on Wednesday night and the windows shook.
P.S. Please tell Nana to send me my tortch.'*

One would hope that his parents had not left him a
whole year without his 'tortch'. Perhaps it had to go
back home everytime for batteries. He reflected the
almost casual attitude to the drama of being bombed
by enemy airships. Home was 'Springfields' at
Playden, near Rye in Sussex. It is just a coincidence
that there is a Springfields nearby at Northaw.
Edward writes of a match where they lost by 13
goals and in May 1917 he was top of the form. But
his health was never good and by the time he was
thirteen he was sent home from the school with
rheumatic fever and anaemia and his formal
education was over.

Northaw Place, c1905. Clement Attlee and Edward Burra both went to school here. Attlee's later achievements were enormous and he virtually ran the coalition Government 1940-1945 whilst Churchill was mainly concerned with the war strategy, in posts as Lord Privy Seal, deputy Prime Minister and Dominions Secretary. The programme of social reform introduced by his Labour Government, 1945-1951, at a time when the nation had a war debt of $20,000m, severe fiscal difficulties and continued rationing, is remarkable.

Writing in a Penguin Modern Painters book on Edward Burra, John Rothenstein says that Edward's comment on the school included the assertion that 'There were a great many strange scholars there,' an observation that echoes in the themes of many of his paintings in later years.

It was after leaving Northaw Place that Edward spent the years until 1921 drawing and painting at home in Rye. He then spent two years at Chelsea Polytechnic and later went on to the Royal College of Art for a year. Perhaps the gaps in his formal education were why he established a unique style early on which can seem grotesque in some works. His watercolours and drawings have great character and always show delicacy and skill in the details.

In an exhibition of his work at the Tate Gallery in 1973 Norman Reid wrote in his foreword, 'Edward Burra stands a little aside from the mainstream of modern art over the last 45 years. It is not easy to categorise his work: it carries elements of the surreal as in Birdmen and Pots 1947, but by 1957 his watercolour of Owl and Quinces, shows none of the unrest of such a picture'. Yet his style continued to chop and change, reflecting the influences of his travels and lifestyle with perhaps here and there a strange character from the Northaw days cropping up in a crowd scene. It was not his habit to sketch on site but to carry images back in his head to work on at home in Rye. The Tate exhibition carried 143 of his works, many on loan from private collections and other galleries.

It is not generally acknowledged how influential Burra was on the 1960s visual styles. 'Storm in the Jungle' (1931), City Art Gallery, Nottingham and reproduced in *The 20th Century Art Book,* might be a still from Yellow Submarine (1968), or an Alan Aldridge illustration, for example. Success in the art world was assured for the Northaw schoolboy. He died at home at Playden near Rye on 24 October 1976 at the age of 71.

Edward Burra, 1905-1976, an outstanding English watercolourist, showed many influences and styles in his work throughout an illustrious career. *Dandies* (1930), for example, could be mistaken for the work of George Grosz, 1893-1959, and his *Storm in the Jungle* (1931), shown here, like paintings by Henri Rousseau, anticipated the distinctive Pop Art paintings and illustrations (such as those by Alan Aldridge) of the 1960s.

Mrs Wilson Fox

Mrs Wilson Fox was a Cuffley writer with many novels to her credit, an interest in the locality and a good historical knowledge. Summed up in the article that follows are the titles of many of her books, some romantic with historical backgrounds, others moral tales and more serious family histories. She wrote from Ridgeway House which remains a beautiful setting for an authoress and retains much of the original exterior structure. Patricia Klijn wrote in the *Hertfordshire Countryside*, July 1987:

Mrs Alice Wilson Fox, author of over a dozen books, is scarcely remembered today as a Cuffley novelist yet from her home on The Ridgeway she wrote popular historical novels as well as a significant contribution to a serious study of the Barclay family between the years 1905 and 1931.

Her earliest book-length works were published by the S.P.C.K. (Christian Knowledge Society) under such titles as 'The General's Choice' (1905),

'Diana's Decision' (1908), 'A Dangerous Inheritance'; or 'Sydney's Fortune' in 1909. The archivist at the SPCK informed me that these titles were books for boys and girls and his records confirmed that Mrs Wilson Fox was a popular writer. The books sold for three or four shillings and 'Diana's Decision' was illustrated with coloured plates by Harold Piffard.

In 1910 her novel 'Hearts and Coronets' was published by Macmillan. This story followed the fortunes of Audrey from a seemingly poor family who was at school with the daughter of a titled family. A series of events, a train stranded in the snow; a stay at the rich house; the older brother; culminated in Audrey being the rightful heiress, inheriting the title and marrying the brother. A very satisfactory novel with clever twists and Mrs Wilson Fox's obvious knowledge of heraldry and titled families well woven into the plot.

It was from her home on The Ridgeway with the

A recent photograph of Mrs Wilson Fox's home on the Ridgeway, Cuffley. She was a distinguished novelist and local historian. We have also reproduced her notes on Cuffley and Northaw between pages 221 and 235 which allow us to also feature many aspects of Northaw, too.

words 'Station Cuffley G.N.R. 1 mile' printed on her stationery that Mrs Wilson Fox wrote to Mr Macmillan delighted that 'Hearts and Coronets' would be published in America. There would, it seemed, be a royalty of 10% on the American edition which she estimates at 'about 6d. a volume'. A charming remark concluded her letter, 'I have always understood it is an advantage to publish in America'.

Her career as a novelist had taken off at this point, for her book was advertised between E. Nesbit's 'The Magic City', Rudyard Kipling's 'Rewards and Fairies' and a Goble illustrated edition of 'The Water Babies' by Kingsley.

It was a connection by marriage with the Barclays of Bury Hill, Dorking that interested Mrs Wilson Fox and she collaborated with Lt. Col. Hubert Barclay of The Orchards, Letty Green, Hertford, in compiling the third volume of the comprehensive 'History of the Barclay Family with pedigrees from

1067-1933'. She concentrated on Robert Barclay (1648-1690), the famous 'Apologist for the Quakers known as 'Urie 11'.

There is only one more novel on record in her name, 'Charmian: chauffeuse', written in 1925. She returned to history with 'The Earl of Halsbury - Lord High Chancellor (1823-1921)' and after that her stories for women's meetings were published by the 'Woman's Magazine' when it was part of 'Girls Own Paper'.

It was some time later that notes by Mrs Wilson Fox on Northaw and District were discovered. Published in the Hertfordshire Transactions in 1923 some of the history is well documented, but did we know Dr Johnson came to take the waters at Cuffley or that Cuffley had caves and a marble fountain erected over the spring of the King's Well? Reproduced in full are her observations and it is easy to imagine how all these things would have had great interest for the successful authoress, see *Notes*

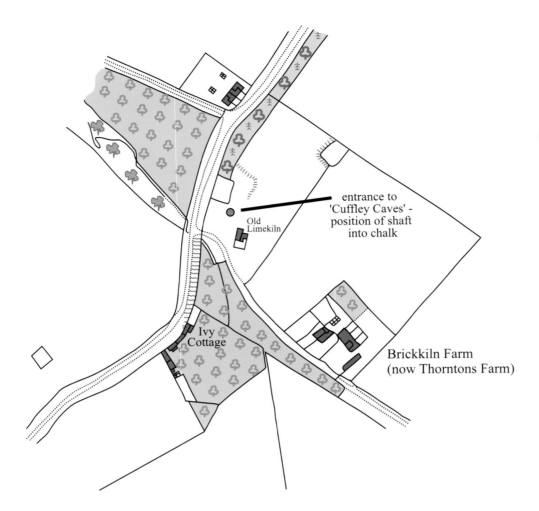

Old Limekiln

entrance to 'Cuffley Caves' - position of shaft into chalk

Ivy Cottage

Brickkiln Farm (now Thorntons Farm)

To the left of the entrance to Thorntons Farm is the site of the way into the 'Cuffley Caves' which is shown in the County Archive. We have re-drawn the details from the exact location given on an old map, (grid ref TL289/032). All traces of the entrance have been lost at the site, which is thought to be on one of the old routes to the King's Well at Cuffley. Entry to the cave may have been offered as a local diversion for the visitors who had principally come to take the waters.

on Northaw and District by Mrs Wilson Fox'
Appendix 3, page 221.

Wally Hammond (W.R. Hammond, 1903-1965)
Cuffley has been home to one of England's greatest cricketers. Walter, better known in his playing days as 'Wally' Hammond, lived for eight years on the Ridgeway following an illustrious career of 1,004 first class innings for Gloucestershire and England. During the 27 years he played at the top level of his sport (from 1920 to 1947). He scored no less than 50,133 runs during this time.

He was 18 times captain of England and has been described as one of cricket's supreme artists. In 1955 he left Cuffley with his wife and three children to emigrate to Durban in South Africa. It was there that he suffered a very serious road accident in 1960 from which he never fully recovered. His last visit to England was in March 1962 when he came to make guest appearances to help increase

membership for his old club Gloucestershire during a three week stay.

The record books tell the story of his great career. Only Leonard Hutton beat his highest English batsman's score of 336, not out, for England against New Zealand. (Hutton scored 364 against Australia at the Oval in 1938). Hammond's most remarkable series was in 1928 when his scores against Australia in the three middle tests were 251, 200, 32 (run out), 119 not out and 177.

In all, he scored 905 runs in the 5 tests that year, with an average of 113.12.

He was also considered one of the greatest slip fielders ever to play for England and held 78 catches in one season. (This is why he was depicted fielding rather than batting on one of the cigarette cards which featured him).

Denzil Batchelor described his approach:

'Hammond did not walk to the wicket - he strode. He stood up after taking guard, and surveyed the

Wally Hammond's house on the Ridgeway, Cuffley. Some of his achievements are described below. Christopher Martin-Jenkins has described Hammond as simply one of the greatest cricketers ever, (see *The Complete Who's Who of Test Cricketers*, Guild, London, 1987).

field. He was not looking to see where the enemy were disposed to catch him: he was looking to see where he could hit those ringing boundaries through the field. He was by nature a positive, not a negative bat.'

Against Australia he hit 2,852 runs at an average of 61.85. Only Sir Donald Bradman and Sir Jack Hobbs bettered that record. Along with his amazing feat of 78 slip catches in one season, Wally Hammond was most proud of scoring 1,000 runs within the month of May - a feat accomplished only by W.G. Grace and Charlie Hallows before him. It was achieved in just 22 days in 1927.

Molly Hughes (1866 - 1956)
Enduring Molly Hughes (page 4) deserves a further note: In *The Echoing Green: Memories of Regency and Victorian Youth*, Gillian Avery includes a whole chapter on Molly Hughes called *'The Modern Girl'*. Molly had been surprisingly well educated for her

time and attended The North London Collegiate School under the formidable Miss Buss before going to Cambridge University. This is just one example of how Molly's books have survived and become social histories of their era thanks to her easily read style and amusing accounts of daily life.

There are little footnotes quoting examples from Molly Hughes in *A Circle of Sisters* by Judith Flanders, (the stories of Alice Kipling, Georgiana Burne-Jones, Agnes Poynter and Louisa Baldwin). The excerpts were taken from *A London Child of the 1870s* although the notes gave the source as *The Victorian Town Child* by Pamela Horn. Here is proof that the works of Molly Hughes are points of reference for serious studies. Her publishers were Oxford University Press and J M Dent.

Kenneth Inns & Vernon Mills
An early illustrator for the famous Ladybird books produced by Wills and Hepworth in Loughborough

Two Player's Cigarette card portraits of Walter Hammond from the 1930s.
Wally Hammond had a major role in the longest ever test match, held in Durban, South Africa, March 1939. It was the last 'timeless' test and after ten days, (43 hours of play), it ended in a draw. The match still holds the record for the highest aggregate number of runs in a test: 1,981.

Unfortunately this last 'timeless' test had to end in a draw because England, by then likely to win, were in danger of missing their boat passage home. It was the last available for several weeks.

was Kenneth Inns. He worked from his home in King James Avenue in Cuffley and several of the religious titles first published in the 1950s carried his full page paintings. For a model he used his own son: *The Shepherd Boy of Bethlehem* and *The Child of the Temple* show the boy who would have been recognisable as a Cuffley child.

Another artist who worked for Ladybird books was Vernon Mills. He moved from his home in Cuffley and went to live in Loughborough to work for the Company where he became a director. He produced a very successful illustrated book on dinosaurs for Macdonald in the 1960s. Prehistoric animals are now a standard part of the school curriculum.

W. Burnard Phillips *(edited from Patricia Klijn's article in Hertfordshire Countryside June '89):*
My pursuit of *'The World's Coarse Thumb'* by W. Burnard Phillips had the librarians searching in vain. I had no idea what the book was about, only that it

was a novel and this particular author was on my list of Hertfordshire writers to be tracked down. I also knew that W B Phillips had lived on Plough Hill in Cuffley and had apparently only written this one book in the 1930s.

The answer came that the only known copy in existence was in the British Museum Reading Room. After form-filling at the Museum and an identity photograph I was allowed to return at a later date to study the book. Eventually I claimed a seat under the famous dome of gold and pale turquoise blue. It was cold. Ornate windows with a central pillar were spaced evenly around, way up in the dome. The doors were faced with mock book spines so as not spoil the sweeping circular effect of solid book shelves. But what of Mr Phillips of Hertfordshire who I had come to see? The book request was put in and shortly after I held the little volume of reddish brown cloth with its dedication *'To Mary who made this book possible'*. I assumed

Two illustrations by Kenneth Inns from one of the familiar Ladybird books of Bible stories, where he used his son as the model for the young Jesus. (See next page for his probable use of the Northaw Church interior). Early Ladybird books are now collector's items.

this was Mrs Phillips, but my immediate problem was how to 'read' a novel in the short time available.

The strange title was explained by a quotation on the fly-leaf. It was from verse XXIV (24) of Rabbi Ben Ezra by Robert Browning and W.B. Phillips had used phrases from this verse as his chapter headings. 'Instincts Immature' for Chapter One, 'Purposes Unsure' for Chapter Two and 'Main Account' for Chapter Three.

The book itself recounted the First World War experiences of a D Company commander. The language of the soldiers, "Put me dahn", "Orlright sergeant", "Get some kip", was deliberately spelled out to emphasise the Cockney accents. Life in the trenches was described and provided one angle of the story.

The other side was the scene at home at Horner's Bridge. No mention here of Hertfordshire and local names. The corn chandler was called Durford and

Pinty was the saddler. The hero's home was Horner House and his two sons attended the Horner's Bridge Grammar School.

I read on and suddenly there was a mention of Coulter's farm. Cuffley has a Coulters Close today and it is just possible that a local name had crept in. During the story the characters waited on Finsbury Park Station and a Station Road was mentioned. It was easy to imagine that although W.B. Phillips had invented Horner's Bridge, a few references to his home village were possible.

A light love story ran through the book with the hero returning to the girl he had left behind at the beginning of the war. But the pain of seeing dead comrades and losing an old schoolfriend was vividly portrayed. The subsequent torture of each Armistice Day as the author described it must have been very real to the readers of this 1930s novel. The moral codes of loyalty and trust and the class structure of the period were well defined and one felt that

As well as painting his son in the Ladybird books when they lived in Cuffley, we have noticed that Kenneth Inns has used the interior of Northaw Church for his altar painting (*facing page*). Mrs Kidston gave the wooden screen for the church in 1913 so that the above postcard photograph must be prior to this date.

contemporary readers would have identified with many of the experiences.

It was time to go. Back went the little reddish brown book to its archives. I wondered how long it would be before anyone else would want to look at it. This Hertfordshire writer had helped me achieve a long held ambition to sit under the dome of the Reading Room at the British Museum. Fancy a writer from Plough Hill prompting me to do that.

Robert Thew

'William Haines, the engraver 1778 - 1848 and painter, studied engraving with THEW at Northaw. He worked later with Scriven on the Boydell-Shakespeare plates'.

It is a sentence like that which opens up so many new avenues as a story just waiting to be explored. Who was Thew? Where did he live in Northaw and was he famous in his lifetime?

Robert Thew (1758 -1802) was, in fact, born at

Patrington, near Holderness in Yorkshire and was entirely self-taught as an engraver, having originally been apprenticed to a cooper and he followed this trade for some years. He then went on to invent an ingenious version of the camera obscura and subsequently took up engraving.

His earliest work 'of a higher class' was a portrait of Harry Rowe, the famous puppet show man. Thew went on to become historical engraver to the Prince of Wales. The Stewards House at Northaw was his home and, although now demolished, it stood next to Northaw House in Pease Lane. Following the production of an exceptional plate of a woman's head (after the artist Gerard Dou) Thew obtained an introduction via the Marquis of Carmarthen to John Boydell. It was in 1786 that John Boydell started a scheme to illustrate an edition of Shakespeare's works with engravings after contemporary artists. The originals were exhibited in his own gallery in London in 1802 and numbered some 102 canvases.

The steps, choir stalls, banner and altar below the stained glass windows of Northaw Church in a Ladybird book illustration by Kenneth Inns. The real Mothers Union banner in the church (*right*) was pictured in 1992 against the exceptional Victorian wall decorations which have been carefully restored in places (see p 163).

John Boydell was Lord Mayor of London for 1790-1791, but by the time of the exhibition he was in financial difficulties and the paintings were disposed of by lottery. Despite this, the engraved edition of Shakespeare was published in nine volumes between 1792 to 1801. It seems very unlikely that Robert Thew benefited very much in his lifetime from his, or his pupils work on the Boydell plates. Thew had engraved in the dot, or stipple, manner twenty two plates after Northcote, Westall, Opie, Peters and others. A listing of engravings and their values published in 1912 put the following prices on the works of Robert Thew:

The Witches and the Cauldron, scene in Macbeth, after Reynolds. £3.10s. Timon of Athens, after Opie. £2.2s. A Winter's Tale (Mrs Jordan as 'Pauline') after Hamilton. 1793. £2.12s.6d. Henry Vlll after Peters. 1796. In colours £4.4s. Plain 10s. The Merry Wives of Windsor after Peters £3.

A Collection of Prints illustrating the Dramatic

Works of Shakespeare in 2 vols (1803) fetched £400 when sold at Sotheby's in 1980.

In 1800 it is recorded that he went to the Cape of Good Hope. The Gentleman's Magazine in 1802 reported the death of Thew at Roxley, near Stevenage, and comments, '*Mr Thew was an artist whose works have been highly approved by the connoisseur and as such well received by the publick.*'

Thus William Haines, the pupil who gave the original clue to Robert Thew of Northaw led us to a story involving the Lord Mayor of London, Shakespeare and a demolished Northaw house.

Janet and John - an everyday story of Hertfordshire folk (*edited from Patricia Klijn's article in Hertfordshire Countryside May 1989*): Many of us, even if we did not learn to read with the famous series of infant reading books, know Janet and John. When I discovered that I had lived as a

(Continued on page 166)

Graham Rust points out a relative's name on an old gravestone in Northaw Churchyard. (During his visit to Cuffley and Northaw in 2002 we passed the house where Wally Hammond once lived and Graham mentioned that his father was given one of Sir Leonard Hutton's cricket bats!)

Above, right: Patricia Klijn & Graham Rust discuss illustrations for this book.

Right, Graham Rust at work.

Restoration work in progress at Northaw Church during July 1992. Dedicated to St Thomas of Canterbury, this, the third church on the site, was built by the firm of John Bentley of Waltham Abbey in 13 months and dedicated on 28 September 1882.

Postcards with deckle edges were the fashion in the early 1960s when this summer time study was on sale.
It has been suggested that a chapel existed on this site in Northaw by 1215 and that the dedication to St Thomas of Canterbury indicated it may have been built in commemoration of the murder of Beckett in 1170 (Gerald Millington and John Higgs, 1983). They reproduce an attractive print by Malcolm of 1805 of the first church which was considered too small by William Strode (who lived at Ponsbourne). He had the building pulled down in 1808 and replaced by 1810 with a severe brick and stucco building and slate roof.
Covered walks to the road are shown in pictures of this and the earlier, attractive brick and flint church. When, in February 1881 the church was completely destroyed by fire, the vicar, Rev William Bonsey, put great efforts into raising the funds to re-build and architects Charles Kirk and Sons of Sleaford, Lincolnshire took on the job. It is a vast improvement on its predecessor and unlike any other North London or Hertfordshire churches. The Victorian decor and the font in the church are of particular interest and familiar local names are to be found, as well as a section of the 15th Century font, in the churchyard.

John Boydell,
Lord Mayor of London 1790-
1791, who employed the
engraver Robert Thew.
Thew worked from the
Steward's House at Northaw,
next to Northaw House in
Pease Lane, (but since
demolished).
The 'Boydell Shakespeare' is
often referred to and is now a
highly valued edition of
engravings and text. Some
cheap editions of Shakespeare
also reproduce these plates.
Top, right: *The Merry Wives
of Windsor* Act II Scene I,
'Before Page's House:
Mrs Ford and Mrs Page',
(after Rev William Peters RA)
and, right: *The Tempest* Act IV
Scene I, 'Before Prospero's
Cell', (after Joseph Wright).

Cuffley artist Hilda Waller's 1949 portrait of a man in fencing costume from about Thew's era, presented as art prize to Anthony Clark at the Guildhouse School, 1951. Hilda's work is also on pages 100, 101 and 229.

THE JANET AND JOHN BOOKS

I KNOW A STORY

BY

MABEL O'DONNELL AND RONA MUNRO

ILLUSTRATED BY

FLORENCE AND MARGARET HOOPES

AND

CHRISTOPHER SANDERS

JAMES NISBET AND CO. LTD.
DIGSWELL PLACE, WELWYN, HERTS.
0 7202 0510 7

Striking cover designs and charming title pages are features of the Janet and John series of books for children, published by James Nisbet and Co Ltd at Digswell Place, Welwyn, Hertfordshire. The firm has since moved to Hitchin and the Mackenzie-Wood family continue to be involved with publishing.

child in virtually the same road as the lady that wrote the books I was even more intrigued. **Mrs Mackenzie-Wood** lived in Cuffley in the 1940s although she had been born in New Zealand. She graduated there having studied with men who were later to become professors at Oxford and Cambridge. Then begun her career in teaching, working in a variety of New Zealand schools. In the 1930s the then Rona Munro visited Europe working as an au pair in Berlin and then Provence. It was while on a visit to Scotland with her father that she met her future husband John Mackenzie-Wood. He went to America soon after the war and returned with the UK rights to the American Reading Scheme *'Alice and Jerry'*. As a result of this Rona Munro wrote her own text books for the British market and *'Janet and John'* were born.

Since then countless children have learned to read with the scheme and Rona Munro's teaching experience enabled her to write further textbooks for phonic reading and practice. Janet and John now have back-up materials of workbooks and cards. The *'Kathy and Mark'* books are another excellent series written by Rona to help children enjoy learning to read.

The *'Janet and John'* series attracted attention when some teachers felt that the family was too stereo-typed and too middle class. It was argued that 'Mother' always washed up and 'Janet' always played with dolls. Whatever the reasons behind the arguments the series is still successful and the books enjoy a steady sale.

Now a director of the Hertfordshire firm that publishes her books *(J. Nisbet and Co, Hitchin)* Rona Mackenzie-Wood is a well-known name in the field of early children's reading. Both her daughters are also involved with the firm and both edit material and write for children. Above all the books are valuable in teaching children to read.

Perhaps it is the characters of Janet and John

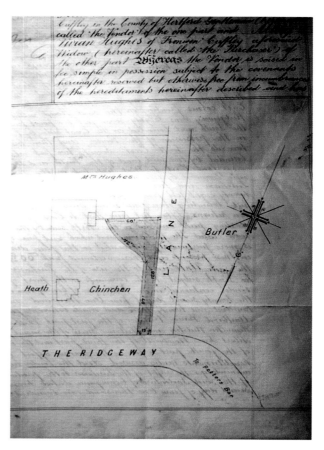

Basil Edmond's nostalgic study of the Cuffley School corridor: "First Day at School'. The deeds of Molly Hughes' home *Fronwen* on East Ridgeway show the access in red where Mr Chinchen built the house. Note the well marked lane between her plot and that of Castle Farm, defined as recently as the 1930s.

themselves and their simple adventures and daily life that give the stories their timeless quality. In years to come the series may serve as social history even if nobody believes that life was quite like that in Cuffley just after the War.

Mary Bourne, (nee Williams), former 42 Hill Rise Cuffley resident, exhibits her paintings, pottery and sculpture at Hertford Heath in her Open Studio. She gained her BA (Hons) at the College of Art, St Albans.

Chapter Twelve

Looking Back

We visited various people in the preparation of this book and particularly enjoyed meeting the present owners of Molly Hughes' house on East Ridgeway where she wrote her account of Cuffley. Entering 'Fronwen', built for her by Mr Chinchen in the 1930s, felt to us to be in some ways an historic moment, after reading her vivid accounts of village life here.

The house itself has been much enlarged, has changed hands several times and is now home to a family with three children which we feel sure Molly would have loved. The gabled roof shape has been carefully copied in the new extension as have the timbered sections of the upper storey of the house. There is now an indoor swimming pool and a

Molly Hughes' home 'Fronwen', built by Mr Chinchen on East Ridgeway next to his own home in the 1930s, and, right, the garden. She shows pictures of its construction in the original hardback edition of her book *A London Family Between the Wars* (1940), in which there is a picture of her in the garden, (see page 264).

billiard room as well as a new lounge and extra bedrooms.

Despite the changes, the shell of Molly's home is there. The little bookroom survives, albeit now equipped with a computer, with rows of shelves, the old beams and similar view from the window. Hedges have grown up, but the garden pond is still there, as well as trees and plants identified by Molly in her book, *A London Family Between the Wars*. Some of the doors are preserved and what was the main living room has the original fireplace surround. Our visit became an exercise in spotting the things Molly might have known. A closer reading of the book identified fir trees, apple trees and shrubs as having been part of the 'Fronwen' garden.

The plans of the house show Mr Chinchen to have divided the land into three plots and it was on one of these that he built his own home, although he disguised the fact that he was a builder for at that time no aspect of 'trade' was welcome on the exclusive Ridgeway.

A further real treat was to see the signature of Mary Vivian Hughes on the deeds of the property. Always known as 'Molly' from an early age, to avoid confusion with her mother of the same name, it was from this house that Molly gathered material and wrote her books, carried on with her examination work and continued to take as active a part in village life as possible with three sons to look after.

The name of the house was also the name of her late husband Arthur's family home in Wales. 'Fronwen' means 'the shining hill' and it was so appropriate for the new house to bear the same name, situated as it was at the top of Plough Hill and looking out over the fields towards Northaw. In later years Molly found it less convenient to carry all the shopping up the hill to East Ridgeway and visitors were a 'rare treat' as the house was so tucked away from the road. It remains quite hidden

Joan McRitchie in her Plough Hill home where she has lived since she was four, (see text). At the time of the photograph Joan was reminiscing about her father's years at the Heal's furniture shop in Tottenham Court Road, London. She has memorabilia from the shop and retained the distinctive curtains, typical of those sold at Heal's in the 1960s. Joan has been a very active member of Cuffley Horticultural Society and maintains a beautiful garden.

and special.

Visiting the house enabled us to fill in yet another link in the Hughes story chain and helped to perpetuate the memory of a remarkable woman.

Chatting to Joan McRitchie about old Cuffley is also a delightful walk down memory lane. Joan's fond anecdotes of family and former residents are vividly remembered as the conversation flows and her stories begin.

Living in the same house on Plough Hill since she was four means that she has seen lots of changes in the buildings, names of roads and the development of the sleepy farming village that was Cuffley in the early days. Plough Hill was originally called Cuffley Hill Road and as such it is named on some of the early village postcards. Confusion with Cuffley Hill which rises to Goffs Oak, led to the change.

Her garden, part of which had to be given over to create the car park at the rear of Cuffley Hall, was originally included in the land of Brickwall farm,

(pages 17 and 31). A pear tree in the garden had survived there since the days of the farm, but sadly fell down after the 16 October storm of 1987. Joan did, however, take photographs of the tree, p 173.

Horace Marvel had a riding school in the field at the back of the house in the old stables (1920s) and later on neighbours, the Westins, kept horses in the same field (1940s). In those days the house numbers started at the top of the hill, at what is now number 32 where Mr Comley lived. He was instrumental in starting the Cuffley Free Church which for many years ran services and a Sunday School in the old Cabin building. It was not until the 1960s that the present Free Church was built on the corner of King James Avenue. At number 2 the Woodhams had a swimming pool, (which was thought to be very special in the 1930s) and nearer neighbours were the Coles. Mr Cole worked at Cheshires the Butchers at Goffs Oak and made rocking horses and push-along
(Continued on page 172)

Joan McRitchie's photograph, taken outside 4 Plough Hill, of a group of 1st Cuffley Guides about 1932 as they walked up Plough Hill for a service at St Andrew's Church on the Green. Joan, then Joan Upton, is at the back where Captain Nancy Marriner is walking. At the front of the group are Molly James, left, and Peggy Baxter on the right. Joan has also distinguished Joyce Bishop, Anita Dia and Pam Haywood. Below: Glass plate contact print from 1925 of Plough Hill in David Whyte's collection (copied 1965 and enlarged at that time to show the detail): *see facing page.*

Enlarged view of Plough Hill from previous page: it would be dangerous to stand chatting in the road today, although a blurred image of a cyclist shows us that someone was also speeding past at the time even then. *Below:* postcard from the 1960s shows the fine field oaks which were later removed from the pavement. The bank on the right side of the picture had yet to be built up as a safe, paved footpath.

Joan McRitchie's garden in the summer of 2002 with the Cuffley Hall complex in the
background. This was the site of Brickwall Farm and the surviving barn, (following the
loss of the farm buildings in a fire in 1900) became the first village hall: the Cabin.

wheeled horses in his spare time.

Joan's maiden name was Upton and many will
remember the family toy shop of that name in
Church Street, Enfield, run by her grandfather. Her
father had worked with Ambrose Heal in the early
days of Heal's, the famous furniture shop in
Tottenham Court Road and very stylishly re-
designed the Enfield shop. 'Shops', she says, 'are in
my blood'. Later Joan and her husband ran a
stationers selling prints, pictures and pottery from
their premises in Bloomsbury, London. Joan has
wonderful memories of the customers there.

Mrs Grace Smith and her son Tony lived at what is
now number 20. Mrs Smith was badly burned by an
incendiary bomb and lost a hand. (She gave the little
girl, Patricia Fenshom, who lived opposite at
number 27, a poetry book for Christmas in 1947).

Mr and Mrs Swinscoe lived with their daughter
Barbara further down the hill. Barbara became
secretary to Clifford Culpin, the architect of the new

St Andrew's Church, whose own home on Carbone
Hill was outstandingly modern for the times. At
number 10 Plough Hill lived Mr and Mrs Crocker
and their daughter Josie. They were all very active
in the work of St Andrew's Church and the summer
garden party was often held in their garden. The
house was called Brookside as the stream that
flowed through the gardens on the opposite side of
Plough Hill crossed under the road to tumble
through the centre of their grounds.

Joan's immediate neighbours were her aunt and
uncle, Mr and Mrs Floyd. Mr Floyd taught at
Belmont School, Tottenham. Their house was
completely destroyed in an air raid. By a strange
coincidence the lady in the centre of the garden
party photograph on page 175, went to the same
Tottenham school: Lilian Knight, who worked as an
embroideress when not helping with the dinners at
Cuffley School or later 'twiddling bits of wire' as
she called it in the temporary building built in front

In the winter snow of 1982 Joan McRitchie took this final picture of the only surviving fruit tree from the original Brickwall Farm orchard: a fine old standard pear. It blew down five years later in the very destructive 1987 gale. Pear trees can live in excess of 200 years.

of the Cabin assembling who knows what for the war effort. At that time she lived at 27 Plough Hill and later helped her sister Olive Fenshom to run Novelties in the late 1940s.

Joan McRitchie travelled to school at Enfield and later in the opposite direction to Ware Grammar School. Joan Clark (nee Gray) was deputed to supervise the girls on the journey to Enfield, but much hilarity took place, the younger Joan (Upton) sometimes ending up on the luggage rack. An early member of the Girl Guides Association in Cuffley, Joan still treasures the little book which records attendance of the Guides and a snapshot shows a parade past the houses opposite her home at the foot of Plough Hill. They were walking to the original St Andrew's Church at the top of the hill. Nancy Marriner was the first Captain of the Guides, a task she continued for many years. She proved to be an inspiration, instilling a love of the outdoors, and tirelessly organising meetings and camps for the

girls that passed through the Company. The 1st Cuffley Guides owe much to her. She lived on the East Ridgeway tending a huge garden as well as caring for elderly parents in later years and working as a physiotherapist at the Clinic at the foot of Tolmers Road.

Memories flowed as Joan even recalled fishing in the local streams in her early days at Cuffley, and enjoying the freedoms of the rural life generally. As a child she played with Freddie Shepherd and the James family: Molly, Dick, Pat and Gordon.

Joan shares a love of gardening with many other Cuffley residents, attends the horticultural society and continues to tend her own delightful garden.

The names recall an earlier Cuffley when entertainment and travel were limited, war years prevented much of either activity outside the village and yet Cuffley provided a secure base for much happy family life within the Parish.

The milkman George and his horse delivered to

A stream once fed the pond where Cuffley Free Church now stands. It flowed under Plough Hill where Patricia Fenshom poses at 'Trelawny' with her father Fred, (in the Pioneer Corps in 1944) to link with Cuffley Brook beyond the station. Vivien and Marion (*above, right*) were two evacuees in 1939 in Plough Hill, with the only picture of one of the horse-drawn Hanyards Farm milk delivery carts we can find.

numerous families from the A1 Dairies, (p 23). Later it was Melvin Bedford who took on the rounds. The baker Cobb from Potters Bar would call with wonderful rice buns and loaves, delivered to the residents of Plough Hill. Another tradesman, Mr Stone 'the fish man' delivered from Goffs Oak with a box on wheels containing a heap of assorted fish.

These last memories have been just one person's story, but conjure up so many other thoughts that a brief record of this kind will always be of value to readers and residents of the Plough Hill of the future.

Jim Roy recorded valuable information on the development of the Ridgeway and the village in general, 1921-1944, in correspondence from Poole in Dorset in 1996. He wrote:

To my mind there were three main events in the history of Cuffley and Goffs Oak: 1. The building of the Northern Railway and Cuffley Station about 1910; 2. The shooting down of the airship in 1916;

and 3. The selling off of the land in plots along the Ridgeways and Hanyards Lane by the Estate Company in 1920 onwards.

The plots were 100 feet wide and varied in length around the 250' mark ie: 1/2 an acre. (Our house, Greystones, was No 17 and was 267'. 6" long). The plots were offered with gas, water and telephone laid on and were advertised in the Enfield Gazette. The plots were purchased by mainly professional people aged between 30 and 40 who had probably saved up whilst living in rented accommodation during the 1914 war. We came from rented accommodation in Chingford; our next door neighbour was Mr. Bennett, Chief Engineer of the Metropolitan Electricity Company. On the other side was Charles Fowler, Chief Engineer to the River Lee Conservancy Board. On the corner plot, the other side of Hanyards Lane, was 'Haytor' set in 2 1/2 acres, owned by Mr. Huggins an importer of bananas. In Hanyards Lane, adjoining our plot, were

St Andrew's Church garden party held in the garden of Mr & Mrs Crocker's home,
10 Plough Hill, in the 1940s. Lilian Knight (see text, page 172) is pictured centre, facing the
camera. She lived at 27 Plough Hill and helped her sister Olive run Novelties in the 1950s.

the Sheperds (Stock Exchange), and further down the Ridgeway, a fine Georgian house was owned by Fairhead, our estate agent. It is interesting that all these first arrivals grew up in the Victorian age. Most of these houses had hard tennis courts, although ours was grass. 'Haytor' had a very fine, fully equipped billiard room. I must admit that my father led a few neighbours to play a trick on Mr Huggins who was a very big, bluff man whilst Mrs Huggins was very wee and ruled him with a rod of iron. It was arranged on his birthday for the neighbours to send him over a dozen postcards from different parts of the country signed in various women's names. As they all arrived on the same day, it was obviously a put-up job, but Mrs Huggins would not believe this and gave him an even harder time than usual! We believe he was secretly flattered and wished it was true!

Most houses were lit by gas; some had small electric generators charging the batteries: the 'pop-pop' noise of the exhaust was irritating to neighbours at times, and one day somebody put a potato up the exhaust pipe of our generator, bringing everything to a halt. Mains electricity came about 1930. Milk was delivered from Hanyards Farm by pony and trap, the latter carrying big 50 gallon churns from which your milk jug was filled. Blaxland the grocer arrived about 1922, a branch of the Chingford shop - in fact we used to say that he followed us, as he didn't want to lose a good customer. Life was the same as any other London Suburb: tennis in the summer and bridge evenings in the winter. Many walked to the station, exactly 5/8th of a mile from no. 17. Only a few had cars at first. All had radios, and television came about 1938, when we had our first set. Reception from Alexandra Palace was good.

The Ridgeway population was remarkably stable: I cannot remember anybody leaving before 1939. Gradually houses were built on both sides of the

The Garden City influence on Cuffley's architecture (see pages 10 and 12) was also reflected in New Park House on the corner of Hanyards Lane and the Ridgeway. It was demolished in 1999 (*above, left*), but the style lives on in the similar *Gables* Restaurant at Newgate Street, (*above, right*).

road towards the Northaw and Newgate Street cross roads. In the late 1930s, the Huggins had to sell up because he lost all of his money investing in Chinese Bonds. That caused a bit of an upset. Every so often no. 17 provided space for a dance, the band being accommodated in one of the hall alcoves.

Our village constable used to occasionally cycle past, but there was no crime that I was aware of and cars were never locked. We children could roam and cycle anywhere across the fields. Our police station was Potters Bar, just on the A1. I do not know what crime they had to deal with, but one morning I took in a packed Air Force parachute that was lying in the road, which I told them had probably fallen off a lorry. Having heard that expression before I think they debated whether to charge me with something and therefore at last put an incident down on their crime sheet. However, sense prevailed, but I think they would have been happier if I had taken the parachute to the Vicar. Their moment of glory came

at last, as some months after the war was declared, we heard that they had raided Wells Farm where they found an illicit still making liquor spirits. We presume that there had been an informant, as we could not imagine that the still was discovered by pure detective work. It did surprise everybody that such an operation was going on in our midst, at Cuffley of all places!

A few bombs fell on Cuffley and no. 17 was slightly damaged, but one bomb, (I would guess at a 50lb weight), dropped in the woods about 300 yards down the hill to the right and in front of No 17, which did not explode. I discovered the hole on one of my 'leaves' and was surprised to see what a clean hole, about 15".in diameter, the bomb had made. I wrote subsequently to Potters Bar police with a sketch of where the bomb was, but I do not know if anything was done about it. I expect the bomb is still there!

Going back to the commencement of the war, a

One last truck stop for Richard

● GOING OUT IN STYLE: The 1940s flatbed truck which took Richard Gentle to his funeral on Friday

Mourners remember village favourite

CUFFLEY: There was laughter among the sadness as hundreds of mourners filled St Andrew's Church for the funeral of one of the village's favourite characters.

Villagers paid their respects last Friday to Richard Gentle, who died on October 24, eight days after undergoing a heart transplant at

Hall secretary worked with him for many years. "He never had any children of his own and he was so good with everybody else's."

At the funeral service, friends shared anecdotes remembering the deceased's kindness and humour. One spoke of the Ten Commandments according to Mr Gentle but gave only nine "because Richard

Richard Gentle's obituary in *The Hertfordshire Mercury*, 9 November 2001. The popular youth worker died on 24 October 2001. He had been a superintendent at New Park House (*opposite*) when it was a childrens' home and later was Youth Centre leader and Manager of Cuffley Hall in Maynard Place.

home guard platoon was formed and contrary to the impression given by 'Dad's Army' shows, uniforms and .303 Enfield rifles arrived almost immediately. At first they drilled in the drive of No 17. We had evacuees, but as months went by and nothing happened, the evacuees went home more or less just in time for the real 'blitz' to begin. The guns at Dunkirk could clearly be heard at Cuffley. I was called up from a reserved occupation in September 1940, and was first stationed in the RAF at Hatfield. I motored there each day on service petrol ration. I was at Hatfield when the workshops were bombed by a low flying bomber, in one corner of the office entrance lobby, whilst in the other corner was Prince Bernhard of the Netherlands and his aide. We had a good view of the action: the plane was shot down by the aerodrome A.A. gun. Unfortunately some people in the workshops were killed.

Most of the houses along the Ridgeway were architect designed and fairly substantial. Obviously the first arrivals chose the best plots, but all had magnificent views south over the green belt land and across empty farm lanes to the railway line, about 1/2 mile away to the north. No 17 (tel. no. Cuffley 17) occupied two plots. The second plot was purchased about 1925. Every house reflected the owners individual requirements, but probably none were more extraordinary than No 17. I ought to say something about the designer and owner, namely my father. He was a typical Victorian, a Jack of all trades, who took a P HD degree in chemistry at Yena University in Germany about 1910, and then added a degree in Electrical Engineering in London a year or two later. He was a very practical man, (a skilled glass blower), and so when it came to building his house, he just sat down and became his own architect and designed every feature exactly as he wanted it. He planned a large hall as a central feature to house his extensive library of scientific books.

177

An enlargement made in 1965 from the 1925 glass plate negative (loaned by David Whyte for the Airship and History Exhibition in 1966) showing the school party in the middle of the Ridgeway and crossing the stile to walk towards Northaw as a pony and trap approaches from the north. Greystones House is to the right of the picture behind the foliage. By kind permission.

He used his doctor's title and because they were scarce in those days, he became universally known in Cuffley as 'the doctor'. This I felt sometimes caused some embarrassment to those who thought he was a medical doctor. However, it caused my father no trouble, as he was quite happy to discourse on medical matters, or any other subject from his vast knowledge.

No building firm was employed to build the house, but at the end of the 1918 war, work was scarce and a number of skilled craftsmen made themselves into small contractors, a gang of 2 or 3, and travelled about the country wherever there was work. Father employed a separate gang for the foundations, brickwork and carpentry. The builders first constructed a long barn, brick built, with a tiled roof. This was sixty-six feet long and provided ample room for all workmen to live in for the next 6 - 8 months whilst the main house was built. The barn was subsequently divided up to become a

double garage, workshop, laundry, coal cellar (housing some 15 tons of coal when full,) and a conservatory at the end. The house was constructed of London yellow stock brick and the corner stones came from a demolished country house near Ware. Hence the house name 'Greystones', and the hall roof (ie the inner ceiling) was supported by steel RSJs 12" deep.

Every room was wood panelled in oak, but one room was beautifully panelled in mahogany, made up in Tottenham. Such a house taxed, I believe, the financial resources of my father as it took some three years to complete, and we certainly lived there before some of the rooms had been panelled.

The staffing of this house portrays the vast difference between those days and today. A live-in maid was essential and various maids came and went, the difficulty being Cuffley was rather remote. One or two were foreign, one being suspected by mother of being a German spy and sent back to

View over Northaw Fields from Greystones House on the Ridgeway about seventy years ago before hedge, scrub and trees obscured the vista. In the 1960s there was a roost of over a thousand starlings in the thorn bushes towards the Dell near here. There are three figures walking up the footpath towards the stile onto the Ridgeway seen in the picture opposite. By kind permission of Jim Roy (see text).

Germany post haste. The gardener was a Mr Luck, working four days a week; the home help was Helenka, who was a niece of Padereski the Polish pianist. For two or three days a month a Mr Dowler would arrive to do the heavy work of floor polishing and finally in later years there was also a young handyman/chauffeur. Mother it seems, was relegated to be the cook, cooking lunch for the staff, (except Mr Luck) at mid-day and then cooking a dinner for the family and maid and home help in the evening. Somehow I think they got things wrong in those days.

Mother sold the house in 1944 on very bad advice. I met the new owner in 1953 and another owner in 1982. He told me he was the son of one of Hitler's generals, which was strange considering father's student days in Germany. The owner's son was paralysed after a terrible road accident on the Newgate Street Hill and this resulted in the owner having a lift installed. I remember giving him a chunk of the 1916 airship that was dug up when the tennis court was made. It had the burnt tips of a man's fingers embedded in it. Not perhaps the most tactful gift.

By 1953 the only alterations were the new entrance drive and the installation of central heating. The original heating was by anthracite burning Esse slow-burning stoves that were dotted about the ground floor and also provided hot water, plus gas fires upstairs. The anthracite came direct from Wales in a 13 ton coal truck. Once a year the Cuffley station master would ring up and say 'Doctor, your coal truck has arrived'. Father would then use one of the firms 5 ton lorries (Leyland ex 1914 RAF vehicle) and two men would bag the fuel in 1 cwt sacks and the lorry would cart some 260 bags up Cuffley Hill in about three trips. The job was done in a day. Finally, I should add that my father died in 1942 from heart trouble as a result of over exertion on a Home Guard field day. (See lists, pp 216-217).

Recent photograph of Greystones House with two interiors (*facing page*) from the 1930s to show the wood panelled library. By kind permission of Jim Roy (see text). Jim describes the construction of the house by contractors for his father on page 178.

Nearly every room at Greystones was attractively wood panelled in oak, but one was beautifully panelled in mahogany, constructed in Tottenham. *Top:* the hall looking back from the gallery and, *below*, the hall looking back from the porch. The house was built in the 1920s and these pictures, kindly lent to us by Jim Roy, are from the 1930s.

Four views of Cuffley roads, this page and facing: the Ridgeway where it dips past Keeper's cottage, about 1910. Loxborough Manor was later moved to a site on the right amongst the trees (see page 261). The Station Master's House (demolished in 1982) and a visiting policeman on his bicycle in Station Road, about 1911.

Two early studies of Cuffley Hill. Top: looking back towards the bridge over Cuffley Brook, when the road was lined by beautiful, tall trees, mostly elms, about 1928. These trees were lost in the 1960s and 1970s due to a fungal disease imported by accident from Canada carried by the elm bark beetle. It continues to kill the trees when they are about ten to fifteen years of age. Below: plate camera study from about 1910.

Northaw.—The Ridge Road

'The Ridge Road, Northaw' Thatched cottage in various postcards from about 1900 to about 1950. Top, facing, has a 1909 postmark. The cottage stood on the crossroads near Northwood (recent colour picture) where Norah Lightfoot typed the manuscript for Gerald Millington's original booklet on the village.

An almost identical thatched cottage stood at the west end of the Ridgeway and is shown with Vine Cottage in the background, (see page 223). This was originally published in Millington & Higgs (1983). They were probably built as cottages for estate workers when the road was made up in 1808 or for residential staff to collect tolls. The head keeper would have been housed in the more imposing building (page 182).

Early housing developments and the styles of the day: Joan Clark, pictured by her husband Bernard William
Clark soon after they were married in 1937, in the lounge of their new home at 44 Hill Rise Cuffley.
Built by Mr Chinchen (see pages 168 and 189) in 1936, the new furniture is a study in Art Deco 1930s style.
Bakelite (named after the Belgian inventor, L H Baekeland, 1863-1944), features on the door handles and key
plate, a bronze figure supports a circular globe light mounted on a marble base next to a silver framed
portrait of Joan when she was Joan Gray (see pages 67, 202 and 204). The steam-curved plywood sprung
chair faces typical rugs, wireless, mirror and curtains which all conform to the 1930s fashions.

'Tintern' on East Ridgeway, built next to the Leefe Robinson Memorial by Joan Gray's parents in 1921.
The vertical wood decoration to the wall is also sported in Melvin Bedford's family home in Theobalds Road (*below, left*) where Melvin (see page 26) stands proudly by the gate.
Yet more stripes, above, right, feature on Alfred and Edith Neill's Cuffley bungalow at 5 King James Avenue. They owned the Daimler featured on page 93.

Left and above: two views of life at
Tudor House on the Ridgeway in the 1950s
from the collection of Clifford Bliss.
Tennis has always been one of the most
popular sports in Cuffley. Edith Bliss is on the
left and Clifford is third from the left. (They
rented a studio in the house to their nephew
Michael Clark during the 1960s and his first
book, *The Mysterious Greatwood* and *Punch*
cartoons were produced here, pp 252-253).
Ken Johns, Rosemary Lemon and Jack Lemon
are amongst the party of tennis players.
The house was angled to catch the warmth
and light on the west side overlooking
The Dell and the Northaw Fields.
Note one of Cuffley's familiar scots pines in
the background on the roadside.

Ken Morter houses have a distinct style to them and we picture two with different roof tile colours from Tolmers Road. Mr Chinchen and, later Mr Morter, became two of the best known and much respected local builders, both of whom made their homes in Cuffley.

Two pictures of the 'Garden City style' cottages once shared by Molly Hughes and the Grays, (see pages 4, 10, 11 and 12). The Grays kept poultry, goats and grew vegetables to the left of the cottage here. Although the windows and the extensions have altered the appearance, the Courtenay Crickmer 1908 trademark 'M' double gable survives.

Bungalows in The Meadway, Cuffley, (with a Ken Morter house in the middle distance), and cottages with attractive roof style and tiles in Tolmers Road which were built on the land where the Gray family kept their livestock between 1917 and when they moved to East Ridgeway in 1921. Molly Hughes later followed them there when Mr Chinchen built her house 'Fronwen'.

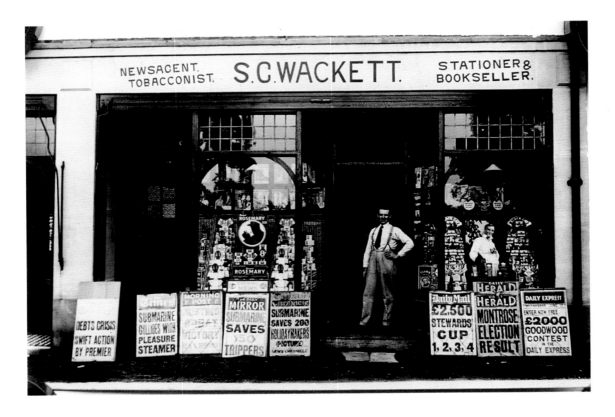

Three generations of the Wackett family have run the same business in Cuffley and supplied the daily news to thousands of people over the years.

Above: Sidney Wackett at the entrance to 40 Station Road with a selection of newspaper display boards from what we have been able to establish is Wednesday 28 June 1933. Cigarettes dominate the advertising: the left window promotes a 'Rosemary' type and the right window has a display of 'Black Cat Craven A'.

Left: Ralph Wackett, Sidney's son, stands in the same entrance some thirty years later. The attractive window style with wooden arches and small panes at the top was common to the first four shops. A different builder took over the development at 34 Station Road. Advertisements for Will's Gold Flake and Players Please have been added and a display of local trophies feature in the right side window. The V. C. initials over the shop were those of Sidney's widow Violet.

(Steve Wackett is featured outside the shop in February 1997 and the family is described in the text on page 124).

Above left: the Physiotherapy Clinic (former Fire Station), for sale in 2004, in Tolmers Road, near Cuffley Station. Len Stokely, (1909-2000), *above right*, was a member of the Cuffley Fire Brigade which originally operated from here. He is also in the group below, second from the left, and the railway station entrance can be seen on the right of the building. The Fire Brigade pictures have been kindly lent by John Higgs.

OLD MILL. GOFFS OAK.

Goffs Oak windmill was once a familiar landmark for people living in Cuffley. Cyril Moore gives full details in his excellent *Hertfordshire Windmills & Windmillers*. Built between 1830 and 1840, worked to about 1898, sales removed 1920s, dismantled in 1953. Millers included: Charles Hart, c1840-1850; Charles Nicolas, 1850-1860; Charles Everitt Nicolas, c1860-1876; Alfred Rayson, c1876-1886; Benjamin Robinson, (after whom Robinson Avenue, the road leading from Cuffley Road to the site, was probably named) c1886-1898.

Views of the garden at 44 Hill Rise Cuffley looking east towards Goffs Oak in early spring, summer, autumn and winter of 1961 and 1962. The major oak which shows partly on the left is featured on pages 23-25.

Manufacturing and light industry has provided employment in the village as the agricultural workforce diminished and has been sited in and around Sopers Road without spoiling the rural scenery. See pages 132-133 for details of the firms, such as Everest, present. This Glade Works frontage was pictured in 2001.

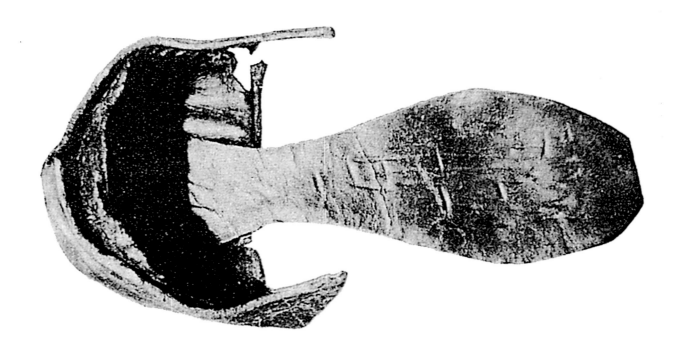

When the new Cuffley Hall and Community Centre replaced the Cabin a section of Roman Road was exposed during the foundation work, (*Herts Archaeology* Vol 9, 1983-1986). The location (TL 305/027) indicates that the straight Cuffley Hill which deviates slightly in Station Road is on the original line of the Roman Road between St Albans and Cheshunt. At the time of this discovery, parts of two leather shoes were found and our illustration is from the same reference. Although these were identified as being similar to shoes excavated at Weoly Castle, Birmingham, about 1220AD, the shoemaker Sarah Juniper considers (from the straight, clumsily cut sole shapes) that they were more likely to be late Tudor, from about 1580.

Appendix 1

Chronological History

The Parish events are listed in chronological order, with reference to Gwennah Robinson (1978), Gerald Millington and John Higgs, the Northaw Great Wood book (1966), The Gentleman's Magazine (1731-1800) and Brian Warren, (2000).

Part of the Roman road which ran between Cheshunt and St Albans was recorded during the construction of the new community centre in Cuffley (TL 305/027), see above.

Written references to Cuffley start in 1228 and appear regularly after 1842. We have added selected events (printed in blue) that took place nationally to help the reader set local dates in their context.

655 Gwennah Robinson notes: *"The division between the Mercian diocese of Dorchester and the*

East Saxon diocese of London ran from Royston down Ermine Street to Throcking, then by the Rib to its junction with the Lea and on to the boundary near Northaw"

948 North Haga (meaning North Wood) given as the name in early records for the area which became Northaw

1130 Religious hermit called Sigar inhabited a cell in the southern part of the Northaw Great Wood.

1201 Dispute between the de Valoignes and the Abbey of St Albans over Northaw Wood settled in the Abbey's favour

1215 Chapel at Northaw dedicated to St Thomas of Canterbury

1228 Cuffley first appeared as Kuffele and two shoes found near the site of Brickwall Farm have been dated to this period, or later, (see above).

1548 Riots against enclosures at Northaw and Cheshunt spread over southern England

1551 Tract of land at Cuffley known as Aviners

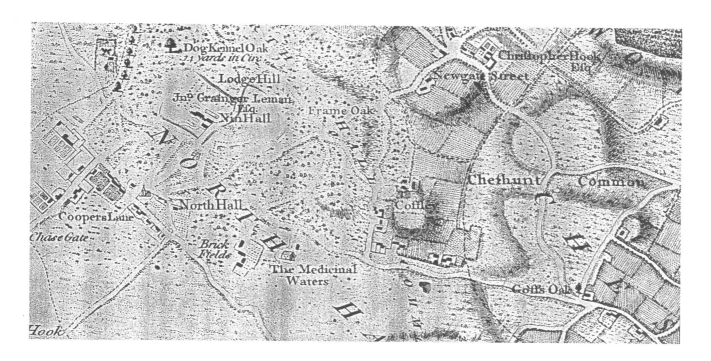

The Dury & Andrews map of Hertfordshire of 1766, by kind permission of Trevor James, shows that there was originally a direct route to Cattlegate before Northaw Road East was constructed. The Frame Oak (see page 37) is named as a great oak even at this date in the middle of the 18th Century. 'Dog Kennel Oak' near the old windmill site, top left, is given as 14 yards in circumference. The open wood pasture character of Northaw Great Wood is indicated, the brick fields named and the Medicinal Waters had The White Horse public house on the site in those days. Hanyards Farm, (above the name 'Coffley'), Hill Farm on the village green, Brickwall Farm (with the Cabin set back from the road) and Lower Hanyards Farms are all shown.

(later Hanyards) granted to the Almoner of St Albans Abbey

1559 Coronation of Queen Elizabeth I

1563 William Cecil, Lord Burghley purchased manor of Theobalds from Robert Burbage and enclosed part of the common fields of Northaw and Cheshunt. (The Cecils later agreed with James I to exchange Theobalds for the estate at Hatfield).

1576 Meeting of the Privy Council met at Northaw on the 30 August

1579 On 16 May commoners of Northaw and Mimms destroyed fences erected on common land. Rioters dispersed by Sir Christopher Hatton

1590 Nyn Hall built by the Earl of Warwick, (demolished in 1774)

1621 King James 1 asked the Earl of Salisbury for a brace of bucks (deer) to be given to the people of Northaw. He took the waters regularly at Cuffley for the restorative properties and the site became known as the 'King's Well'

1625 Death of King James I at Theobald's Park, Cheshunt, Hertfordshire (referred to as the 'wisest fool in Christendom' and accession of his son as Charles I on 27 March. He had been born at Edinburgh Castle, the only son of Mary Queen of Scots and Lord Darnley on 19 June 1566

1654 Commencement of Northaw Parish register

1660 1 January: Samuel Pepys began his diary that continued until 31 May 1669

1661 Postmarks introduced in Britain by the Royal Mail, 19 April

1667 *A sad little episode recorded in the County Archives Sessions Books:* Order that the inhabitants of Northaw shall provide a convenient habitation for Mary Shaw, a poor inhabitant. *The following year:*

1668 Edward Hayward is 'committed to gaol on 1st November until he finds sureties to save harmless the Parish of Northaw concerning a bastard child of Mary Shaw, whereof he is the reputed father'

1690 Northaw Place built as dower house for

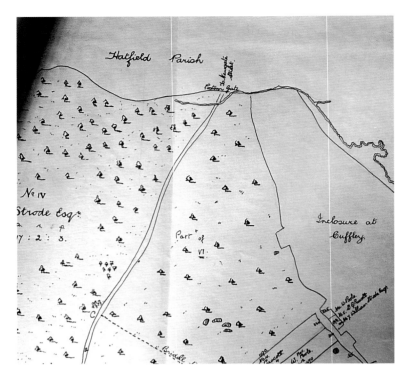

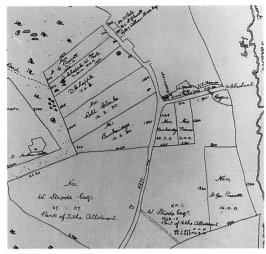

Great Wood, Carbone Hill and Home Wood details of the enclosures illustrated on the 'Inclosures' Map of 1806 showing Cuffley Brook, the portion of the Parish lost here (above the stream by Postern Bridge), and bridle path through Home Wood. This was used by one of the authors and others in the 1950s to get to Guildhouse School, part of which is now known as Homewood Lane.

The east side of the 1806 'Inclosures' Map and (*facing*), south portion showing the route of Cuffley Brook, the 'Northaw Waters' site and ownerships by Messrs W Poole, S G Prescott, William Strode, (who lived at Northaw and later at Ponsbourne), D Chapple, Robert Clarke, Buckeridge and Thomas. The line of the Theobalds Wall is clearly seen as a curve and described as *'Part of Theobalds Park taken off from Northaw Common'*. All these details by kind permission of Trevor James.

William Leman's daughter, Sarah

1698 Northaw House (formerly known as Nyn Lodge) built for Mrs Angin

1732 Death of a Mr Pheasant, at Northaw in Hertfordshire, Turkey merchant, 23 March; Mr Petit, gardener to Sir William Leman of Northaw in Hertfordshire Bart, *"presented to His Majesty a ripe melon, the first produced this year, as he has done for these ten years past"*, 22 April

1739 Marriage of Christopher Wyvil, Esq, Comptroller of Cash in the Excise Office, to Miss Asty of Northaw, with £12,000, 14 March

1749 The Dower House (Fairlawn), Northaw built for Mrs Lucy Alie, Lord of the Manor; death of Richard Leman Esq, at Northaw, Hertfordshire, 6 July

1750 Increasing enclosure by Act of Parliament

1753 Death of Mrs Alie of Northaw, Hertfordshire. She left £500 to Foundling Hospital, 24 September

1756-1758 Accounts for Theobald's Park Estate

includes a listing of tithe charges for lands in the Parish of Northaw

1757 Marriage of John Leman of Northaw, Hertfordshire, Esq to Miss Worth, July

1762 6 January. *"A lady in Bond Street, said to be nearly related to the young officer who was wounded in Hyde Park, shot herself through the head with a pistol, and died in great agonies. She was the daughter of a family of fortune at Northaw in Hertfordshire, and had married against her friend's consent"*

1768 16 October. A farm house belonging to John Leman Esq of Northaw in Hertfordshire, was maliciously set on fire, and entirely consumed, together with the barns and a great quantity of grain

1768 21 October. Marriage of Rev Dr. Hollingworth of Northaw to Miss Clayton

1771 August: Bankruptcy of Benjamin King of Northaw, Hertfordshire, dealer

1772 25 August: Marriage of Lt-Col Townsend, of

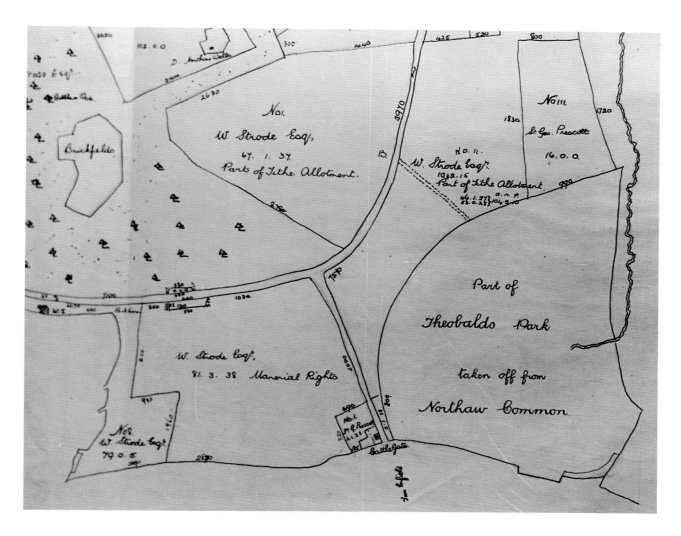

the 34th Regiment, to Miss Ford of Northaw, Hertfordshire

1775 Charles Lamb, English essayist, born in The Temple, London, son of a clerk, 10 February

1777 Death of Thomas Cotton, Esq, at Northaw, Hertfordshire, 8 May

1781 Death of Mrs Vincent, aged 74 at Northaw in Hertfordshire. Widow of the late Robert Vincent Esq 15 April

1783 Marriage conducted by the Archbishop of Canterbury. William Strode, Esq of Northaw, Hertfordshire, to the widow of the late William Leman, Esq of the same place, 9 December

1784 Death of J Pope Esq aged 75 at Northaw, 7 May

1785 Marriage of Thomas Blachford Esq of Northaw, Hertfordshire to Miss Moore, 27 January

1785 Mr John Heathfield, vicar of Northaw. From list of Parishes with incumbents, June

1786 Death of Mr Blackford, goldsmith and refiner,

nephew of the late Mr Alderman Blackford at Northaw, Hertfordshire, January

1786 Death of Mrs Butts, formerly of Fleet Street, at Northaw, Hertfordshire, December

1789 Marriage of William Hall Esq of Northaw to Miss Cooke of Aldersgate Street, 14 May

1794 Death of Mr George Dasent, son of the Hon John Dasent, deceased, late chief justice of the Isle of Nevis, at Northaw, 5 October

1794 About 10 o'clock at night a fire broke out in the stables of Mrs Vincent, in Cooper's Lane, Northaw, which in two hours destroyed them, with two saddle horses, a third was saved, but 'terribly singed'. It is supposed to have been occasioned by a candle, left while the servant went into the house to fetch some gruel for a sick horse, 28 November

1795 Northaw Place, in child-bed, the lady of A Watt Esq: a birth recorded, 8 January

1797 £1 notes first issued by the Bank of England, 26 February

NORTHAW SCHOOL WINTER 1964-1965

Northaw School, built for £600 in 1851 and extended in 1879, was the subject of a student project when Michael Clark was invited to photograph there during the winter 1964-1965. The following six pictures are from the same source. The school (see 1845 print of proposed school on p 214) originally had places for 60 boys and girls with 40 infants at a fee of one penny a week. It replaced teaching in Northaw from 1816 at the Vicarage and then, in 1824, by John Binyon in Church Lane. His school was then made into four cottages.

1799 Northaw Statute Fair held. (Hiring fair for farm workers), 28 September

1800 Death of Mr England at Northaw, of the injury he received from two footpads, labouring men in the neighbourhood, who had waylaid him, knowing he had been receiving the Duke's rents. Mr England was steward to the Duke of Leeds. One man has since been executed at Hertford, and the other transported for life, August

1801 General Enclosure Act

1809 May: Norman church at Northaw demolished by the Lord of the Manor Mr William Strode and a new one built

1811 Death of William Strode. Sale of Northaw Great Wood and part of Nyn Manor. Bought by Patrick Thompson

1839 'Bradshaw's Railway Companion' became the first national railway timetable to be published, 25 October

1840 First British adhesive stamps, the penny black and two-penny blue introduced by Sir Rowland Hill, officially issued by the GPO, 6 May

1842 Cottage opposite Hill Farm, Cuffley licensed as a beerhouse. (The Plough)

1850 Sir Ebenezer Howard, originator of the Garden City movement, born London, 21 January; first tractors appear on British farms

1851 Northaw School built

1851 Britain's first pillar boxes erected in St Helier, Jersey brought into public use, 23 November

1855 London's first 6 pillar boxes were installed, painted green, 11 April

1857 Lord Baden-Powell, founder of the Boy Scout Movement in 1908, born in London, 22 February

1862 Cuffley communal pump installed on the village green at the top of Plough Hill

1869 Austria issued the first postcard, 1 October

1870 Britain issued its first postcard for inland use only, along with the introduction of the half-penny postage stamp, 1 October

Children running in the playground at Northaw school, with Vineyards Road in the background. This was an entirely unplanned event and the headmaster, Mr Thomas, had told the children to treat the photographer as if he was not there throughout his visits. They obliged and always ignored both the visitor and his camera.

1871 School built of white brick erected at Cuffley (on the site of the present St Andrew's Church)

1876 Graham Bell filed his patent for the first telephone 3 hours ahead of a similar one by Elisha Gray, 9 March

1876 Nyn Park built by John Kidston

1880 First telephone directory published by The London Telephone Company with 255 names ('up to 16 January'), 15 January

1881 Northaw church burnt down

1882 New St Thomas the Martyr at Northaw designed by Kirk and Sons of Sleaford (Lincs) in an unusual style for Hertfordshire, August

1894 Parish of Northaw formed, known as the Parish of Northaw and Cuffley from 1982

1895 Earliest demonstration of a celluloid cinematograph film given in Paris by Auguste (died 10 April 1954) & Louis Lumiere, 22 March

1900 Daily Express newspaper first published in London, founded by C Arthur Pearson, 24 April;

Count Ferdinand von Zeppelin (born 8 July 1838 in Constance, died in Charlottenburg, near Berlin, 8 March 1917) flew his first airship from a field on the outskirts of Berlin, 2 July

1901 Death of Queen Victoria at Osborne House, Isle of Wight, aged 81, on 22 January after reign of 63 years and accession of eldest son as Edward VII.

1902 Postmaster General sanctioned divided back postcards. (Germany accepted these in 1905 and North America allowed them in 1907)

1903 Walter Hammond, Gloucestershire & England cricketer born in Dover, 19 June, (died in Durban, South Africa, 1965, 2 July)

1904 Vehicle registration for first time in Britain: A1 to Earl Russell for his Napier automobile, 1 January; books of stamps first issued in Britain by the GPO, containing 24 at 1 penny each, 16 March

1909 Old Age Pension paid for first time: 25p a week for over 70 year-olds, 1 January

(Continued on page 218)

Left: Head teacher Mr Thomas maintained a disciplined and happy atmosphere at Northaw School.

Formal Cuffley School photographs of the last century featured in *Cuffley in Old Picture Postcards* by Patricia Klijn (1995) and John Higgs has a 19th Century group outside the original Cuffley School, a 1916-1918 register from which is on the next two pages, by kind permission of *Hertfordshire Archives & Local Studies*. Nellie Wharf is shown in 1964 and was listed as 'Ellen', one of 19 Wharf children from Sopers Farm. Only Nellie could write and only Charlie, Ted and Mabel also lived into adult life. Mabel and Susie Richardson from Sopers Farm and Joan Gray from Hill Farm are also shown.

Admission No.	Date of Admission [or Re-Admission.]			Date of Birth.			Surnames.	Christian Names.		Address.	What, if any, Claim to Exemption be made?
1916	Day.	Mon.	Year.	Day.	Mon.	Year.		Child's.	Parent's.		
306	24	1	16	13	11	10	Whewhall	Frank E	William	New Cottages, Cuffley	
307	20	3	"	29	9	08	Robinson	Herbert-Sydney	Walter	Cuffley Hill	
308	3	5	.	15	4	11	Butler	Elsie M	Hubert	Verdun, Cuffley	
309	9	4	.	2	3	12	Carpenter	Edward	Chas.	Hill Farm "	
1917 310	8	5	.	5	9	10	Graves	Elsie	Frank	Cuffley Station	
311	19	6	.	9	10	09	Shepherd	Constance	Augusta	New Cottages	
312 R	19	6	.	14	6	09	Halliday	Victor	Louis	School House Cuffley	
313	3	7	"	21	3	10	Goodyear	Leslie	Robert G	Hanyards Farm	
314	25	9	"	21	6	11	Gray	Joan	John	Cuffley Hill Farm	
315	14	5	17	10	1	09	Richardson	Susie		Cattlegate	
316	24	9	17	8	2	12	"	Mabel		"	
317	19	10	17	15	2	11	Halladey	Derek	Bernard	Cuffley	
1918 318	3	7	18	16	11	07	Freer	Samuel	William	Tops Farm	
319	"	"	.	28	1	11	"	Norman	"	"	
320	9	9	.	22	8	09	"	Ernest	"	"	
321	"	"	"	30	"	13	Shepherd	Jack Wm	Harry Aug	New Cottages	
322	7	4	19	26	12	06	Drury	Alfred	Fred	Cattlegate	
323	"	"	"	4	9	10	"	Fred	"	"	
324	5	5	.	17	5	06	Dennis	May	William	Tops "	
325	"	"	"	13	10	09	"	Lizzie	"		
326	"	"	"	13	1	13	Dennis	Horace			
327	13	.	.	4	1	13	Drury	Walter	Fred	Cattlegate	
328	"	"	"	3	2	13	Parker	Florrie	Harry	"	
329	"	"	"	4	2	15	"	Charles	"	Cuf...	
330	27	"	"	9	10	10	Halliday	Lonnie	Louis	Cuf...	
331	23	6	.	28	7	14	"	Stanley	.	"	
332	30	.	.				Carpenter	Iris	Ellen	"	
333	15	9	"	23	7	14	Sell	Leonard	Tom	"	
334	15	9	"	20	3	16	Kendal	Grace	William	"	
335	21	1	20				Taylor	Joy	Tom	"	
336	"	"	"				"	Eric	"	"	
337	12	.	"	4	2	14	Walmsley	Trevor	Robert	"	
338	2	2	.	.			Goodyear	Clifford		"	
339	31	5	.	4	2	14	Burrell	Thomas Wm	Thomas	"	
340	31	5	"				Brown	George	George	Cattlegate	
341	"	"	"				"	"	Joseph		

NAME IN FULL	Admission No.	NAME IN FULL.	Admission No.
Williams George	5	Webb Fred: Chas.	221
Wharf Milly	6	Webb Harold Frank	222
Wharf Mabel	14	Webb Gladys Maud	223
Wharf Edmund	21	Whybrow Ivy Clara	225
Wharf Alice	38	Whiting Daisy	226
Willingham Henry	39	Whiting Elsie	227
Willingham John	40	Worboys Herbert	228
Willingham George	41	Wharf James	232
Wharf Ellen	55	Whybrow Lucy	237
Wilkinson Alfred	56	Weatherly Thomas	240
Warboys Frances Louisa	73	White Hilda	245
Warboys Elizabeth	74	White Florence	246
Wilkinson David	77	White Rose	247
Ward Alfred	78	White Fred	248
Warboys James	90	White Ernest	249
Wharf Maud	101	Worboys Dorothy	250
Williams Violet	102	Whybrow James Fred.k	257
Wharf Charles	112	Wilshire Emma	260
Whybrow Arthur	125		
Whybrow Ernest	128		
Weatherley Gertrude Maud	141		
Lilian May Weatherley	142		
Whybrow Ellen	149		
" Florence Mabel	155		
" Doris	160		
Wharf Edith	174		
Woodhams Sidney	177		
" Frances	178		
" Harold	179		
" Charlie	180		
Worboys Maud Ellen	184		
Worboys William Joseph	185		
Worboys Henry	195		
Whybrow Ernest	208		
Whybrow Ellen	209		
Whybrow Florence	210		
Whybrow Doris	211		
Whybrow Else			

An aerial view of Cuffley School by kind permission.
'Dinner Ladies' who helped at Cuffley School: left to right, Mrs Greenwood, - , Mrs Baker, Miss Knight, with, seated, the Headmaster's wife Mrs Holmes and Mrs Green, the school cook, late 1940s.

Poltimore School class pictures by kind permission of Alan Gill. This was a private school in Tolmers Road. Among the groups are Mary Gill and Dorothy Hubble. Note that the roof of the school could be opened in fine weather. The picture was taken by 'Pauleste, Cuffley'.

Miss Harriet and Miss Mary Smith, Guildhouse School headteachers, at Anthony and Christine Clark's wedding, Northaw Church, 1962. *Below:* a group of boarders at Guildhouse School in the summer of 1956.

Guildhouse School's 76 pupils, Cuffley Playing Fields 1952: including Robert, Michael & Elizabeth Hall, John, April & Julie Reynolds, Anthony & Michael Clark, Brian & Stuart Meeke, Carole & Angela Fitch, Evan, Bridget & Sarah Morgan, Graham & Paul Cable, Elizabeth Ogborn, Wendy Perry, Pamela & Maxine Lemon, Bridget Petherbridge, Richard Briggs, Anthony Madsen, Christine and Stella Jones, John Bean, Angela & John Ripley, Richard Lightfoot, Susan Meads, Christopher Seager, Peter Lock, Rodney Slatford, (see page 143). Rodney's father is on the far left, top picture. Peter Lock lived at Greystones, (see page 180), at this time. John, April and Julie Reynolds lived at The Crown in Newgate Street. (Apologies to those not named!)

Two school groups from 1946 not already shown in *Cuffley in Old Picture Postcards* by Patricia Klijn: the Reception Class teacher, Mrs Steventon on the same day that her daughter Mrs Allingham's class of leavers was taken and reproduced in the Postcard book, *top*, and the Guildhouse group, Carbone Hill. The father of Janet Duncombe, (in top picture) ran the Kiosk Cafe by the station. Anthea Beverley is also shown.

Uniform :

Girls.   *Summer*—Navy blue blazer or coat, white panama
hat with navy blue ribbon.

Winter—Navy blue coat, navy blue beret.

Boys.   Navy blue cap and overcoat, navy blue or grey
knickers, navy blue blazer.

Badges may be obtained at the School, price 1s.

*(Uniform is not essential except in the case of school
expeditions and school functions.)*

PHYSICAL TRAINING CLASS.

Boys and Girls.   Navy blue knickers, white blouse, navy blue
tie, white socks and black gym. shoes.

Day pupils are required to bring :

Knife, fork, spoon, table napkin if mid-day dinner is required
daily.

A towel.

A mug.

A pair of indoor shoes.

A pair of black gym. shoes.

A shoe bag.

A pencil box and coloured crayons.

A rug, small pillow if required.

Everything should be clearly marked.

Boarder's list on application.

THE GUILDHOUSE

Kindergarten and Preparatory School.

Carbone Hill,
Cuffley,
Herts.

Telephone : Cuffley 2482.

PRINCIPALS :

Miss MARY ELIZABETH SMITH.

(B. of E. Teachers' Certificate),
(Physical Training Certificate, Reading Univ.)

Miss HARRIET SMITH

(Cambridge Teachers' Diploma).

The education given provides a sound moral training and
ensures a suitable groundwork on which children may build
later.

Preparation for all entrance and scholarship examinations.

The Principals are assisted by a qualified Staff.

School Curriculum :

Divinity, English, History, Geography, Mathematics,
Elementary Science, Latin, French Grammar and Con-
versation, Singing, Ear Training, Educational Handwork,
Needlework, Drawing and Painting (R. D. S. Exams.),
Drill, Dancing, Organised Games, Wolf Cubs and Brownies,
Acting and Voice Production.

Hours of Attendance :

Morning	.	.	.	9.30—12.30
Afternoon	.	.	.	2.15— 3.45

FEES :

	£ s. d.
Full Board, per term	20 0 0
Weekly Board, per term . . .	15 0 0
Laundry	10 0

(This does not include tuition.)

Tuition :

	£ s. d.
Children 4 years and under . . .	4 4 0
„ from 5 years . . .	5 5 0
„ from 6 „ . . .	6 6 0
„ from 7 „ . . .	7 7 0
„ from 8 years and over . .	8 8 0
Stationery and use of books, per term . .	10 0

Optional Subjects :

(Per term.)

	£ s. d.
Dancing (by Miss Stewart) . . .	1 1 0
Piano (by Miss Withers, L.R.A.M.), £2 2s. 0d.—3	3 0
Violin (by Miss Withers, L.R.A.M.), £2 2s. 0d.—3	3 0
Eurhythmics and Percussion Band . .	10 0
Elocution	1 1 0

Day Pupils :

	£ s. d.
Hot Milk each morning, (per term) . . .	3 6
Cold „ „ „ „ „ . . .	2 6
Dinner, per day	1 0
Tea, per day	6

A Term's Notice is required before the removal of a Pupil.

Fees will be chargeable if this notice is not given.
Continued provisional notice cannot be accepted.
All Fees are payable in advance.

The Guildhouse prospectus: both sides of the same folded card. Some pupils walked from the village to the
school via the Home Wood footpaths, although the initial form of transport for very young pupils was pony
and trap, driven by Harriet. By the 1950s cars and bicycles became the norm. One of the most popular
teachers was Jone (pronounced Joan) Burgess who cycled to Cuffley from West Street in Hertford each day.

Poltimore

20·3·40.

Dear Mother,

We close School
on Thursday March 21 st.
at 3.30 p.m. and return on
Wednesday April 17 th.
There will be no detailed
Reports this Term as

Mr & Mrs Gill
from
Miss Munckton
Poltimore School
Cuffley
Herts

Above: this delightful scene is on the site of Cuffley School by kind permission of Melvin Bedford, who notes: 'I still have the crow egg I got by climbing the elms in the right background to this picture. It shows, in about 1936, left to right: Arthur Bedford, Madge Toladay, Beatie Toladay, Pat Toladay and Barry Appleby'. Alan Gill has kindly let us reproduce, *facing, left,* the first page of a letter he wrote from Poltimore in 1940 and his Cuffley College report from the following year. It is doubtful if many readers knew there had been a 'Cuffley College'. It was held at Wells Farm from 1939 by Mr Fretwell and lessons were sometimes run in a converted barn. Pupils remember counting dandelion heads during lessons and the image of sticky tape across the class room windows of war time. The Blass boys and David Myers also went there. Another pupil, John Hussey, went on to work for Shell and was awarded the OBE.

Cuffley College.

Report of the Christmas Term, 1941   Form "II"   Average Age of Form 9.1 Years.
Name Gill A. L.   House " — "   Age 8.5 years.   Side " — "

Group Subjects.	Marks obtainable	Highest Marks obtained	Marks obtained	Place
English: Literature, Grammar, Composition, Reading, Spelling, Writing, History, Geography.	500	399	389	2
Mathematics: Arithmetic, Algebra, Geometry, and Higher Maths.	300	279	262	2
Science: Chemistry, Physics, Mechanics.	300	289	270	2
Classics: Latin, Classical History.	300	not taken yet		
Languages: French, German.	300	120	110	2
Drawing: Freehand, Model.	100	82	82	1
Term's Work: Total	1000	not added this Term		
Total	2500	1165	1113	

Place in Form 2   Conduct Very good   Absent 3 half days
No. in Form 5.   Application V.G.   Late — times

• Next term will begin on 15 Jan. 1942

N.B.—Notice of unavoidable absence through sickness, or other urgent cause, should be sent to the Head Master BEFORE School begins.

Analytical Report.

Subject.	Marks obtainable	Marks obtained	Position
English: Literature	150		
General		125	2
Grammar	50	40	2
Composition	50	35	2
	50	44	1
	50	29	3
	50	36	3
	50	38	3
Mathematics: Arithmetic	100	82	2
Algebra	100	83	2
Geometry and Higher Maths.	100	90	2
Science: Chemistry	100		
Physics	100	270	2
Mechanics	100		
Classics: Latin	150		
Classical Hist.	150		
Mod. Languages: French	150	110	2
German	150		
Drawing: Freehand	50	40	1
Model	50	42	1

365

Remarks.

Games:	Football 9	Tennis —
	Cricket —	Swimming —

Music: He shows great interest

I am pleased to note Alan's high place in Class.

He deserves praise for he is very steady & painstaking

— Fretwell, Form Master.

— Thrussell, Head Master.

Proposed Schools and School House Northaw, Herts
S S TEULON ARCT

G. CHILDS LITH   M & N HANHART IMPT

Compared with the solid Victorian architecture of Northaw School shown in this delightful 1845 lithograph, the Cuffley School Room was a rather like the 'tin' St Andrew's Church, but many happy times were spent in both, as this lower picture shows:

Christmas Party for the Brownies in the Cuffley School Room about 1958. It was demolished in 1964 when the new St Andrew's Church was built here. The picture includes Marilla Kelly, Gillian Gathercole, Rhona and Wendy Gentle, Vivienne Allingham, Lynne Harty, Susan McEvoy and Paula Lince. Brown Owl Mrs Blackford with her helper Mrs Staines and her daughter Pat. Patricia Fenshom is second from the right at the back.

The Old School Room was replaced by the new St Andrew's Church, (dedicated on St Andrew's Day, 30 November 1965, and pictured here by Trevor James in September 1967).

Top: Northaw Road East in 1925, from a postcard, showing the new bungalows before pavements were constructed on both sides of the road. At its junction with Plough Hill, an earlier school house had been built in white brick in 1871. It was replaced by the one featured opposite in 1901. On the right of the Old School Room stood the School Mistresses' House. A police box was later sited here on the roadside.

Clark. B.W.
Oak Cott.
44 Mill Rise

18.11.40.

HERTS HOME GUARD.

No.2.Sect.   3rd.Platoon.   11st Coy.

PATROLS - LIST OF DUTY.

Wednesday 20th November   James, Clark,B.W.
Thursday   21st   "   Cpl.Hopkins, Stevens.
Friday,   22nd.   "   Longley, Wood.
Saturday.   23rd.   "   Mackintosh, Holmes.

        Commencing Sunday 25th November 1940, Sub-Sections as under will
provide the Patrol in sequence of A.B.& C.

Sub-Section A.	B	C.
Cpl.Tolworthy I/C.	Cpl. Gifford, I/C.	Cpl. Hopkins, I/C.
Cpl. Roy.	Vol. Clark, H.E.	Vol. Knight.
Vol. Bath.	Baldwin,	Willcocks.
Harty,	Chipperfield,	Wood.
Yuill.	Holmes,	Horstead,
Robb,	Richardson,	Ruthven,
Watson,	Williams,	Stevens,
Thrussell.	Clark,B.W.	Bartlett,
Marriner,	Longley,	Greenland,
James,	Mackintosh,	Hyland.
Boyle.	Large.	

Section Orders in future will be distributed through N.C.O's I/C Sub-Sections.

RIFLES.   N.C.O'S I/C Sub-Sections will arrange for all rifles and S.A.A. to be
brought on parade on Sunday next at 09.45.hours at Greystones without
fail. Any shortages in S.A.A. should be reported as soon as possible
and rifles must be handed over in properly clean condition.

INSTRUCTORS -   are required in the following subjects, and anyone who feels
competent to act as an Instructor is asked to report to N.C.O.I/C
viz. Musketry, Fire Control, Indication of Targets, Judging Distance,
Automatic Weapons, Squad Drill, Bayonet Training, Signalling, Gas,
Messages and Reports, Patrols and Guides, Map Reading and Field
Sketching.

LEWIS GUN.   A refresher course will be commenced on Thursday 28th November at
19.00 hours at the Masonic Hall, Stores Building, Welwyn Garden City.
Also a course in the Browning Medium M.G. will be held at the same
place and time but commencing 25th November.   Anyone prepared to attend
is asked to report at once. Transport can probably be arranged.

RECRUITING. is still open and Members are asked to suggest to friends that they
join in suitable cases.   In the case of persons who are not sufficiently
well known by Members to enable a direct approach to be made, the names
and addresses should be sent in.

PARADES -   Wednesday, November 20th. Scout Hut. 20.00 hours.   Lecture.
(Subsistance allowance will be paid out to those who have not
already had it).
Sunday 24th November 1940. 09.45. hours at Greystones.

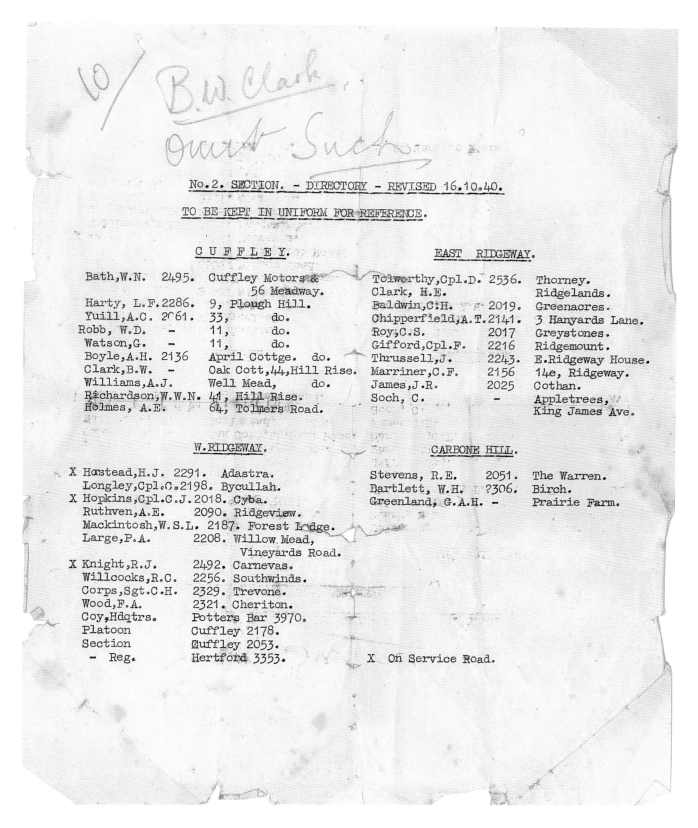

No.2. SECTION. - DIRECTORY - REVISED 16.10.40.

TO BE KEPT IN UNIFORM FOR REFERENCE.

C U F F L E Y.

Bath,W.N.	2495.	Cuffley Motors & 56 Meadway.
Harty, L.F.	2286.	9, Plough Hill.
Yuill,A.C.	2061.	33, do.
Robb, W.D.	–	11, do.
Watson,G.	–	11, do.
Boyle,A.H.	2136	April Cottge. do.
Clark,B.W.	–	Oak Cott,44,Hill Rise.
Williams,A.J.		Well Mead, do.
Richardson,W.W.N.		41, Hill Rise.
Holmes, A.E.		64, Tolmers Road.

EAST RIDGEWAY.

Tolworthy,Cpl.D.	2536.	Thorney.
Clark, H.E.		Ridgelands.
Baldwin,C.H.	2019.	Greenacres.
Chipperfield,A.T.	2141.	3 Hanyards Lane.
Roy,C.S.	2017	Greystones.
Gifford,Cpl.F.	2216	Ridgemount.
Thrussell,J.	2243.	E.Ridgeway House.
Marriner,C.F.	2156	14e, Ridgeway.
James,J.R.	2025	Cothan.
Soch, C.	–	Appletrees, King James Ave.

W.RIDGEWAY.

X	Horstead,H.J.	2291.	Adastra.
	Longley,Cpl.C.	2198.	Bycullah.
X	Hopkins,Cpl.C.J.	2018.	Cyba.
	Ruthven,A.E.	2090.	Ridgeview.
	Mackintosh,W.S.L.	2187.	Forest Lodge.
	Large,P.A.	2208.	Willow Mead, Vineyards Road.
X	Knight,R.J.	2492.	Carnevas.
	Willcocks,R.C.	2256.	Southwinds.
	Corps,Sgt.C.H.	2329.	Trevone.
	Wood,F.A.	2321.	Cheriton.
	Coy,Hdqtrs.		Potters Bar 3970.
	Platoon		Cuffley 2178.
	Section		Cuffley 2053.
	– Reg.		Hertford 3353.

CARBONE HILL.

Stevens, R.E.	2051.	The Warren.
Bartlett, W.H.	2306.	Birch.
Greenland, G.A.H.	–	Prairie Farm.

X On Service Road.

Bernard Clark (1908-1994) kept these two Hertfordshire Home Guard duty lists in the pocket of his old uniform (as instructed) and there are many familiar old Cuffley names in the columns here. He lived at Oak Cottage, 44 Hill Rise with Joan and soon after this (18 November 1940) he joined the RAF. He was quickly promoted to Squadron Leader before returning to Lloyds Bank after war service which included a term in Norway. Greystones, on the Ridgeway, was a meeting point and Jim Roy refers to this and his father at this time, from page 174. By 1940 telephone numbers ran from 2000.

The Catholic church, St Martin de Porres, *above*, (1962). At the end of Church Close, it forms a triangle of centres of worship in this part of Cuffley.

Above: the familiar red 242 bus in Station Road pictured by Trevor James in September 1967. Before cars were more available the London Transport 242 was the main link to Potters Bar where the 134 in the bus station would take you on to Hadley Highstone, Barnet and beyond. Perhaps the most popular users in the evenings during the 1940s, 1950s and 1960s were the film goers to the Ritz, Potters Bar or the Odeon, Barnet cinemas. Alternatively, the bus takes you via Goffs Oak and Cheshunt on into Essex and Chingford. The train gave the easiest access to the Rialto cinema in Enfield.

1910 Cottages built in Oak Lane for McAlpine site executives who built the railway as part of the Cuffley Garden City Estate

1910 Cuffley & Goffs Oak station built. First train ran on 4 April

1910/11 Temporary St Andrew's Church built at top of Plough Hill. Nicknamed the 'Tin Tabernacle', it survived for 55 years

1913 Benefits for sickness, (50p), unemployment (30p), and maternity (£1.50 a week) introduced

1914 Cub scouts founded in Sussex, 2 February; Britain entered First World War, 4 August, (ended 11 November 1918); first Zeppelin appeared over the British coast, 29 December

1915 The first casualties in an air raid over Britain were sustained on 19 January when bombs were dropped on Great Yarmouth in Norfolk by German Zeppelin L3; passport photographs were first required in Britain, 1 February; Women's Institute organisation founded in Britain in Anglesey, Wales,

11 September, following start in Canada, 1897.

1916 British military tanks had their first trials at Hatfield, Hertfordshire, 29 January; daylight saving, advocated by William Willett, was introduced in Britain, 21 May, (made permanent 1925, 7 August)

1916 3 September. SL II airship brought down at Cuffley during largest raid of the war by William Leefe Robinson (who was awarded the VC)

1917 Formation of the Northaw Women's Institute. The first in Hertfordshire. President Miss Poland

1921 The last postal delivery on a Sunday, 12 June

1922 Wireless licences introduced in Britain at ten shillings p.a., 1 November

1923 Northaw Great Wood sold to Albert Wombwell of Lower Hanyards Farm, Cuffley for £8,500

1924 Agricultural Wages Board set up

1929 Britain's largest (777ft) airship R 100 (built at Cardington, Bedfordshire, and designed by Barnes Wallis, b 26/9/1887,) first flew on trials, 14 October

The Parish featured on BBC 1 TV in 1966 at the publication of the book on Great Wood. It was the work of the *Hertfordshire & North Middlesex Branch of the British Naturalists' Association*, published by HCC and edited by Bryan Sage. He discussed it on air with Richard Baker, (*above*). It soon sold out and was re-printed. Photographed from the live television in 1966.

1930 Poltimore private kindergarten school opened in Tolmers Road; Scout Hut built by 1st Cuffley Scouts, Plough Hill, Cuffley. (Demolished 1964)

1930 Tractors, combine harvesters, milking machines more widely used on farms

1935 30 mph speed limit introduced for towns and built-up areas in Britain

1935 Guildhouse School opened on Carbone Hill, Cuffley, (closed 1955)

1936 Death of King George V at Sandringham, Norfolk, aged 70, with accession of eldest son as Edward VIII 20 January, but abdicated in favour of his brother, the Duke of York who became George VI, 11 December

1936 Albert Finney, British actor, born in Salford, Greater Manchester, 9 May. (Filmed in *Night Must Fall*, made in the C. of E. Parish vicarage, 1963).

1937 Telephone Exchange built at Cuffley

1938 Cuffley Primary School built at the end of Theobalds Road. Headmaster G C Holmes; Tolmers

Scout Camp started, adjoining Home Wood

1939 Britain and France declare war on Germany after the invasion of Poland, 3 September

1940 Food rationing began (ended 1954, 3 July)

1942 Soap rationing began in Britain (ended 1950, 9 September)

1945 Clement Attlee became Britain's Prime Minister after a landslide vote for Labour in the general election, 26 July, following the end of WW2; Home Guard defence force was disbanded, 29 December

1946 First television licences issued in Britain at cost of £2 p.a., and bread rationing began, 22 July, (ended 1948, 29 July)

1947 Floods in Britain were the worst on record

1947 Nyn bought by St Bartholomew's Hospital

1948 British Railways nationalised, 1 January and first supermarket opened in Britain (London Co-Op) 12 January

1949 Start of first Scout 'Bob-a-Job' week, 18 April

John Carter has kindly lent us pictures from his archive of Cuffley photographs and we have identified, *left to right*, Nicky McEvoy, Gordon Maynard, Avril Sare, possibly Richard Titford. *Front row:* Kitty Wiltshire, Joan McEvoy, (Nicky's mother), Margery Briggs, W. James Paine and Katie Wiltshire in the Cabin.

1950 Petrol rationing ended in Britain, 26 May

1950 Cuffley Free Church built at junction of King James Avenue with Plough Hill (now the hall to the Church)

1952 Death of George VI at Sandringham, aged 56 and accession of his daughter Elizabeth, 6 February

1953 Sweet rationing ended in Britain, 4 February; Coronation of Queen Elizabeth II, 2 June; sugar rationing ended, 26 September

1955 Richard Baker presented the late-night summary on BBC to become the first television newscaster to be seen in vision, 4 September

1956 Third class rail travel abolished on British Rail to conform with continental practice, 3 June

1958 Building development 'Cuffley Hills Estate', (Cranfield Crescent and Bacons Drive) begun, followed by further housing development at the end of Tolmers Road with Bradgate, Coulter Close, Warwick Avenue, Farm Close and continuation of Hill Rise, Wood View and Hanyards End to follow

1961 Large black & white £5 paper notes ceased to be legal tender, 12 March

1962 Roman Catholic Church dedicated to St Martin de Porres built at Cuffley.

1963 On Good Friday 12 April, Nyn Manor house was gutted by fire

1964 Stansted in Essex provisionally chosen as the site for London's third airport, 24 March

1964 Scout Hut on Plough Hill demolished as part of the St Andrew's Church development

1965 St Andrew's Church, Cuffley built on site at top of Station Road. Architect Clifford Culpin, consecrated St Andrew's Day, 30 November

1966 British Post Office issued the first special Christmas stamps, 1 December

1967 Separate school for Infants added at Cuffley Primary School

1968 5p and 10p decimal coins introduced in Britain, 23 April, in advance of new system in 1971

1968 Nyn Manor purchased by Major Russell Dore.

This is also from John Carter's file of photographs and is of Avril Sare, *left*, and Nicky McEvoy at Cuffley Playing Fields during what he guesses was one of the Cuffley Carnival celebrations of about 1958-59. It appears to be during the procession before or after the Cabin photograph on the facing page. (We would, of course, be grateful for any corrections to our captions and text).

Hanyards Farm Dairy shop closed on 7 September
1971 Decimal currency system introduced in Britain, 15 February
1971 Hanyards Farm demolished for housing development
1973 Redevelopment of old Cabin site at Cuffley for Village Hall, Library and Clinic
1982 Cuffley incorporated in the Parish name for first time and demolition of stationmaster's house at Cuffley (now Laurel Court)
1983 £1 coins went into circulation and replaced paper notes in England & Wales, 21 April
1996 Millennium Committee established by Peter Birch, Chair of Residents' Association
2000 Cuffley chapter by Brian Warren in book by *Hertfordshire Association for Local History Recorders' Group* on Community Life in the County in 2000 describes Millennium Garden, Tapestry, Fair, Flower Festival, Photographic Display and Time Capsule with a brief history of Cuffley.

Appendix 2

Notes on the Parish by Mrs Wilson Fox (1923)

At the Conquest, Northaw was probably a trackless waste of swamp and forest, and was not, therefore, mentioned in Domesday Book.

But William the Conqueror is recorded to have granted the Manor of 'Northholt, Nynne and Cuffeley' to one of his followers, Peter de Valoignes, during the life of the Abbot of St Albans, to whom it had belonged. Peter de Valoignes was a robber baron, and made himself a stronghold in the heart of the forest, then called Berevenue, from whence he harried and ravaged the countryside. The house now called 'Barvin's' still preserves the name. At the death of the first baron, the then Abbot attempted to recover his rights, but the son of Peter resisted him, and the lawsuits

Swaine del 1796.   Etched by J.B.S

NINN HALL, HERTS.

The second house in Nyn as 'Ninn Hall' in a 1796 print, (see text below). Note the ha-ha or sunken walled fence. Despite the artistic licence shown with sheep here, a ha-ha gives uninterrupted views from a country house and its cultivated garden across pasture *without* allowing the livestock onto the lawns and flower beds.

resulting lasted for several generations, and were not finally decided until the reign of Henry I, in favour of the Abbot. At the Dissolution it became Crown property, and was granted by Henry VIII to Sir William Cavendish, a faithful adherent of Cardinal Wolsey. In exchange for lands mostly in Derby, his descendants gave it back to Edward VI.

The first Nynne Hall was built by the Earl of Warwick in Elizabeth's reign, and was demolished in 1774. The first road across Northaw Common was made in 1757 by Mr Leman, the Lord of the Manor.

Northaw is spelt in many different ways in the old maps and chronicles. 'Northaga,' or North hedge, points to its having been a boundary in Danish days. 'Northolt,' or North wood, is a Norman variation. Northalt, Northall or North corner, Northalgh, Northole, and finally Northaw, which last has been accepted to-day. There used also to be a Southaw in the neighbourhood.

Northaw Place was built by James I, as a hunting lodge for Enfield Chase. The King enclosed a portion of Northaw Common within the wall of the Chase, in exchange for which he gave some roods of land near Barnet, which now being built over, produce a certain income, which is administered by Trustees for the benefit of the parishioners of Northaw and Cuffley, and is known as King James's Fund.

Northaw House is said to have been built out of the materials of the old house of Nynne.

The church is a modern edifice, built about thirty years ago, to replace the one which had been burnt down. The old church held the tomb of the wife of Sir Thomas More, and had succeeded a yet earlier building, of which no traces remain, except an old stone font.

There is an interesting staircase at the Hook, Northaw, which was taken from the house of Gobions, the residence of Sir John More, father of

Trevor James' March 1977 study of the Parish boundary marker and Coal Tax Post, where Well Road meets the Ridgeway, opposite the site of a cottage that once stood in front of Vine Cottage (*below, right*, via John Higgs). In 1972 Trevor James also pictured the milestone on the bridge which is dated as built in 1726, at the dip in Vineyard Hill (formerly known as Handpost Hill) as it becomes Vineyards Road.
Vine Cottage may have been linked to The Vineyard when an actual vineyard once ran across the Nyn estate to here. The little cottage is a twin of the one at the crossroads (see pages 184-185).

the celebrated Chancellor, Sir Thomas More, who is said to have written his *Utopia* when staying there. Gobions was situated in Brookmans Park, and was pulled down about 100 years ago.

A small house, called Vernon's, has windows of early eighteenth century type. There is an old manuscript at Woodfield, which gives the names of several gentlemen's residences in Northaw in the seventeenth and eighteenth centuries. A red brick house, with a 'hog-backed' roof, now divided into cottages, is reported to have been the residence of the personal attendants of King Charles II, when he came to drink the waters at Cuffley, and is still called 'Muscombs.'

The Caves, now called 'The Chalk Arches'

Between upper Cuffley and Northaw there is a high chalk ridge. There is a tradition that a chain of eleven or twelve caves run under it, following the formation of the celebrated Chislehurst caverns. In the memory of old inhabitants, two or more caves have been explored, and about thirty years ago there used to be excursions organised from the surrounding towns to visit them.

But as is the habit of excursionists, they did so much damage to fences and trees that the farmer closed up the entrance, and forbade trespassers. Since then the ground, which is of a light sandy character, has slipped and fallen in, effectually concealing the old entrance, and bringing down large trees.

About ten years ago, however, some men were engaged in digging out a badger, and uncovered a narrow opening. A party of friends penetrated into the first of the caves, but found no way into another.

There is a curious subterranean passage out in the chalk, probably at one time communicating with the caves, and some twelve feet below the ground. It was lighted or ventilated by several shafts, two of

(Continued on page 228)

Previous page: 19th Century line drawing of 'Nyn Hall, the seat of John Leman Esq, Northaw, Herts' by kind permission of the *Hertfordshire Archives & Local Studies*. The Hall which had new wings added after the 1796 engraving, was demolished in 1876 and rebuilt by the distinguished architect Reginald Blomfield (subsequently knighted) for John Kidston, with a mock tudor style and beautifully maintained gardens. There were circular flower beds and borders to paths below a walled kitchen garden retained from the earlier days.

Above: a 1920s drawing of Nyn by a Mrs T Hardman when Mrs Kidston's son was given as resident: 'J P Kidston'.

Mrs Kidston continued to live in the house until 1929, following her husband's death in 1895. The estate was bought by a Mrs Arthur who lived here until 1947. She then moved to Vernon's House in Northaw village. Nyn was then sold to St Bartholomew's Hospital who at one time wanted to establish a convalescent home here. It was only being used for the storage of bedding and other hospital equipment at the time of the fire, *facing page.*

Left: the Lodge Gate to Nyn in 1964, just prior to Major Dore's purchase of the estate.

Nyn Manor House burnt down on Good Friday, 12 April 1963. Michael Clark was returning home from Totteridge with his father and saw the light in the evening sky. He retrieved his camera from home and ran across the fields to obtain a few colour slides of the event before the film ran out. He returned in the snow in January 1968 to picture the scene again. The original walled garden is in the foreground. It is thought that a hunting lodge probably stood on this site prior to 1535 and Elizabeth I and Cavendish are likely to have stayed here on their recorded visit to Northaw. The Earl of Warwick had the first Nyn Hall built about 1590.

Watercolour of Corner Cottage, School Lane, in Northaw by Vivian Hughes, about 1922, (Catalogue 34). The cottage was first recorded in 1786 as occupied by a Robert Clarke, 'bachelor of this Parish', buried in the churchyard close by. See also facing page, *top*, a C B Bray postcard, and a recent photograph, *facing, below.*

which are still visible, though nearly filled in with earth and rubbish. This passage was said to have been made by the chalk-workers, who had a flourishing trade some hundred or more years ago, burning the chalk for lime. An old kiln still remains.

But it seems unlikely that, where the chalk lies so near the surface, it should have been thought necessary to excavate such an elaborate passage, supported by brickwork arches, of which the tops were visible when the last shaft fell in (about 1912) and it is thought that the chalk workers were more likely to have utilised a much older passage, which they found there.

It has also been suggested that the passage was of still earlier origin, being a Roman military road. Investigation of the brickwork might help to fix the date, but it seems unlikely.

If permission could be obtained to open up the caves once more, it is possible that interesting discoveries might be made.

The 'King's Well' Cuffley

Early in the sixteenth century, a medicinal spring was opened at Cuffley, the discovery being due to a tradition among the peasantry of the district, who had found the water efficacious in the cure of gout and rheumatism.

It soon became popular, and being within easy reach of London, was resorted to by people of rank and fashion. James I was supposed to have drunk the water, and as he was frequently in residence at his magnificent palace of Theobalds, in the centre of Enfield Chase, about four miles distant, it is very probable.

It was at this time that King James enclosed a portion of the common of Northaw, referred to before. During the Commonwealth the Palace of Theobalds was demolished, and the materials sold to pay the soldiers of Cromwell's Army. The Castle Farm, Cuffley, was a keeper's lodge to the Chase,

Above: Hilda Waller painted School Lane in the snow from below Corner Cottage, (see Vivian's painting, *opposite*). It shows the old vicarage, originally known as The Parsonage, (now owned by Cecil Parkinson), and Northaw Church in the background. By kind permission of the artist and her sister, Grace Lawrence, who very kindly allowed us to photograph the picture.

and the old post-office at Newgate Street another.

Until about three years ago the Castle Farm stood among a very picturesque group of Scots firs, which are supposed to have been planted to show the Jacobite sympathies of the owner in later days, and as a signal to other Jacobites. The present owner, however, has had these interesting memorials of the past cut down, and prefers a small crop of cabbages to any historical associations.

When Charles II was restored to the throne, he also patronised the Cuffley spring, and was followed by so many ladies and gentlemen of the Court, that he is recorded to have given orders to Sir Thomas Bowles, the Keeper of the King's tents, to erect marquees near the spot for their accommodation.

In later days the great Prime Minister, William Pitt, and Dr Johnson 'took the waters' at Cuffley, and, doubtless, many other well known personages of that period. When in the height of the fashion, the King had a marble fountain erected over the spring,

and had it called 'The King's Well' under which name it is still to be found in the ordnance maps.

There were three entrances to the field. One past Wells Farm, another by the Castle Farm, Cuffley, and a third is believed to have been approached past Thorntons Farm, through a field of daffodils, which grow wild, but are not indigenous, being indeed the 'Van Sion' variety and must have been originally planted. As these daffodils were introduced into England in the seventeenth century from Holland, it seems possible that some sort of garden or pleasure grounds may have been laid out at the entrance to the 'Spa.' Two of these approaches are now closed, but the field can be entered through a 'blind' lane past the Castle Farm.

Cuffley is also famous for a later historical event, when the first German airship was brought down on British soil, by Captain Leefe Robinson, VC, fell there on the night of 3 September, 1916. An obelisk, commemorating the fact, stands near the spot.

Facing page, top: a 2003 view of the paddock at Northaw House looking towards Nyn. Below: Northaw House from the rear. (A tall monkey puzzle tree once stood here).
This page, above: Graham Rust's previously unpublished original sepia drawing of Northaw House in 1960.
Left: part of the old piggery next to the outstanding walled garden and orchard, Northaw House, 2003.

1905 postcards: The Garden House in Nyn Cottage. (Miss Harriet Le Blanc, a governor of St Pancras Workhouse, and Mrs Kidston converted Nyn Cottage, which stood opposite the church in Vineyards Road, to take children from the workhouse for short holidays). *Below:* Northaw House before it was painted white.

There were several different postcards printed of the children outside Nyn Cottage and six young people at a time were brought here during the summer from the workhouse in St Pancras, (*facing page, top picture*). It was known as 'Mrs Kidston's Convalescent Home for Destitute Children' and one postcard includes Mrs Carey, the Matron. The welfare of horses as well as children was clearly paramount, exemplified on this page, *top:* the splendid Riding School, Northaw House, (used as a mobile unit in World War 2, see p 250), and *below:* the Yearling Boxes, also Northaw House. ('C B Bray, Potters Bar', pictures).

Above, left: 'John's Hole' in the Great Wood, (dated 1883 over the brickwork), apparently with a cottage in background, from 'Mr Butcher's lantern slide, copied by MC 8 July 1966'. It looks like an ice-house entrance. *Right:* the 'Switchbacks' on the Ridgeway, 1977, by kind permission of Trevor James.

Cathale

The hamlet of Cattlegate is said to derive its name from the long vanished ecclesiastical foundation of Cathale Priory.

It shared with St Albans the reputation of being one of the greatest religious centres of the Middle Ages. It was said to stand on high ground, overlooking three counties (Hertfordshire, Middlesex and Essex).

There are no traces left of the Priory, except a large pond or small lake of some five acres in extent, near Sopers Farm, which is still known by the name of the 'Fishponds.'

Some authorities dispute the origin of the name, and maintain that Cattlegate was only one of the entrances to Enfield Chase kept for the drovers of cattle. As it stands on the line of the old wall, as do Northgate and Southgate, there is some support for this view.

The Great Wood

The Great Wood is all that remains of the extensive forests that used to cover most of this district, and afforded such good hunting ground for so many of our sport-loving monarchs.

There is an interesting legend connected with it which may not be generally known. In the sixteenth century a manuscript was found among the archives of St. Albans, which related that in the thirteenth century, a holy monk, called Sigar, (who flourished in the time of Abbot Geoffrey, 1119-1146) asked permission of the Abbot, to retire 'into the wilderness' to offer up his devotions, undisturbed by the crowd and clamour of the city. He built himself a cell near a well of pure water, in Berevenue Forest, and prayed for the sins of the world, walking daily to hear Mass in the Abbey.

It was a long walk, and he found his evening prayers were disturbed by the songs of the

Two views of the ex YWCA Hut, Northaw, from Richborough, Kent, which increasingly took on the contour of the hill after being reconstructed here in 1919. It served as the village hall until it was replaced in 1969. One use was as a drill hall for the pupils of Guildhouse School who would walk here from Carbone Hill each week for their gym exercises which included skipping as Miss Mary Smith vigorously swung the rope around with the help of a pupil.

nightingales, which abounded in the wood. He therefore prayed that the nightingales should be silent during his hours of prayer. So holy was this hermit, and so efficacious were his petitions, that for many hundreds of years no nightingales were ever heard in the Great Wood of Northaw.

A few years ago the wife of the present owner was asked by an old woman for some of the water from 'John's hole' for her rheumatism. It was explained that this was the Hermit's well, and the story was told. Soon after the lady heard a nightingale singing. She told the old woman, who said: 'Oh yes, it's all right, now that the gentleman who owns the Wood is a Roman Catholic'

So once more the nightingales can be heard in the Great Wood. The tomb of the holy hermit Sigar can be seen in the Abbey of St. Albans with the following legend inscribed on it: 'Vir Domini verus jacet hic heremita Rogerua, et sub eo clarus meritus heremita Sigarus.'

The hill that leads to Newgate Street from here is called 'Carbone Hill', which seems to suggest the presence of charcoal burners in the past.

(A similar story is told of the nightingales that disturbed the devotions of St. Edward the Confessor, at Havering, Essex, and St. Thomas of Canterbury, at Otford Park, Kent; a recluse in St. Leonard's Forest, Sussex, also suffered in the same way until his prayers, or curses, silenced the strains of Philomel. The Medicinal Waters are referred to elsewhere, including locations on our maps, and there is a Shire Publication, *'Discovering Spas'* by R & D Jowitt, 1971, which mentions Northaw along with Barnet).

(We are pleased that Mrs Wilson Fox's history of the Parish has given us a chance to illustrate many aspects of Northaw as well as Cuffley in this appendix).

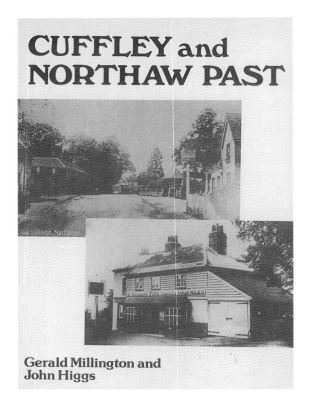

CUFFLEY and NORTHAW PAST

Gerald Millington and John Higgs

Left: the front cover of Cuffley and Northaw Past by Gerald Millington (below left) and John Higgs (centre). The local photographer Ron Warner is shown on the right and they are pictured at the 1986 exhibition of village history by a display of Cuffley airship relics.

Gerald retired to Budleigh Salterton in Devon and John continues to give talks on the history of Cuffley from his unique archive of pictures. Ron produced many sets of postcards of the village and was always ready to help with the preparation of material for displays and publications. He died in 2004 after a long illness.

The book brought together pictures from various sources and the text has helped with our captions in many parts of this publication.

Gerald contributed articles to *Hertfordshire Countryside* and by 1969 he had written at least thirty for Cuffley Free Church's *Focus* magazine, previously *Signpost*, including: Issue 11, 'Zeppelin'; 12, 'Public Houses'; 13, 'Water & Northaw'; 15, 'Hatfield'; 16, 'Wesleys', 'Baptist Hymn book', 'Church in Northaw Parish', 'Non-Conformity Church', 'Fenson-Leman'. 1968 'Potters Bar History'; 1969 'Northaw Village and Kingswell'.

Cuffley Courier

Free to Residents of Cuffley and Northaw
Edited by Brent Cheetham   No. 32

Brent Cheetham (*left*) in 2004 at one of the popular talks on the history of Cuffley given by John Higgs. Brent's *Cuffley Courier* is delivered to every house in Cuffley and took on the lively style of what could be described as a local *Private Eye* magazine. With a strong conservation message and regular features on local history, the *Courier* is also a forum for letters that show how strongly many people in the community feel about Parish issues. Brent stands for Third Way at General Elections and was elected to the Parish Council in 2003.

After Don Hayes took over editorship of Focus magazine, Gerald went on to write about 'Cuffley Farms', 1969; 'Cuffley before the railway', 1969; 'Hatfield Church' and 'Music in the Church', issue 30; 'St Mary's Church, Essendon', 45; 'Place Name Derivations', 46; 'Hanyards Farm, part 1', 49; 'Hanyards Farm, part 2', 50; 'Roman Remains found in Cuffley', 51; 'Hanyards Farm, part 3', 52; 'St Albans Abbey', 57.

Right: Cuffley news is included in the Northaw & Cuffley Parish Council's *Update* and the Cuffley website is http://www.cuffley.co.uk

This September 2000 issue of *Update* described the background to the purchase of Peter's Wood, on behalf of the people of the Parish, by Russell Thomas. Reference is also made to the Millennium Garden, Parish walks and local Societies such as the Cuffley Horticultural Society which was founded in 1942 as part of the wartime 'Dig for Victory' campaign. It has over 600 members and three shows a year.

UPDATE
ISSUE 13 SEPTEMBER 2000

The Newsletter of Northaw & Cuffley Parish Council

Peter's Wood - The People's Wood

I doubt if there are few residents of Cuffley and Northaw who are unaware of the story surrounding the purchase of 27 acres of woodland between the Scout Camp, the railway line and Brookside Crescent. However as it illustrates the community spirit I make no apology for repeating it here.

Railtrack Plc offered by auction a land locked wood of 27 acres subject to a lease to the Scouts at a rental of £600 p.a. There was a claw back of up to 80% should the land receive planning permission. It was mentioned in the auction catalogue that there was a potential for development subject to planning permission.

The Parish first became aware of the auction at the end of June and helped organise a public meeting on the 3rd July for the residents to discuss the situation and for the council to appreciate the feelings of the community. I was amazed at the response, primarily because about 130 people attended and secondly I have never attended a gathering where every question and statement, without exception, was constructive and all to one aim.

It was the Parish's wish to facilitate the purchase of the woods. However, with limited funds it would be unable to justify fully financing it where only a few residents would directly benefit. It was therefore proposed that Cuffley residents should pledge funds to purchase the land in the name of the Northaw and Cuffley Parish Council for the benefit of the community.

With only 9 days to raise the money we were all pressed for time. A circular was distributed to about 75% of Cuffley explaining the situation and requesting pledges, within 5 days we had £55,000 pledged and by the auction on the 12th July there was £80,000. Subsequent donations have raised that to £86,000, which included an anonymous donation of £25,000. Every penny pledged was duly received!

PARISH COUNCIL MEETINGS

Parish Council Meetings are open to the public and are held on the third Wednesday of each month at Northaw Village Hall starting at 7.30pm everyone is welcome to attend.

Questions have been asked as to why the press and public are excluded (quite legally) from part 2 of the meetings. The answer is that at this part of the meeting confidential matters, for example rents etc. are discussed, and which the residents concerned would like to be in confidence to protect their individual privacy.

Maureen Cullimore

Whilst the fund-raising was going on we contacted the tenants, the Scouts Association, who expressed a wish to purchase the woods for the Association but felt it was not in either party's interest to bid against each other. A meeting was arranged for 6th July with their solicitors and surveyors to discuss our mutual aims and interests. Unfortunately they were unable to contribute any financial help.

On 5th July we received a call from Broxbourne Borough Council in who's borough the wood rests, stating that they would wish to purchase the land and issue a new lease to the Scouts. At first sight this appeared to achieve the aims of the community, however we were a little uneasy, as they would be the owner and the local planning authority. This land is the "other side of the tracks" and would have the least impact on Broxbourne if it were allowed to go for development.

The Parish circulated a letter to nearly all of the people who pledged funds to ask them if they would be happy with Broxbourne's offer. We had 100% support that the Parish should go it alone if possible.

The Parish hastily organised a special meeting of the Council on Saturday 8th July where it was resolved that we would bid for the woods using the appeal pledges and some Parish reserves.

On 12th July the auction was held at the Cafe Royal in London. Four councillors, the clerk and a number of local residents were also present.

The bidding went quickly to £50,000 when we entered the fray. It was then a battle between us, - representing the local citizens and the Scouts - against a local resident of Northaw, whose obvious lack of community spirit, pushed the bidding to £111,000.

We must all be philosophical of the outcome, the wood is now owned by the residents and a little piece of green belt is protected from the developer.

The Parish felt that the wood required an identity that focused the ideals of this community action and the future of the land. Peter Sanderson was a resident of Homewood Avenue and an active figure in the village, his interest in the woods was reflected in his tireless involvement as warden of Homewood and committee member of the Broxbourne Wood Liaison Group. It was therefore decided to name it "Peter's Wood" as a tribute.

Finally we, the local community, must sincerely thank the people who contributed towards the purchase of the wood, the people who devoted considerable time and effort and also Broxbourne Council for their support. *Russell Thomas*

There have been seven public houses recorded in the Parish including *The Plough*, here, (Catalogue 19, page 241), drawn by Vivian Hughes on Cuffley's village green: *The Chequers* on Potters Bar Causeway, *The Sun* and *The Two Brewers* in Northaw Village, *The Hand in Glove*, which stood in Vineyards Road, (later 4 cottages known as The Wilderness, now demolished, close to the entrance to Thorntons Farm), *The White Horse* which stood at the site of the King's Well, Cuffley, (and shows how popular that site must have once been), and *The Cuffley Hotel* in Station Road, now a *Harvester* Restaurant.

Appendix 3

Catalogue of Vivian Hughes' Northaw & Cuffley pictures

The Cuffley & Northaw Paintings & Drawings of Vivian Hughes (1900-1954). Born in Barnet.

Vivian Hughes' illustrations to this book are from the pictures of the Parish in the collection of Joan Clark and Jack Gray, given to them by Arthur Hughes, Vivian's younger brother. When an original title was given to one of his pictures by Vivian, this is shown in inverted commas. Otherwise descriptive titles have been provided. Shape is given, (either as 'landscape' or 'portrait'), followed by dimensions and the date, if this was known. If the picture is reproduced in this book, the page number is given in brackets with the measurements and description.

Vivian produced a large number of watercolours on arrival in Cuffley in September 1920, and he kept these in a folder marked 'Cuffley: September 1920'. A second folder was made, called 'Views of Cuffley: Spring 1921'. He was prolific and seemed to use much of his Easter break from Oxford in 1921 to walk along the footpaths and roads in the Parish with sketch pad and watercolours. He carried out other work in Oxford and St Albans, for example, but these are not included in the Cuffley and district collection of 44 pictures.

He returned to the same places repeatedly to work from different angles rather than paint each village feature and there are no less than 13 views of Lower Hanyards Farm and the same number of the Plough Inn and village green. Upper Hanyards Farm only appears in a distant view, (see page 20, catalogue 40). There are 3 pictures of Cuffley Station; (trains were another of his hobbies). 14 other subjects are known from pictures he made around the Parish.

An ancient felled tree and logs appear to have been left to provide fuel for The Plough's open fires in this pencil drawing by Vivian Hughes, (catalogue 21, page 241), from Spring 1921. Vivian not only exhibited fine draughtsmanship, but had an eye for detail and all appear to have been carried out from life. The only possible exception is a pencil study he made of Hill Farm (which faced The Plough) which resembles a photograph of the farm with two figures, (page 34). By the time Vivian moved to Cuffley the building had been clad in black Hertfordshire weather boarding, but he shows it in the original brick state.

He attended a local painting club, worked in either watercolour or coloured pencils and his later pictures show a sense of design with flat paint in more confident areas of colour. His mother, Molly, also drew well (as can be seen from drawings in her books) and we have been left with a unique insight into how rural Hertfordshire once looked. Vivian found the village much the same as it had appeared for centuries. He died in 1954, aged 54, before the major changes to the Parish took place.

1   *Lower Hanyards Farm* Watercolour, landscape 177mm x 128mm. September 1920. Tall elms surround the farm, viewed from Station Road.

2   *Lower Hanyards Farm* Watercolour, landscape 250mm x 177mm. About summer 1921. The tall elms are more clearly defined. Confident use of flat areas of watercolour.

3   *'Lower Hanyards Farm'* Watercolour, landscape 252mm x 174mm. About summer 1921.

Excellent detail of the buildings and the best view of the old farm house. (Page 27).

4   *Lower Hanyards Farm from Tolmers Road* Watercolour, landscape 252mm x 175mm. About summer 1921. Distant view of the buildings across the field from Tolmers Road.

5   *'Hanyards Farm, Cuffley'* Pencil and coloured crayon, landscape 230mm x 157mm. Dated 2 April 1922. Lower Hanyards was the farm nearest his home down Tolmers Road and he would pass it on an almost daily basis when going to the station or when cycling or walking through the village via what became Station Road.

6   *Lower Hanyards Farm* Watercolour, landscape 172mm x 128mm. September 1920. Painted from the exit to the station where the path divides for the short-cut to Tolmers Road. A similar, but elevated view from the station is the title page photograph in *A London Family Between the Wars* by Vivian's mother, Molly Hughes. (Page 28).

Vivian Hughes clearly delighted in the rural character of his new surroundings when he arrived in Cuffley from Barnet in 1920 and this watercolour he made of Lower Hanyards Farm buildings from Tolmers Road has much charm as well as carefully observed detail of the buildings.
(See Catalogue 7, below).

7   *Lower Hanyards Farm gateway*
Watercolour, landscape 172mm x 125mm. 1920.
Painted from Tolmers Road. (See above).

8   *Lower Hanyards Farm from Tolmers Road*
Watercolour, landscape 176mm x 125mm. 1920.
Tall elms and very much the same position as that used by an early photographer. (Page 29).

9   *Lower Hanyards Farm with cart*
Watercolour, landscape 176mm x 125mm.
September 1920. Painted facing north from next to the station master's house and showing haystack, cart, barns, tall elms and Tolmers Road leading away up the hill behind. (Page 15).

10   *Lower Hanyards Farm barns* Coloured pencils, landscape 225mm x 177mm. Spring 1921. Drawn from the same position by the exit to the station where the path divides for the short-cut to Tolmers Road, but with bare trees in spring the following year. There is some foxing (brown staining) on the paper.

11   *'Lower Hanyards Farm April 1921'*
Coloured pencils, landscape 225mm x 172mm. With one haystack. Tolmers Road is seen rising northwards behind the farm and both of the 'railway cottages' are shown in the distance. There is some foxing on the paper.

12   *'Lower Hanyards Farm'* Coloured pencils, landscape 225mm x 172mm. Spring 1921. The station master's house is just visible from Station Road. (Page 16).

13   *Lower Hanyards Farm showing red roof*
Watercolour, landscape 250mm x 175mm. Summer 1922. With two haystacks and green tarpaulin in centre. Tolmers Road is seen facing north with an indication of the roof of one of the 'railway cottages' in the distance. (Page 14).

14   *Cuffley Station from the east platform*
Watercolour, landscape 176mm x 125mm. September 1920. Painted facing north from the platform for trains travelling towards London and

The first houses in Plough Hill appear with the foliage of one of the two oaks on the roadside in Vivian Hughes' sketch of The Plough, about 1925. Vivian called this drawing *'Theobalds Park from Cuffley'*, (see catalogue 29, page 242) and he demonstrates the free use of coloured pencils also found in his view of Northaw Great Wood: 'On the way to Newgate Street', (Catalogue 38, page 244). The rapid hatching is not, however, haphazard and he indicates changes in foliage in both studies to good effect.

showing the Cuffley and Goff's Oak station sign, waiting rooms and 'railway cottages' on hill behind. There is very accurate detail on the platform structure. (Page 84).

15   ***Cuffley Station from the north***
Watercolour, landscape 176mm x 127mm. September 1920. Painted from the hill above Vivian's home and showing the waiting rooms and railway bridge beyond the platforms. There is a path across the field towards the cutting. (Page 84).

16   ***Cuffley Station with train*** Watercolour, landscape 176mm x 127mm. September 1920. Painted from the fields on the south-west side of the station and showing a train pulling carriages over the bridge. Goff's Oak is in the background and the station master's house is in the centre. (Page 81).

17   ***Cuffley Village Green with pump and Plough Inn*** Watercolour, landscape 176mm x 127mm. September 1920. Painted from the start of Hill Rise, looking south. Tall elms and oaks.

18   ***The Plough Inn from Plough Hill***
Watercolour, landscape 176mm x 127mm. September 1920. Painted from below and facing the public house. Tall elm, part of St Andrew's Church roof and chalk or rubble heap indicated. Low west sun indicates Vivian painted this picture about 4.00pm in the afternoon. Vivian's initials 'I.V.H.' in lower right corner.

19   ***'Cuffley Village September 1920'*** Coloured pencils, landscape 223mm x 170mm. From Plough Hill and including one of Hill Farm's barns in front of the tall elms. St Andrew's Church roof and chalk, straw or rubble heap is indicated. (Page 238).

20   ***'The Plough Inn looking towards Enfield'*** Pencil and coloured pencils, landscape 226mm x 144mm. Spring 1921. Drawn from the village green and chalk, straw or rubble heap still present.

21   ***The Plough Inn with tree trunk*** Pencil and coloured pencils, landscape 241mm x 145mm. 1921. Possibly straw for pump and tree by inn. (Page 239).

No views of Northaw Stores by Vivian were included amongst those Arthur Hughes gave to the Grays, although he would have known the very old building. The window bricked up at the time of the window tax (1691-1851) indicates its considerable age and by 1887, H Cox, who owned a shop in Potters Bar, had taken over here. E A Cobb, also of Potters Bar, was proprietor by 1930. It is shown in 2003 after closure.

22   *'Cuffley Village April 6th'* Pencil and coloured pencils, landscape 230mm x 170mm. 1921. View from Hill Farm fields through trees including The Plough and Hill Farm buildings. Badly foxed.

23   *The Plough Inn and houses from the village green* Watercolour, landscape 250mm x 175mm. Summer 1922. Painted from the centre of the green and facing south with Theobalds in the distance. (Page 18).

24   *'The Plough Inn looking south to Theobalds Park'* Pencil and coloured pencils, landscape 235mm x 155mm. Spring 1921. Showing the water pump and Hill Farm barn on the left side. Drawn in the evening, with deep shadow on the nearest chimney, from the entrance to Hill Rise.

25   *'Cuffley Village April 1921'* Pencil and coloured pencils, landscape 225mm x 172mm. Badly foxed paper. Cottages, haystack, tall bare elms and chalk heap, straw to wrap the pump in frost or rubble in front of the entrance to Hill Rise.

26   *'The Plough Inn, Cuffley April 13th 1921'* Pencil and coloured pencils, landscape 225mm x 172mm. Badly foxed paper. A striking two-point perspective, showing inn from below, facing north.

27   *'Firs, Cuffley Village April 13th 1921'* Pencil and coloured pencils, landscape 225mm x 172mm. Slightly foxed paper. Drawn at the sharp bend from the Ridgeway onto the village green where Hill Rise commences. The drawing shows that the road was once fenced here. (Page 19).

28   *Cuffley Village from Castle Farm fields* Watercolour, landscape 250mm x 175mm. About summer 1922. An interesting view from the west showing the line of the hedge where the airship fell, (to the extreme left), St Andrew's Church, the rear of the Plough and a house in Plough Hill. (Page 66).

29   *'Theobalds Park from Cuffley'* Pencil and coloured pencils, landscape 220mm x 160mm. About summer 1925. In his later style, showing houses built in Plough Hill. (Page 241).

The coloured version of two studies Vivian Hughes made of 'Corner Cottage', East Ridgeway, (Catalogue 36, next page, later owned by the Parrs) where the road makes a sharp right turn into The Ridgeway. The new family home *Fronwen* was built opposite this house at about the time of the drawing and the fir trees also show in the background of a picture of Molly in the garden of her new home, (see page 264).

30   **'The Triangle, Cuffley April 7th 1921'** Pencil and coloured pencils, landscape 227mm x 177mm. Behind the grassy triangle stands the Cabin and the road sign spells out 'Cheshunt'. (Page 17).

31   **'Our first home in Cuffley September 1920'** Pencil and coloured pencils, landscape 228mm x 172mm. Although Vivian wrote this title and date on the back of the drawing it is clearly from the spring of 1921 series of pictures with bare oaks. (Oaks usually retain their leaves well into November). The Hughes family moved into the left side of the cottage as viewed here, next to the Grays who vacated this half to provide space for them. Drawn from Oak Lane. (Page 11).

32   **'The Wood, Cuffley April 7th 1921'** Pencil and coloured pencils, landscape 230mm x 175mm. Badly foxed paper. It is interesting to note that a barn stands in the clearing at the brow of the hill on the wide track through Home Wood. The building had been removed by the time land here became the Scout Camp and was fenced in the 1950s. The tree in the left foreground is typical of the oaks in this old oak/hornbeam woodland. (Overleaf).

33   **The Cabin and Station Road** Water-colour, landscape 174mm x 127mm. September 1920. Painted looking towards the station with Goffs Oak on the horizon. The group of three oaks feature in a later postcard view of the station. The distinctive shape of the roof as it extends over a side section makes it easily recognisable and there is a 'wigwam' structure in the centre which also appears in a photograph of the building with Mrs Martin and her family in 1918. The pond shown (and the original farm building) also appears on the 1898 Ordnance Survey map. (Page 245).

34   **Corner Cottage by School Road, Northaw** Watercolour, landscape 250mm x 177mm. About summer 1922. Facing east at the road junction. A very much older 'Corner Cottage' than the one on East Ridgeway, (see next entries). (Page 228).

Vivian Hughes' coloured pencil study of the track through the Home Wood, 7 April 1921. A barn clearly existed in the clearing at the brow of the hill at this time. Although the drawing is badly foxed, the character of this fine oak and hornbeam woodland is well shown. (Catalogue 32, page 243).

35   **'Corner Cottage', East Ridgeway** Pencil, landscape 170mm x 144mm. About 1930. Drawn with the very confident line work of his later pictures. The group of pines also appear in a second drawing of this house and in the background of a photograph of Molly Hughes in her East Ridgeway garden in the 1930s, p 264. (There is a sketch of a train pulling carriages, with steam billowing, on the reverse of this drawing).

36   **'Corner Cottage, East Ridgeway with Pines'** Pencil and coloured pencils, landscape 232mm x 155mm. About 1930. Drawn from a more head-on position facing the building than the previous picture so that the strongly coloured pines cast shadows over the roof. Vivian observed the trees as well as the buildings in Cuffley with great accuracy. (Page 243).

37   **Scots Pines, Northaw Fields** Pencil and coloured pencils, portrait 156mm x 232mm. About 1930. It is uncertain where, between Cuffley and Northaw, this particular pair of pines stood, but the fence and background suggest the artist was facing Cuffley, looking towards the general direction of Cattlegate and Theobalds.

38   **'On the way to Newgate Street'** Coloured pencils, portrait 160mm x 220mm. About 1930. Drawn adjacent to the lower entrance to Tolmers Park, facing the Great Wood. A telegraph pole is centre left and a cart is suggested on the road, but the vigorous line work of foliage illustrates a scene which is much the same today. (Page 46).

39   **'The Coach & Horses, Newgate Street'** Coloured pencils, portrait 160mm x 220mm. About 1930. Drawn at the approach to the road junction with a road sign and telegraph pole either side of the view through to the public house.

40   **'Fir Trees and Cottages, Cuffley, March 17th 1930'** Watercolour, portrait 262mm x 347mm. The largest watercolour in the Cuffley collection with confident blocks of colour. Painted at the

Vivian Hughes' watercolour, September 1920, looking towards Cuffley station with Goffs Oak on the horizon. He describes painting this, (see page 12), and shows the Cabin, (before it was the village hall), part of Lower Hanyards Farm, the Station master's house, the railway bridge and pond. (Catalogue 33, page 243).

entrance to Hill Rise, it shows the old farm cottage with distinct chimney from ground to roof level and Upper Hanyards Farm buildings in the distance. As well as the Scots Pines, an oak is indicated lower down the hill. (Page 20).

41   ***Tolmers Road and Oak Lane Cottages***
Watercolour, landscape 180mm x 128mm. About 1922. Railway fence and hedge shown, as well as the cottages built for railway staff in the style of Courtenay Crickmer's Letchworth work. (Page 13).

Other pictures by Vivian Hughes:
42, 43, 44, 45   We also have reproductions of four other pencil drawings and watercolours: Hill Farm (pencil) with 'I.V.H.' initials in corner; 'Fronwen' under construction, (pencil); farm fields, (pencil); Castle Farm (watercolour), page 40, all made between 1920 and 1940, not in the original collection. Vivian's drawing on page 10 is from Molly Hughes' *A London Family Between the Wars* and not in the collection of originals.

Appendix 4
Mesolithic & Neolithic Sites

Two very well illustrated papers on the locations of flint hand tools in Cuffley were published in Hertfordshire Archaeology in 1977 (Vol 5) and 1983-86 (Vol 9). They were the work of John William Collins Lee and describe five sites: three surrounding Cuffley Hill and Hemps Hill near Thorntons Farm, one at the School Camp badger sett near Postern Bridge and one by Tolmers Road.

An example of one of the flints is reproduced on page 39, but he shows many others in the papers.

During the early 1960s flint scrapers had been found in The Dell, but only recorded in the personal diaries of Michael Clark. Features were confirmed by Tom Clarke, who had publications on flint tools issued by the British Museum. They were found between the farm sites later described by John Lee.

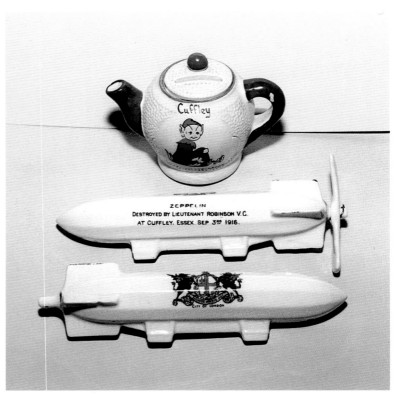

Above, left: Mrs Ruth Leefe Irwin visited the Daily Express Memorial to her brother, William Leefe Robinson VC in 1966 and gave us pictures and the account reproduced below during a visit to her home in Hove. She was the most charming and friendly of visitors during the 50th anniversary year of the event. Cuffley souvenirs, *above, right,* include 'Zeppelin' models made in 'Savoy China, Stoke-on-Trent', (Cuffley is erroneously described as being in Essex), and a Manor Ware teapot with slot for coins. The latter were very popular with children when staying at the School Camp during their visits to the Novelties shop.

Appendix 5

My Brother, William Leefe Robinson
14 July 1895 - 31 December 1918

William Leefe Robinson's sister Ruth Leefe Irwin gave us this account in 1966 when she lived in Hove, Sussex. She visited his memorial as our guest and we have edited her notes with additional information that was kept with her text on his service in the Royal Flying Corps. We think this is the first time it has been published.

Among these chapters it may be permitted to add one picture which, as we grow older, acquires a sharper outline than the contemporary scene. As one ages, the memory seems to be invested of present events to grow dim in the same proportion as ancient happenings become clear.

My brother William was at the end of a family of seven: four girls and three boys. He was sent to school in Oxford from India, returned to India for four years and then went to St Bees School in Cumberland. This school later had three winners of the Victoria Cross amongst its ranks of old boys.

On leaving school he entered the Royal Military College at Sandhurst. When war broke out in 1914, William obtained a commission in the Worcester Regiment and transferred into the Royal Flying Corps in March 1915. He gave the impression that he was born for the first Great War and entered upon the task to which he was dedicated with enthusiasm.

He had a remarkable gift for managing men, especially bad characters, and endeared himself to all who served with him. He never appeared out of temper or depressed, and wherever he was he diffused an air of confidence and hope. He always managed to get the best out of everybody and won a general affection because he himself gave so much.

My parents were in India at this time and his

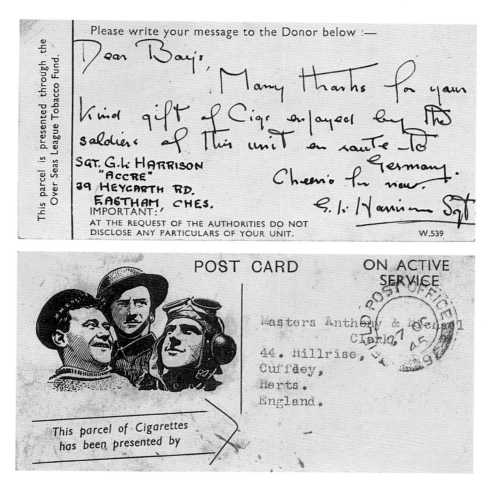

This parcel is presented through the Over Seas League Tobacco Fund.

Please write your message to the Donor below :—

Dear Boys,
Many thanks for your kind gift of Cigs enjoyed by the soldiers of this unit en route to Germany. Cheerio for now.
G. L. Harrison Sgt

SGT. G. L. HARRISON
"ACCRE"
39 HEYGARTH RD.
EASTHAM, CHES.
IMPORTANT:—
AT THE REQUEST OF THE AUTHORITIES DO NOT DISCLOSE ANY PARTICULARS OF YOUR UNIT.

W.539

POST CARD   ON ACTIVE SERVICE

This parcel of Cigarettes has been presented by

Masters Anthony & Michael Clark
44. Hillrise,
Cuffley,
Herts.
England.

Two sides of a 27 October 1945 thank-you card from Sgt G. L. Harrison to Anthony and Michael Clark (aged 5 & 2) for sending cigarettes to the forces. Ironically, the Clarks have always been non-smokers.

guardian was a Lady Alabaster. When war was declared, he was living in Boscombe and announced that he was going into Bournemouth to see the fun. At that time a great German flier was known to be in England on a visit and when William appeared every one took him for this man. He returned to Lady Alabaster quite bleeding. The mob had given him such a hammering. Little did they know that in two years or so's time William was to do that daring feat and bring down the Zeppelin over Cuffley on September 3rd 1916.

He had initially trained as an observer, but gained his wings on 15 September 1915. After three months with No 19 Squadron at Castle Bromwich he was seconded to the London Defence and then posted to the newly formed No 39 Squadron at Sutton's Farm, Hornchurch in Essex.

Despite poor weather, the Germans had prepared for their biggest airship raid of the war, 2nd - 3rd September 1916. For the first time both the Army

and Navy airships joined forces and that afternoon 16 left for England, amongst them the newly commissioned Army craft, SL 11. Under the command of Hauptmann Wilhelm Schramm, SL ll flew over the River Crouch at 10.40pm and then took a circular course in order to approach London from the north. After dropping some bombs on London Colney, Enfield and Potters Bar, the SL ll was engaged by the Finsbury anti-aircraft guns.

After taking evasive action the airship continued to bomb Ponders End when it was attacked by three BE2c aircraft of No 39 Squadron.

At Sutton's Farm that night, William had been instructed to carry out normal patrols. He took off at 11.08pm and proceeded to patrol the area between Sutton's Farm and Joyce Green. At 1.10am he sighted a Zeppelin illuminated by searchlights south-east of Woolwich. He approached to attack, but the airship, the LZ 98, slid into cloud. After a fruitless search for the Zeppelin, William returned to

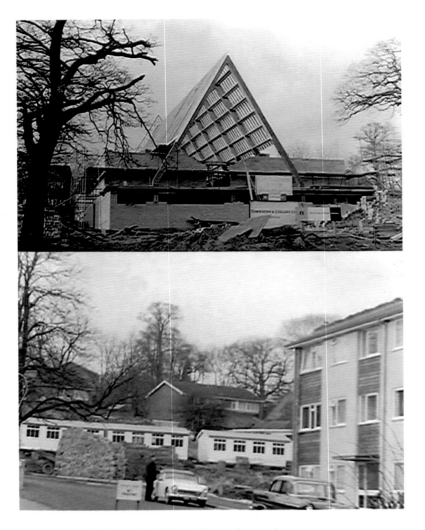

his patrol height and within a few minutes he spotted a red glow north-east of London and rushed to investigate.

A few moments after 2am he spotted the SL ll and dived to attack. Approaching to within about 300m, he flew up and down the hull of the airship, firing two full drums of tracer bullet ammunition without visible result. The crew of the airship did not return his fire. With only one drum left he closed in and concentrated his fire on a small section of the hull. As he fired this section began to glow and within seconds the rear of the hull burst into flames. The SL ll plunged to the ground, with William hastily manoeuvering out of the way.

The glow from the airship could be seen for 35 miles and, as it crashed, London celebrated. People ran into the streets cheering and clapping. Train whistles and factory hooters added to the noise. William became, much to his dislike, a national hero. He was showered with gifts, received prize money totalling approximately £4,200 and, at a special investiture on 8 September at Windsor Castle, he received the Victoria Cross from King George V: the first one awarded for acts within the United Kingdom. After an inquest in Cuffley, the crew were given a military funeral at Mutton Lane Cemetery in Potters Bar.

William continued to serve with his No 39 squadron for a further five months, during which time he married Joan Whipple. He then joined No. 48 Squadron and was sent to France. On 5 April 1917 he was shot down whilst leading a flight which was attacked by five Albatross DIIIs led by Manfred von Richthofen. He was captured and remained a prisoner of war until the Armistice. During this time he was victimised for his feat and very badly treated. On his return to England he was thin and in poor health. Sadly he soon succumbed to the pandemic of influenza which was sweeping the world at the time.

"Who are these men that rush on death ?" and the answer comes: *"Cadets of Sandhurst are we"*. He did not dream that it would be his fate to die after release from a German Prison in 1918. During his incarceration he had tried to escape four times and was caught over the Dutch border each time. On English soil his life slowly ebbed away. He died on the last day of 1918 and was buried with full military honours at Harrow Weald.

It is a bitter thing, when mind and spirit are on high, to surrender youth and the hope of achievement. My brother faced his sacrifice with a splendid fortitude. I have known many brave men but I have never known braver.

I have seen many devout servants of their country but I have never known any so single-hearted. I have known many gentle hearts but none more fitted with the supreme Christian virtue of courtesy.

Ruth Leefe Irwin

Appendix 6

Grace Lawrence has kindly allowed us to reproduce her copy of Vida Slatford's notes on their life in the Mechanised Transport Corps during World War 2 (when she was Grace Marie Seamer Waller):

Cuffley 1939-1945
by Vida Slatford

Volunteer drivers were called for by the Hatfield Rural District Council and asked to report to Hatfield Park with large white discs stuck onto mudguards to enable us to see other vehicles in the black-outs. All types of cars, vans and lorries turned up. Evacuees arrived at Hatfield House from London. The car drivers picked them up and delivered them to their new homes in the district.

Hatfield RDC were then asked by the Mechanised Transport Corps to recruit women drivers with their

A famous night-fighter ace from WW2, 'Cats-eyes Cunningham', 1918-2002, (*left*), came to Cuffley at the time of the seventieth Cuffley Airship anniversary in September 1986. He lived at Harpenden and was a distinguished test pilot for de Havilland, Hatfield. He is pictured in the undercroft at St Andrew's Church with Audrey Curson and Bernard Clark, (see page 217).

own cars to enrol into the Corps. A company was formed with members from Hatfield, Brookmans Park, Northaw and Cuffley. Khaki uniforms were distributed and prospective officers went to Headquarters Training School in London. It meant hard graft every day for three weeks!

The subjects taken included company management, car maintenance, first aid, drill and public speaking. I became an officer with the rank of Captain in charge of No 12 Company. We had our own HQ at Brookmans Park Golf Club and an office from which we operated. The members from Cuffley and Northaw who worked from there included Grace Waller, Lally Shepherd, Mick Ferret and Peggy Rosewell.

We had a Mobile Unit equipped with First Aid and we worked in conjunction with the Red Cross unit trained by Dr Gardner. The stable block at Northaw House was the centre for the Mobile Unit and 'sitting case' cars were garaged there, (page 233).

Members manned the post at night on a rota system and slept in the small cottage in the grounds of Vernon's House which was owned at that time by Mr and Mrs Philip Hamilton. Mrs Hamilton was also an MTC member.

There was a memorable night when two of us drove down to Nyn to collect a fellow driver on duty as incendiary bombs were falling like rain - it looked like fairyland, but was very frightening.

West Hall was taken over by Hatfield RDC to house evacuees - those small boys who were not so well behaved!

Many bombs fell in Cuffley, including oil bombs in the Home Wood which left large holes, and a mine on Mr Cope's front hedge. All his neighbours got out quickly, leaving their windows open, and went to stay with friends in roads further away. The Briggs family housed us in Hill Rise! The mine was detonated by the army. Another mine fell in the fields behind The Meadway. A bomb fell in Northaw

Arthur Hughes returned his late brother Vivian's pictures to Cuffley from Ireland in 1981 and is shown at the history exhibition in Cuffley Hall on Saturday 24 October 1981. Arthur is with his family on the left. Far left is Marie Gray, wife of Jack Gray, who stands at the back between Arthur and Hilda Waller. Anna Clark and other members of her family are on the right, with T Gordon Jones, second from right. Some of Vivian's paintings and drawings can be seen on display in the centre.

Road East and another in Station Road. An incendiary fell on a bungalow on Plough Hill giving Grace Smith an injury to her hand. ARP wardens were busy and Fire Watchers all did their turn of duty.

Many social events were held to make money for the Red Cross, including whist drives and dances. One dance in particular was held at Cuffley School as the sirens went off and bombs were falling on London and as far out as Enfield. The glow from the fires was visible for miles and Cuffley School was a high vantage point.

Cuffley and Northaw were lucky to have few casualties, especially as we learnt afterwards that we were one of the 'most bombed' areas in these parts. We had a unit of the Observer Corps stationed on the Northaw Road, opposite Mr Dallyn's farm which was manned by, among others, Leslie West, Jack Lemon, Gordon Laird and George Large. I think in retrospect one remembers the

wonderful spirit of friendship there was in the village at that time.

Grace Waller added a note: '*During the school holidays I drove for the Observer Corps when I had day time as well as night time duties. At night I stayed at Vernon's House with Phil and Phillip Hamilton.*'

When Grace (Waller) later married, (see page 100), she wanted to call their first child Vernon after the house, but they had a daughter and she became 'Vernonne', (who has kindly done much to help us copy their pictures reproduced in this book). The Waller family owned Paradise House, Park Lane Paradise and were once famous London costumiers. Grace has a Victorian double picture of this large, exceptional family house for stereoscopic viewing which gives a three dimensional effect.

Grace explained how the family firm of London costumiers had flourished until WW2 when the premises were bombed and stocks destroyed.

We have used articles and our pictures elsewhere in this book and were diffident about including more examples of our own Cuffley work, but we decided that some of our own memories might find echoes in certain other readers' minds: Patricia's poems, *below*, and Michael's first book here are from 1989 and 1972. The peregrine attacking a partridge, *next page*, was produced at Tudor House on the Ridgeway for *The Guardian* newspaper to illustrate a review of J A Baker's new book *The Peregrine*. It appeared on Saturday 4 March 1967 and had been commissioned by the then Features Editor, Christopher Driver.

Appendix 7

Two poems by Patricia Klijn of her Cuffley childhood, both written on 22 May 1989. Many will remember the ancient yew tree and attending school at Ware. Patricia compiled the fascinating *Cuffley in Old Picture Postcards* book (facing) in 1995.

The Yew Tree in the Home Wood
Up in the yew tree thick and knotted
Many an hour was idly spent
Higher, higher, beat the others
Be the boldest, dare again
Climb and hide there, dark and gloomy
Glorious freedom
Thought intent.

Back to ground now
Mind the scratches
Through the ferns and fallen leaves

Learn the pathways
Know the turnings
Fearless pleasures
Timeless ease.

The School Bus from Cuffley
Some days we went through Hoddesdon
Past Amwell down to Ware
Not the other way through Bayford
or Brickendon more winding
And longer to get there.
At lonely spots a cottage would mean a pupil too
The wiggly way would widen as our coach went charging through.
We squashed three to a seat now
We argued, fought and sang
Some knitted lots of sweaters
Some studied, tried to write
The blotchy bits of homework
They'd forgotten overnight.

"When you've finished playing with the children . . ."

J A Baker's earlier book, *The Goshawk*, is highly regarded for its description of the dedication needed for successful falconry. At the time of the above drawing Michael Clark was employed to produce cartoons, illustrations, maps and diagrams at *The Guardian*. He nearly caused a strike by the printers (who produced the *Sunday Times* in the same building in Gray's Inn Road) by introducing *Letraset* dry transfer lettering on a map. *Above, right:* a *Punch* cartoon published in the 8 May 1968 issue and in the book *Pick of Punch* by Hutchinson in 1969.

It taught us much of Hertfordshire
The names of pubs, some rare
The daily trip to learning in
The other world of Ware.
Then back again to Cuffley
To pass the farms and fields
We knew the places backwards
From our home up on the wheels.

Appendix 8

People Called Cuf(f)ley

We are indebted to David Cufley, (spelt with one 'f' in his case) davidrcufley@btinternet.com for most of the information and for the pictures in this section. David runs the Cuf(f)ley One Name Group and is always pleased to hear from people who share the name.

The earliest reference to someone with the name is from a Manor Court roll dated 1429 which states 'John Cuffele surrendered into the hands of the Lord one messuage with a curtilage late of Thomas Fostere lying between the land of Thomas Lowyn and land late of John Fletcher and one croft of land called Lecroft. John Attele knight of which the heriot is priced 3s 4d'

The name of Cuffley survives away from the village: there is a Cuffley Avenue in Watford. Hemel

David Cufley has given us considerable help with information on the Cuf(f)ley name and granted us permission to use three pictures from re-union visits to the village: here in 1993 outside *The Cuffley* public house. (For a time the Charrington's original *The Cuffley Hotel* sign was retained inside). David tells us that the current UK Cuf(f)ley population is around 326 with about twice as many spelling their name with two 'f's.

Hempstead has a Cuffley Court and in Luton Bedfordshire you will find Cuffley Close. In North America there is a cloth cap called the 'Cuffley' cap. Just recently, in 2004, a circular from the local Cuffley Co-operative stores gives the Regional Operations Manager as Eddie Cufley. In fact, in the UK alone there are 326 people with the surname: 32 families spell it with one f and 52 with 2 fs. Many Australians share the name and USA and Canada have branches, too. Our memorable picture of the American soldier on Cuffley Station during the Second World War, on page 86, was of Henry Leroy Cuffley in 1943 and this scene was re-enacted by Mike and Chad Cuffley from Baltimore USA with David Cufley from Dartford in Kent fifty years later in 1993. The original 1943 picture had been taken by Wayne Douglas Cuffley (1951-2002) who also attended the Cuffley gathering in 1993 with his brother Mike and their sons Bryan and Chad. Wayne had been a captain in the Baltimore Fire Service and

the family are descended from the same line that originated in Enfield where David's relatives came from, despite the different spelling.

In October 1999 the 'Cuf(f)leys' 3rd World Gathering took place at the historic town of Beechwood, Victoria, Australia: one of the centres of the 19th Century goldrush. The author Peter Leonard Cuffley (born 1944) lives in Australia and one of his titles is 'A complete catalogue and history of oil and kerosene lamps in Australia'. In Canada there is a small town named after its postmaster called Cuffley near Saskatchewan.

William Cufley (1768-1828) was the Beadle of Enfield for 14 years. He and his wife had 9 children. David recently traced Benjamin Cufley to the first fleet to sail to Australia, but has found that this mariner from Northampton was actually called Cusley: the indexer had misinterpreted the 's' in old English spelling for an 'f'. There is a large group of Cuf(f)leys in Northamptonshire and it may be that

The Cuf(f)ley family gathering in 1993 also visited Enfield and included families from Baltimore, USA, Portsmouth, Dartford, Sussex, Spain, Plumstead, Coventry, Birmingham, Eltham, Folkestone and Chatham. On the next page is the third picture provided for us by David Cufley, which includes him with American visitors on Cuffley Station.

this surname is a deviant rather than a separate name.

John Cuffleys have made their mark: John Robert Cuffley (1800-1858) founded the Commercial Travellers School in 1845 and manufactured looking glasses. He was also a cabinet maker and upholsterer. John William Cuffley was born in 1939 at Kensington, London, and played for a time with Emile Ford and The Checkmates. He went on to join the Climax Blues Band (for a time known as the Chicago Climax Blues Band) between 1973 and 1980. John was further involved with the group 'Tarney Spencer' in 1978. It was as a designer for Portmeirion Pottery in Stoke-on-Trent that John literally made his mark. He designed a coffee set of gold on black in the late 1960s called Phoenix. The radical cylinder shape sold in fairly substantial numbers and has become a collected item of 1960s memorabilia. John was assistant to Susan Williams-Ellis at Portmeirion. He also designed a mug to

commemorate the Apollo Moon landing in 1969 and a 'Mayflower' mug for the 350th anniversary of the 1620 sailing of the Mayflower in 1970. Another range of 'Zodiac' mugs bears his name. Aries and Pisces are examples that are stamped: 'Zodiac by John Cuffley, Portmeirion Pottery, Stoke-on-Trent, Made in England', (pictured below).

There is a Janet Goodchild-Cuffley who illustrates fairy tales, a Robert Cuffley from Calgary who makes videos and directed 'Turning Paige' in 2001.

Above, left: Mike and Chad Cuffley from Baltimore, USA, with (*right*) David Cufley from Dartford, Kent, pose on Cuffley Station to recall the 1943 picture (see page 86). Above, top: John Carter's pictures of past Tolmers Roads residents at the 28 February 1993 reunion in Cuffley Hall: David & Isobel Rushbrooke (nee Hawkes) with Valerie Rodgers (nee de Gerdon) on left and, below, Michael Paine, left, with Martyn and Susan Bittlestone (nee Hawkes). See page 264 for other pictures from John of this evening.

Acknowledgements

We have had considerable help from the County Archive in Hertford and individuals such as Vernonne Allan, Melvin Bedford, Trevor Bentham, John Carter, Anthony Clark, Joan Clark, David Cufley, (David's branch of the family of Cuffleys spell their name with one 'f'), Jack Gray, John Higgs, Arthur Hughes, Trevor James, Stella Jones, Betty Lanham, Sir Cameron Mackintosh, Diana Mackintosh, John McCarthy, Joan McRitchie, Graham Rust, Emma Pitrakou, Rodney Slatford.

We welcome further information, corrections and any archive pictures you might like to let us copy for any future editions of this book.

Many of our pictures are simple family snapshots, but hopefully this demonstrates that you might also have images that will give future generations an idea of life in Cuffley.

The authors have tried to obtain permission for all the pictures used, other than those taken by themselves, but we apologise if any have unknowingly been used without agreement. Please contact us through the details given at the start of the book, (facing the Contents page), if you have any concerns in this area. A number of the pictures we have copied exist as postcards and occur in several different collections. There were some previously published old photographs that we have left out because we wanted to show as many new images as possible.

One of the most exciting aspects of the book preparation was having the watercolours and coloured pencil drawings of Vivian Hughes to reproduce for the first time. This was entirely due to the generosity of his brother Arthur and Jack and Joan Gray. Vivian's pictures captured over a decade of Cuffley - between 1920 and the mid 1930s - before the hamlet changed irrevocably from farming community to commuter village.

The open air seating in the School Camp, Cuffley in 1963. Muriel (*left*), who helped found Cuffley Camp, became head teacher at Tewin Cowper Junior Mixed Infants School between 1943 and 1961. Sadly she died just a year after she retired with James to live in Salcombe, South Devon.

James and Muriel Grant were remembered in *Two Hundred Years of Tewin School, 1792-1992,* compiled by Stephen James, from which the above portrait of them came. James Grant was given the task of establishing Cuffley Camp and their daughter Sheila Heggs wrote: 'I lived at Cuffley Camp for the whole of the first summer when my father was seconded from St Audrey's School in Hatfield to set it up. The first thing he had to do was build a bridge over the tank trap in order to get on to the site. It was quite nerve-racking when he drove our car over it to test the strength! Everything was under canvas except for my parents' small caravan and, eventually, a very basic kitchen building. It was my idea of heaven'. The camp had originally opened in May 1943 as a holiday camp for young war workers and youth groups.

We urge all readers to help conserve the buildings and countryside of the Parish by their strong support for all the local organisations active in the community. Wildlife recording is emphasised in our chapters devoted to the natural history of the Parish and the **HBRC** - (*Hertfordshire Biological Record Centre*) - is c/o Environment, County Hall, Pegs Lane, Hertford SG13 8DN (Telephone 01922 555220) biorec.info@hertscc.gov.uk

Membership of the **Hertfordshire Natural History Society** links all wildlife interests in the county and recorders for the Society compile the distribution and status for such subjects as the birds, insects, wild flowers, mammals, reptiles and amphibians encountered by members, often through observations given to them, in turn, by the general public. Membership contacts will vary over the years, but you will find details on the websites: www.hnhs.org and www.hertsbirdclub.org.uk

The **HMWT** - Hertfordshire & Middlesex Wildlife Trust manages our nature reserves and has a network of volunteers and full-time staff all working for the conservation of wildlife in the two counties. You can enquire at info@hmwt.org. **HALS** - *Hertfordshire Archives & Local Studies* is a treasure trove of material on the county. It is based at County Hall and access to the archives is being made far easier with Heritage Lottery Funding to enable material to be put on the web. For further information you can telephone 01438 737333 or call in at County Hall between Monday and Saturday each week. The general opening hours of 9.30am to 5.30pm will vary through the week, so visitors should check before arranging their visits. You can e-mail on hertsdirect@hertscc.gov.uk or visit the website www.hertsdirect.org/hals

We have found the expert staff in the archives very helpful and the chance to examine original material invaluable. Our special thanks to all the people who have guided our searches over the years.

John Carter has kindly sent us a picture from a youth group dance in The Cabin from 1959 and has picked out Gillian Gathercole (on left side), Tony Burnell with Andrew Nevell, (centre, behind dancers), and Paula Lince, in party dress (right side of picture).

The oldest bookplate reference to Cuffley we have found is in Patricia Klijn's collection, from 1875, (*left*). We believe George King later lived at 10 Hill Rise.

The Lemon's house, in Hanyard's Lane, features behind the knife-grinder, (*facing page*), who regularly toured the Parish between the 1950s and 1970s. This photograph was taken in 1964 and there was a colour postcard by Mrs E White issued through the Northaw Womens' Institute of the same subject in Vineyards Road. It was first published in the 1970s as a calendar, from which postcards could be detached.

George King.
Cuffley School. 1875.
Prize for Examination
in Religious Knowledge.

'THE WAY I SEE IT'

Cliff Sings & Talks about his faith

CUFFLEY FREE CHURCH

8.00 p.m.

FRIDAY 4th MAY 1979

25p

Bibliography

Banks A. (1989) *A Military Atlas of the First World War* Heinemann, London

Clark M.B. (2001) *Mammals, Amphibians & Reptiles of Hertfordshire* Hertfordshire Natural History Society & Training Publications Limited, Watford

Gray J. H. (2002) *Jack's War* Training Publications Limited, Watford

Hughes M.V. (1940) *A London Family Between the Wars* Oxford University Press, Oxford & London

Hughes M.V. (1981) *A London Family 1870-1900* Oxford University Press, Oxford & London

James S. (Editor, 1992) *Two Hundred Years of Tewin School* Tewin, Hertfordshire

Klijn P. (1988) *A Cuffley & Hertfordshire Miscellany* Jack Edwards, Goffs Oak, Waltham Cross, Hertfordshire

Klijn P. (1995) *Cuffley in Old Picture Postcards* European Library, Zaltbommel, The Netherlands

Miller M. (1989) *Letchworth* Phillimore, Kent

Millington G. (1975) *Northaw with Cuffley* Author, Cuffley

Millington G. & Higgs J. (1983) *Cuffley & Northaw Past* Jack Edwards, Goffs Oak

Rimell R.L. (1984) *Zeppelin!* Conway Maritime Press, London

Rimell R.L. (1989) *The Airship VC* Springfield Books, West Yorkshire

Robinson G. (1978) *Hertfordshire* Barracuda Books Limited, Buckinghamshire

Sage B.L., Editor, (1966) *Northaw Great Wood* B.E.N.A & Hertfordshire County Council, Hertford

Warren B. (2000) Cuffley chapter in *Community Life in Hertfordshire 2000* Hertfordshire Association for Local History Recorders' Group, Hertfordshire

Facing page: Cuffley Free Church's Rev John Lambert, seated on his Maxi bonnet with his family on a delightful and original Christmas card, wrote regular articles for the *Hertfordshire Mercury*. John died in 1999.

The Church was host to enduring popular music celebrity Cliff Richard in 1979 and this was ticket 75. Cliff had lived in Cheshunt and Anthony Clark recalls attending one of his first concerts when he was still known as Harry Webb.

The model vans sold through the Novelties shop depicted local scenes around Cuffley and came from an idea by John Parkes.

Jill Insley wrote of Loxborough Manor (*right, this page,*) in *The Observer*, 16 March 2004:
'This sixteenth-century manor house has proved so popular with previous purchasers that it has been moved and rebuilt twice. Originally built as a manor house in 1530 in Great Ilford, Barking, the timber-framed building was moved across the estate and reconstructed on a similar scale in 1830 to become the bailiff's house.
'In 1930,' (when Bernard Clark's picture here was taken), 'it was dismantled and bought by a Mr Russen of Cuthberts, the seed company, who rebuilt the property for his own use on the south side of Cuffley Ridgeway. The Russens were keen gardeners and laid out magnificent grounds over three acres of land which the current owners enjoy today. It was on sale through Lane Fox in 2004 for £3m'.

Index

A celebration lunch was held on the 'turnaround' in Oak Lane, Cuffley to celebrate the wedding of Prince Charles with Lady Diana Spencer. The 'street party' took place on Monday 27 July 1981. Shown in the picture are Oak Lane residents dressed in red, white and blue. Olive Fenshom is on the extreme left.

The same event, (*facing page*), with Fred Fenshom to the rear of the partygoers and
Oak Lane, leading down to Tolmers Road, in the background.
The Royal Wedding took place two days later on 29 July 1981.

John Carter, *above right*, with Stella Jones, helped organise the highly successful 1993 Cuffley Reunion which featured Buster Miekle's band in Cuffley Hall and included such guests as Peter Smiley, *above, left*, with Alec Gibb. The band can be seen in the background. Alec lived in Tolmers Road and Peter lived in Molly Hughes' house *Fronwen* on East Ridgeway at this time.

We end the book as we began it with Molly Hughes, here in the garden of her new home on East Ridgeway, *Fronwen*, about 1937, from *A London Family Between the Wars* (1940), Oxford University Press.